YOU
ALREADY
KNOW
WHAT
TO DO

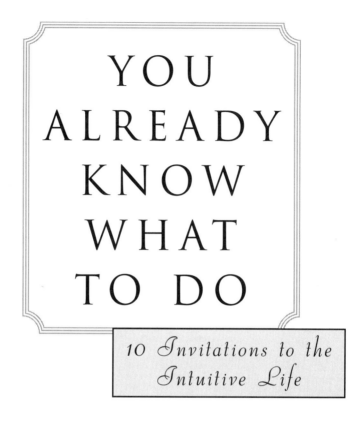

YOU ALREADY KNOW WHAT TO DO

10 Invitations to the Intuitive Life

SHARON FRANQUEMONT

JEREMY P. TARCHER/PUTNAM *a member of*
Penguin Putnam Inc. *New York*

Most Tarcher/Putnam books are available at special quantity
discounts for bulk purchases for sales promotions, premiums,
fund-raising, and educational needs. Special books or book excerpts
also can be created to fit specific needs. For details, write or telephone
Putnam Special Markets, 375 Hudson Street, New York, NY 10014.

Jeremy P. Tarcher/Putnam
a member of
Penguin Putnam Inc.
375 Hudson Street
New York, NY 10014
www.penguinputnam.com

Library of Congress Cataloging-in-Publication Data
Franquemont, Sharon.
    You already know what to do : 10 invitations to the intuitive life /
by Sharon Franquemont.
        p.   cm.
    ISBN 0-87477-946-4 (alk. paper)
    1. Intuition (Psychology)   2. Intuition (Psychology)—Problems,
exercises, etc.   I. Title.
BF315.5.F73   1999   98-51437 CIP
153.4'4—dc21

Printed in the United States of America

10   9   8   7   6   5   4   3   2   1

This book is printed on acid-free paper. ∞

Book design by Lee Fukui

ACKNOWLEDGMENTS

I come from a long line of seekers. My paternal great-grandfather's probing books rest on my bookshelves along with the spiritual life story of my maternal grandfather and grandmother. I give thanks to my ancestors whose lives left a path for me to follow. With the loving support of my mother and father, Max and Claudia Franquemont, and the constant encouragement of my joyful Dakota father, Harry F. Byrd, I have been able to stay on the road. I am also grateful to my brothers, Ed and Gerry, and their families, who have always championed me.

My children, Christine, Megan, Erik, and Mark, have shared the laughter, excitement, and labor pains necessary to birth a book. They stood beside me like a rock. The thought of them, and others like them, often inspired me; it has been my intention and hope to write a book that would be useful to present and future generations.

I am thankful to Joyce Searls for providing the impetus to write, to her husband, David, for suggesting the name of this book, and to my colleague and friend, Colleen Mauro, for putting me in contact with Tarcher. Thanks also goes to my beloved soul sister, Lorrie Eaton, who willingly read and commented on every version of this manuscript. Constant support and love flowed to me from my life partners, Betsy Stang and David Berry, and all my Washington, D.C., colleagues. I will always cherish the intimacy that developed during the final months with my fellow author and cherished friend, Joan Kenley. My thanks goes to Marcia Scott, Kathleen Brittle, and Marsha Isley who contributed their talents to the original graphics. Thanks also goes to Anne Dosher, Roger Harrison, Margaret Harris, and the Maypole Group for inspiration and spiritual sustenance.

Wendy Hubbert, my editor, provided the guidance and the organizational suggestions that helped make this book a reality. Without her, my shelf would still be littered with mutually unsatisfactory manuscripts. My thanks also goes to Jeremy Tarcher, Joel Fotinos, and the entire staff of Tarcher for their trust and confidence in my work. My thanks go to copyeditor Timothy Meyer for his thoughtful suggestions. Thanks also goes to Irene Prokop.

Intuition is my passion. It has introduced me to a world of marvelous people: Robert Gerard, Willis Harman, Buck Charlson, Nancy Rosanoff, Marcia Emery, Jeffrey Mishlove, Georg Feurstein, Barbara Schultz, Daniel DalCorso, Roger Frantz, Barbara Marx Hubbard, Bill Kautz, Helen Palmer, Mike Arrons, Rhea White, Alan Vaughan, Marilyn Schlitz, Dean Radin, Stanley Krippner, Gary Zukav, Belleruth Naparstek, Jean Houston, Cindy Seigel, Loyd Auerbach, Bill Roll, all my colleagues at The Intuition Network and in the field of parapsychology, and the people at the Life Science Foundation and Sounds True. These individuals, and others, are part of my learning community; they have helped give shape to my dream.

I am thankful for the many students with whom it has been my privilege to work. Each of them is precious to me. They are central to my education, and I am grateful for the numerous stories they have shared with me. Without my students, there would be no book.

Finally, throughout the past fifteen years I have spent many days and nights curled up next to the fireplace in my office reading books, listening to music, and praying and/or meditating in order to acquaint myself as best I could with the great Teachers and Masters of eternal wisdom. They are the meaning behind everything I do. This book is written in their honor.

DEDICATED TO:

The Soul

CONTENTS

INTRODUCTION

Whether you know and recognize what intuition is or not, believe me, at some point in your life you have experienced its miraculous powers. Intuition is a sense, just like sight or smell, a perception that brings you information. It comes to you as a still small voice, an instinctive action, a flash of creativity, or a moment when you are one with the world. You suddenly know something without the use of analytical processes; the knowledge is just there. You *know* it. While the word itself comes from the Latin *intueri*—meaning to consider, to look on—intuition implies something deeper than simple perception and is best described as *apperception,* the ability to "take hold of" knowledge in one glance. *Webster's Unabridged Dictionary* sums up intuition as "the immediate knowing or learning of something without the conscious use of reasoning; instantaneous apperception." Simply stated, intuition is direct knowledge. It tells you what to do.

In my work as a teacher, coach, and intuitive consultant, I've seen intuition touch many lives in amazing ways. For example, Susan[1] and her husband needed a new home for their family because in a few days they had to vacate the old one. Mentally distracted by the problem, Susan wasn't paying much attention one day as she walked her son to preschool. Suddenly, her whole body knew that her son's teacher, a relative

> Most of us are living at the periphery of consciousness while intuition invites us into the center.
>
> WILLIS HARMAN

stranger, had the answer. She instinctively asked the teacher if he knew of any available properties, and his answer provided her family with a wonderful home for the next twelve years.

Similarly, Tom had experienced several business failures and was wondering if he'd ever succeed. An inner voice urged him to apply for a routine government job. He reluctantly decided to listen to that voice, and within two and a half years of obtaining the government job, an after-hours interest group he had formed blossomed into a full-time position in the highest offices of the land. He experienced success beyond his wildest dreams.

We all have the power of intuition within us, and by learning to tap into that power, you can take care of your pragmatic needs as Susan did, realize an inner dream like Tom's, and achieve a more fulfilling life. This is because intuition arises out of your richest resource—your soul. Intuition is the language of the soul. When you are called by intuition to make a different decision, follow a greater vision, or make a creative breakthrough, the voice you hear is that of your soul guiding you to what is deeply right for you. One woman who was attending a talk given by my Intuition Network colleagues and myself summarized this by saying, "Now I get it. Intuition is 'soul speak.'"

We are just now beginning to recognize the power of intuition. As the spotlight of traditional scientific research turns onto intuition, it's become more and more acceptable for us to talk about our intuitive experiences. The author of *Emotional Intelligence,* Daniel Goleman, has done research which suggests that your gut is "intelligent"; it knows things ahead of your rational mind. Dr. Antonio R. Dimasio of the University of Iowa College of Medicine and his colleagues have actually identified the part of your brain—the frontal lobe—that specializes in intuitive decision-making. Their research shows that you intuitively know what isn't working "best" for you, and that you have the power to heed this inner advice.

This book tells you how to bring this power—the power of "soul-speak" in your body, mind, and spirit—into your life right here and now. While most books on intuition treat this unique power as primarily a tool or a technology, I take a different approach. Twenty-eight years of working with in-

> *Intuition is the voice of the Real Self, a sure guide toward ultimate perfection.*
>
> LEONARD BOSMAN

tuition have taught me that intuition thrives best as a way of life rather than just a tool one picks up and puts down. Intuition's value extends far beyond simple problem-solving, decision-making, or creative break-throughs. Intuition serves our deepest purpose and places us in harmony with what the universe and our soul intend.

The East Indian sage Patanjali, writing thousands of years ago, provided a model which helps us understand why intuitive knowledge flows best at these deep bedrock levels. Briefly, he stated these four different ways of knowing something: (1) you know what it looks like (its form); (2) you know how it makes you feel (its quality); (3) you know its meaning (its purpose); and (4) you know its soul (its essence). Intuition, which makes random appearances at the first two levels, thrives at levels three and four. This is why life automatically becomes more intuitive when you seek to put meaning or purpose in your life. Meaning feeds intuition and vice versa.

Let's go back to Susan and her housing dilemma. Note that she was not alone in that situation: although it was her intuition that first identified her family's future home, it was through her husband's subsequent visualizations and trust that the home became a reality in twenty-four hours. The partnership of Susan and her spouse clearly illustrates what collaborative intuition can accomplish. This incident highlighted a potential meaning for their partnership—united spiritual action—which they had the ability to actualize or not, depending on their choice and awareness.

Tom's story also goes deeper than professional success. Tom was seeking his place in the world, a place which would release his passion and inner purpose. Ever since he embraced intuition as a way of life, he has

> *Intuition is the language of light through which men and God "intercommunicate."*
> WALTER RUSSELL

lived a highly synergistic and connected existence where everything works in harmony with his illuminated soul mission. As busy as his days get, he is always able to stop and drink from a deep well of inner peace. This is because Tom knows who he is: an embodied soul.

When we know who we are at the core of our being, we know what to do. So when basketball superstar Patsy Neal describes a basketball performance by saying, "I know what people mean when they speak of a 'state of grace,'" he is speaking of flowing with intuitive knowledge. When business man Jagdish Parikh speaks of creating a "synthesis . . . beyond selfishness and selflessness, beyond collectiveness and competitiveness, to a cooperativeness based on selfness," he is calling on intuition. In the early nineteenth century, when writer Samuel Taylor Coleridge awoke with the "distinct recollection of the whole" of "Kubla Khan," he demonstrated the effectiveness of intuition.

Intuition takes us beyond our small self into our best self, into our soul. The bottom line is that your soul knows what to do in every situation. All you need to do is identify and follow its suggestions. You achieve this through practice, but, unfortunately, for most of us this is not as easy as it sounds.

The first challenge we face is inexperience. Intuition is a language unto itself, and you probably have not had more than a few hours of intuition training in your life, if that. It's very difficult to follow the guidelines and suggestions of any language you do not understand. A second challenge is trust. Anyone who learns a new language doubts his or her skill at first, and intuition is no different. As our intuition develops, we have to learn to trust our skills and, ultimately, our soul. This is especially true when, like Tom, we think intuition's suggestions take us away from our goals. A third challenge is transformation. An intuitive way of life changes us forever. Most people tend to choose the status quo, the familiar patterns, or the lesser callings and skip basic training rather than risk confronting an inner urge to change.

Our work together in this book addresses each of these issues as well as the difficult challenge of separating authentic intuition from projections and wishful thinking. Projections are inner images or ideas we construct, often unconsciously, on the basis of a past interaction. We carry these images or ideas

> *We are having this conversation about intuition because we all want to become real.*
> ROB RABIN

around with us and *literally* project them onto the "screen" of present circumstances. Think of this as a double feature at the movies, but the projector is running both features—your past and present—on the screen at once. It is hard to figure out what is going on, so most of us choose the most familiar image—the past. Whether this past movie is a good one, bad one, or something in between, it keeps us from having an undistorted interaction with the present. Wishful thinking functions in a similar way, although it focuses on the future. Your inner movie projector busily cranks out ideas or images of what you hope or fear will come true, rather than staying with the truth found in the present moment.

When the subtle plane of intuition, which can appear as images or ideas, gets activated, it challenges us to stay in the present, to bring our unconscious projections and wishful thoughts to light, and to recognize what we already know to do. One simple criterion for distinguishing authentic intuition from ego projections or wishful thinking is that the real stuff is delivered as *invitations,* not demands. The words "You should do . . ." or "You must do . . ." are not part of intuition. Rather, intuition is your soul saying, "Please consider. . . ." or "Will you . . . ?"

Your soul is kind, gentle, and patient. It doesn't give up, or, as my colleague and friend Nancy Rosanoff, author of *Intuition Workout,* says, "Your intuition is not going to go away." Even if you've denied your intuitive experiences in the past, rest assured: your invitations will continue to come.

I've designed this book around what I consider to be ten basic "invitations of the soul." Each invitation establishes an aspect of your intuitive development and builds a foundation for the next invitation. An overview

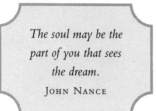

The soul may be the part of you that sees the dream.

JOHN NANCE

of what you have to look forward to follows. As you read it, remember what the purpose behind each invitation is— *your soul wants you to be fluent in intuition so that you know what to do in every situation.*

Invitations	Purpose
1. Just Say "Yes"	Turn on your intuition and your life.
2. Open Your Senses	Experiment with your intuitive body. Know what it knows.
3. Cultivate Silence	Court the inner quiet which allows you to listen for your intuition.
4. Nurture Joy	Open your intuitive pathways with laughter and joy.
5. Set Time Free	Free yourself from your ideas about time. Experiment with intuitive time.
6. Shift Space	Know your identity goes beyond your skin. Explore how intuition and space interact.
7. Discover Your Purpose	Align yourself with the intentions of your soul. Bring power to your life.
8. Mate with Soul	Experiment with soul-to-soul knowledge on journeys into love and healing.
9. Partner Exponentially	Explore collaborative intuition in group settings. Learn about intuitive vision and intuitive leadership.
10. Connect the Dots	Discover a Big Picture view of life on Earth.

Each invitation is explored in a chapter containing background information, stories, challenges you may face, and practice exercises, which are the cornerstone of intuitive development. There are many, many exercises in this book. You do not have to com-

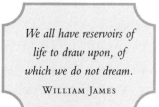

We all have reservoirs of life to draw upon, of which we do not dream.
WILLIAM JAMES

plete all of them! If you don't want to do a particular exercise because you are tired, bored, not committed, or avoiding issues that a particular exercise evokes, trust yourself. Skip it. The time will come when you will want to do the very exercise you are skipping now.

In general, consistency is more important to intuitive development than thoroughness. You have not "failed" because one or more exercises is not completed. Do the ones which attract you. You can always go back later and complete the ones you skipped.

When you've finished these ten invitations and their exercises, you'll know that you do not need to be a mystic, channel higher entities, believe in God, abandon your logic, or be rigorous in your discipline to achieve an intuitive life. Curiosity and intention are the only requirements.

To increase the long-term benefits of these attributes, purchase a spiral-bound, composition, or loose-leaf notebook. Some people prefer a loose-leaf notebook because it allows them to insert new pages as they wish. The advantage to other types of notebooks is that the pages are bound and thus more secure with frequent use. Whatever you choose, be sure you are comfortable with it because it will be your Intuition Journal. Your Intuition Journal is very important: *you may use it the rest of your life.*

Label your journal. "My *(year)* Intuition Journal." It is important to label the year of your journal, e.g., 1999, because over the years you may build up a collection of Intuition Journals and need to distinguish them. As you work with this book, you'll fill your Intuitive Journal with guiding images, the results of your practice exercises, records of your intuitive experiences, flashes of insight, and wild, intuitive possibilities. Your journal will become a gold mine. Its pages will contain the wealth of your intuitive development, ideas for new projects, moments of truth, insights

> Intuition is one of the
> most important abilities
> we can cultivate . . . It is
> becoming necessary for a
> comprehensive personal
> and global perspective.
>
> JAGDISH PARIKH

into relationships, strategies, and entertaining stories. You'll mine its nuggets for years to come.

In addition to all of this, an Intuition Journal provides the objective record necessary to assess your intuition's accuracy. Although the purpose of such a record is not to "validate" intuition, you have every right to expect pragmatic results from your inner work. Sometimes the meaning of a journal entry won't be clear for months or even years to come. You deserve a tangible record of your intuition's wisdom.

One last tip: it is rich to work with this book in a group setting. Every person develops his or her own style and short cuts to knowing. When you work with others, the pool of your intuitive skills is available for all.

Whether alone or with others, you will learn that intuition is always at your fingertips. For example, try this short experiment right now. Ask yourself, "Why is it important for me to invest in my intuition?" When you are comfortable with the question, flip randomly through the pages of *You Already Know What To Do* until you want to stop. Next, let your fingers or eyes identify a phrase or sentence on the page which has relevance to your question. This simple exercise may or may not reap results right at this moment; if it does not, be assured that your capacity for receiving quick guidance and making decisions will flourish as your intuitive adventure progresses.

My own adventure with intuition began many, many years ago. My formal training and work began when I was twenty-eight, but my earliest intuitive recollections are bound up with the sights, sounds, and smells of childhood.

Fortunately for me, I received permission from my mother to know

what I knew. One day after a particularly vivid night dream came true precisely, I sought my mother's advice. I
was nine years old at the time and assumed everyone had such experiences.
From my perspective, all I lacked was
the ability to categorize and talk about
what was happening. My mother was
the perfect person to ask because she
had told me some of her dreams, which later came true.

> Sell you cleverness and
> buy bewilderment.
> Cleverness is mere
> opinion. Bewilderment
> is intuition.
> RUMI

"Mom," I said, "I had a dream that came true at the bus stop this
morning. What is this?"

"Tell me about it," she responded.

"In my dream I saw the others girls and myself talking to a new girl.
This morning the same girl I saw in my dreams came to the bus stop. Her
family moved to our neighborhood this weekend. I recognized her immediately, and we started talking. I knew exactly what everyone was
going to say before they said it. Everything moved in slow motion. I felt
like I was watching a play I had already seen."

My mother was silent for only a moment and then said, "This is
a natural part of life. Many people have these experiences. Don't be
worried."

Many years later, after I had become a university professor of intuition, I asked my mother if she remembered this crucial conversation. She
had no recollection of it at all, but the abiding comfort her words gave me
that day were a priceless inheritance for my life to come. They told me,
"Sharon, intuition is a natural part of your inheritance."

This book is about that inheritance. Borrow the meaning of my
mother's words. Say to yourself as often as necessary, "Intuition is a natural part of my inheritance." Claim your inheritance. Let yourself choose
to do this. The harvest of a more passionate, purposeful, and powerful life
awaits you.

CHAPTER 1

Intuition:

TELL ME MORE

Whether in my college classes or in other settings, people want me to tell them more about intuition. They repeatedly ask me to answer these five questions:

1. Can I really improve my intuition?

2. How can I keep my logic from putting down my intuition?

3. Doesn't this stuff make you weird?

4. What is the difference between psychic and intuitive events?

5. In the Big Picture, what purpose does intuition serve?

These are excellent questions which actually address deep issues in human experience. Throughout the centuries, philosophers, scientists, Indigenous cultures, psychologists, and spiritual people have asked themselves these questions and, as a result, have developed a variety of ways or models for understanding what intuition is and how it might work. In fact, questions two through five are best answered by exploring four of these models. This exploration is important for two reasons: (1) the models move your understanding of intuition from a flat dictionary definition to a four-dimensional perspective and (2) you'll discover which of the ways is most natural for you and be able to turn to it whenever you need to throughout this book.

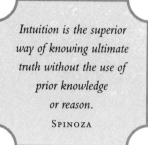

Intuition is the superior way of knowing ultimate truth without the use of prior knowledge or reason.
SPINOZA

In addition, exercises which help you apply the ideas behind the models follow each discussion. Important hint: If you find yourself by-passing the exercises, examine the answers to these two questions: (1) Am I so left-brained oriented that I invalidate intuition by not investing in the exercises? If you answer yes to this question, practice by *acting* as if you believed in intuition. Invest in a new adventure. (2) Am I so right-brained oriented that I am reading the text for moral support but think the exercises are unnecessary for me? If your answer is yes to this question, humble yourself and recognize that there is always room for growth and improvement.

Application is everything in intuitive development. In both cases, give yourself over to the experience by doing the exercises.

In contrast to questions two through five, question number one doesn't require any model; it is easy.

1. Can I Really Improve My Intuition?

"Absolutely!" I always answer. "You are designed to know what you know."

Unfortunately, many people don't realize this. They accept that their analytical skills can be improved upon but believe their intuitive abilities are limited at birth to some kind of intuition allotment. Some people are born with lots of intuition, they think, some with less, or some with none at all. Or they believe that if you are born a man you don't have much intuition, but if you are a woman, you have a lot. Both these beliefs, in my opinion, are nonsense. Regardless of your gender, you have plenty of intuition, although it may be true that you are not using it. And, as with any

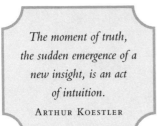

The moment of truth, the sudden emergence of a new insight, is an act of intuition.

ARTHUR KOESTLER

other skill, intuition is strengthened by use, stays dormant with disuse, and varies with expertise.

It is not surprising that people believe in an intuition allotment theory because, unlike analytical skills, public school curriculums do not try to improve children's intuition or identify their particular area of intuitive expertise. Multiple-choice questions designed to help students evaluate when and how they intuit best, rewards for essays such as "My Greatest Intuitive Experience," or college courses labeled "Intuition 101" don't exist. People have to decide to do these things for themselves.

When they do, they don't regret it, because intuition is part of healing. Most people raised in Western culture are divided within, separated from their deepest knowledge and wisdom. Our long and fruitful journey into science and technology now begs for an end to this inner division and a return to ancient knowledge methods which are not bound by superstitions, but revealed by expanded consciousness. It is important that we journey to this consciousness as a species not simply out of fear for our collective survival but because we love and are committed to all Life. Commitment requires changes and, while changes motivated by fear are fleeting, changes impelled by love last.

Because the word "intuition" is not very illuminating, people often wonder, "Precisely what is this thing called intuition?" When I use the word, I am referring to a specific skill in consciousness for obtaining knowledge. I believe intuitive awareness exists on a continuum within us, although we use different words to describe it. For example, we call non-rational knowledge in our bodies, "instinct," in our emotions, "psychic," in our minds, a creative "A Ha," in our vision, "precognition," and in our experience of the Absolute, "mystic or spiritual." Naturally, people get confused because, like the mythic Prometheus, our right to know what we know changes forms according to our present awareness.

To get around this nomenclature problem and to capture the breadth of intuitive abilities, I often use the phrase "intuitive intelligence" or what I call your InQ. We are all familiar with IQ (intelligence quotient), a number which represents people's ability to provide predetermined correct answers to questions focusing on a variety of analytical skills. In contrast, your InQ (intuition quotient) reflects your ability to go inward, respond to a variety of intuitive skills, perceive connections, and thrive in the unknown. While IQ is as-

> *Intuitive knowledge is an illumination of the soul, whereby it beholds in the light of God those things which it pleases Him to reveal to us by a direct impression of divine clearness . . .*
>
> René Descartes

sociated with the brain, InQ is distributed throughout your body because we literally do know with our minds, emotions, and bodies. In short, your InQ describes a huge piece of inner territory. This can complicate people's confidence in the learning process until they realize what their intuitive strong suit is. Working with this book gives you an opportunity to know where your greatest intuitive abilities lie (in your body, emotions, visions, silence, or joy) and to begin mapping your InQ strengths.

Another problem people encounter is the multi-tasked nature of the word "intuition."[1] The word is a noun, yet it is used to describe a process (the arrival of knowledge in unique ways) much like a verb is used. The real verb, *intuit,* is rarely used. So, most people choose to say, "I used my intuition to know the answer" rather than "I intuited the answer." This subtle distinction robs intuition of its action in the world and makes it a thing to understand rather than an action to take. By the end of this book, I hope you are as comfortable with the word "intuit" as you are with the word "intuition."

You will also notice that I frequently refer to intuition as a living force, saying things like, "Intuition is calling you." Whenever I say that, remember it comes from a belief that this "living" intuition serves as a communication bridge, a language, for the soul. Therefore, this book engages you in enchancing a skill (intuition as process), making friends with your intuition (as a living force), and learning the language of your soul.

> The discovery of the significance of the two hemispheres is clearly of momentous importance.
>
> CHARLES HAMPDEM-TURNER

All of these things begin when you turn on your intuition (Invitation One), and I'll do my best to lead you through a step-by-step acquisition of intuition's inner wealth.

One last thing about your entitlement to know what you know. The wealth of intuition flourishes in the context of purpose and soul. This provides an ethical dimension to its information, which is often sadly lacking in the domain of knowledge. Take, for example, this story of a man whose inner development had a magnetic effect on others. The man, a salesperson, liked the money he earned but wanted more. On one sales call, unhappy not to have met his financial goals, he decided not to correct one of his customers when she mistakenly thought an item cost $150 more than its actual price. Driving home with the extra money in his pocket, he was mentally distracted by justifying his decision to himself and accidentally bashed in his front bumper. When he later received a repair bill for precisely $150, he recognized the folly of his thinking and its inevitable outcome. Intuition is powerful, and a sincere commitment to intuition makes it impossible for you to abandon ethical behavior for long. This is a bonus in your development package.

2. HOW CAN I KEEP MY LOGIC FROM PUTTING DOWN MY INTUITION?

As people begin to work with their intuition, often their inner analytical voice berates them, saying things like, "This isn't real" or "You can't trust this stuff. It isn't logical." This voice can be so destructive that it cripples or invalidates intuitive information *before* you are even able to completely receive, act on, and evaluate your intuition. It appears that logic loves to checkmate intuition. An answer to why logic puts down intuition is found in the first of our four ways of understanding intuition: The Scientific Model.

Important background for this model comes from philosopher Alfred North Whitehead, who in 1925 declared the absolute dominance of the scientific revolution, which he defined as "a vehement and passionate interest in the relation of general principles to irreducible and stubborn facts."[2] Intuition, which is not an irreducible stubborn fact and is experimentally unreliable, non-repeatable, and uncontrollable, went out as the scientific tide came in.

> *The healthy understanding . . . is not the logical, argumentative, but the intuitive; for the end of understanding is not to prove and find reasons, but to know and believe.*
>
> THOMAS CARLYLE

The tide didn't start turning until 1972 when Robert Ornstein popularized scientific research on the difference between the left and right brain. The research, which was based on studies of people with severed connections between the two hemispheres, suggested that each hemisphere has its own area of expertise.[3] The left brain is an expert at verbal, linear, detailed processing. The right brain excels at non-verbal, spatial, wholistic, and symbolic processing.

This discovery partially, but not entirely, sanctioned intuition, which usually uses non-verbal, symbolic methods to communicate. The sanction remains partial because most Westerners have been educated *about* right-brain expertise in a left-brain manner. Immersion *in* right-brain learning styles is rare and, in fact, the few educational subjects which emphasize right-brain skills—art, music, dance, some aspects of sports—are considered optional or eliminated first in budget cuts. For most of us, the right brain remains the technical but silent partner of the left. It is this silence and little direct experience with intuition which foster logic's ability to put intuition down.

Nowhere is this more evident than in the Great Brain Debate exercise I conduct in intuition seminars. Participants begin by sharing with each other a "wildly" creative plan they haven't dared to follow. I then ask, "What does your left brain say to your right brain about your plan?" There is never a moment's hesitation. People mimic it saying things like, "You don't know what you're doing!" "Who do you think you are? You

FOUR WAYS OF UNDERSTANDING INTUITION

The Science Centered Model: The Left/Right Brain Theory

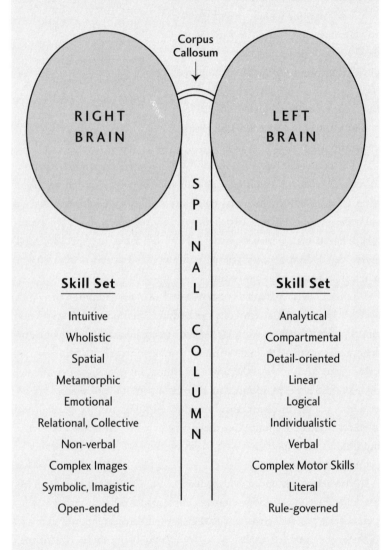

Corpus Callosum

RIGHT BRAIN

LEFT BRAIN

SPINAL COLUMN

Skill Set

Intuitive
Wholistic
Spatial
Metamorphic
Emotional
Relational, Collective
Non-verbal
Complex Images
Symbolic, Imagistic
Open-ended

Skill Set

Analytical
Compartmental
Detail-oriented
Linear
Logical
Individualistic
Verbal
Complex Motor Skills
Literal
Rule-governed

can't do that," "You're just a dreamer,"
"You're a fool for believing that," and
"How are you going to explain why?"
When I ask people how their right
brains defend themselves, usually silence fills the room. Most people's right
brain becomes paralyzed in a debate
with the left. In my latest workshop, the
silence was explained by someone calling out, "The right brain isn't verbal."

> *When intuition operates,*
> *information flows* not
> *from the conscious mind*
> *we are so used to dealing*
> *with, but from somewhere*
> *beyond that mind, from a*
> *place we normally have*
> *no control over.*
> WILLIAM KAUTZ

When I ask people what they imagine the right brain might say if it talked,
they always begin with statements like, "You [left brain] don't know
everything!" "You are so short-sighted," "My perspective has more meaning than yours," "My images are colorful and caring compared to yours,"
and "You miss the Big Picture completely." At this point, the debate
sounds like two egos locked in combat over who is going to "command
operations." This ego combat must stop in order for you to end your
logic's ability to put down intuition and vice versa.

A key to a truce is understanding that *combativeness is not a right-brain
quality.* The right brain loves connections and relationships. When people
realize that combative statements are not natural to the right brain, healing sentences such as "Let's work together," "Our partnership can contribute to the world," "You can show me what things comprise something
and I'll show you the overall result," and/or "Enumerate something for
me and I'll reveal its elegance" emerge. People then feel the potential of
whole brain thinking—intuition working with logic, not against it or as a
substitute for it.

This is our goal, and it can help us monitor ourselves. If your life is
feeling dull and uninspired, you know you need to go out dancing, take
up art or poetry, or find other creative outlets. On the other hand, if creative projects surround you, but nothing is getting done, you need a
course in time management or other organizational skills. You need your
whole brain to actualize your talents. Those of you who still want to learn

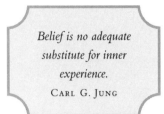

Belief is no adequate
substitute for inner
experience.

CARL G. JUNG

about intuition in a very organized, left-brain manner can consult Dr. Marcia Emery's *The Intuition Workbook*.

In summary, when your logic tries to put down your intuition, go to inclusive and cooperative statements. Remind yourself that (1) the acquisition of knowledge is not only a linear process; (2) the right brain processes information in symbolic and spatial ways; (3) whole brain thinking allows you to access more talents; and (4) science supports learning in ways other than analytical.[4]

Exercise: The Science Centered Model: Left/Right Brain

1. Turn to the *fifth* page of your journal. You'll be using the first three to four pages of your journal for exercises in the next chapter. Label the top of the fifth page "The Great Left/Right Brain Debate." Create two columns by drawing a line down the middle. Give the left side to the Left Brain and the right to the Right. Begin by listing all the arguments your left brain is famous for when it encounters an objectionable right-brain suggestion. Then create the same list for the right brain. Be creative and let everything come out.

2. Add to your right-brain list the responses of the natural right brain (non-competitive, spatial, symbolic). If you already have some listed in exercise number one, circle or highlight them.

3. Write down how *whole* brain thinking will assist your daily activities.

3. DOESN'T THIS STUFF MAKE YOU WEIRD?

Some people are afraid that intuition will make them crazy. They worry they'll end up talking to themselves, seeing things that don't exist, making bad things happen, or being seen by associates as weird. In fact, I encountered so much of this in the late 1970s and early 1980s that I started calling it "The Clark Kent Syndrome." At parties or professional gatherings, as soon as people knew of my interest, any number of them would find me, ask me to step aside, and in a hushed voice confess an interesting intuitive experience. Their descriptions were always so enthusiastic that I came to believe many supermen

> *For the goal is always psychic totality, the ideal solution in which at least three of the four functions and both reaction [attitudes] types are made as conscious and available as possible.*
>
> JOLANDE JACOBI

and superwomen in consciousness were dressed inside street clothes and waiting, just like Clark Kent, for the moment when their inner selves were needed and could safely appear. In response to their fear, I often introduced them to the thoughts of C. G. Jung, the psychologist who provides us with the second way of understanding intuition: The Psychological Model.

Unlike his mentor, Sigmund Freud, Jung did not believe intuition, religion, or transcendent experiences were due primarily to compensatory behavior for psychic loss, e.g., loss of the safety of the womb, the protection of the father, etc. In fact, Jung listed intuiting as one of the four primary ways human beings process reality. He placed intuiting and the other three modalities—sensing, thinking, and feeling—on an equal armed cross (see diagram on page 20) to show how these functions interact.[5] Notice that Jung places intuition and sensate on opposite ends of the vertical axis, and thinking and feeling on the opposite ends of the horizontal axis.[5]

For Jung, sensing and intuiting belonged on the same axis because *both* methods of perception directly apprehend something rather than using thought (thinking function) or feeling (feeling function) to judge and evaluate it. The sensate uses his or her body to apprehend; the intuitive uses his or her psyche to discern what is so. Jung also noted that for most people the four functions were not balanced. People tended to have

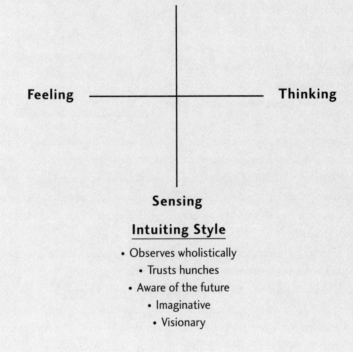

Four Ways of Understanding Intuition

Psychologically Centered Model: Carl Jung

Intuiting

Feeling —————————— **Thinking**

Sensing

Intuiting Style

- Observes wholistically
- Trusts hunches
- Aware of the future
- Imaginative
- Visionary

a favorite function and its opposite, a "shadow" function which they didn't use or understand very well. The shadow function is key to understanding people's fear of weirdness surrounding the intuitive process.

For example, if you are a strong sensate and your intuiting perception is *underdeveloped,* you base your life on concrete reality, dismissing subtle realities such as intuition. On the other hand, if you *overdevelop* your intuitive style, you dismiss the physical world, always looking "through" it for deeper meaning. A perfect example of this is the mystic who is so absorbed in the ephemeral world that he or she cannot function in the day-to-day world and, therefore, often earns the label "weird." Jung's warnings about distancing oneself from the physical world are important; your readiness to explore intuition must be based on the desire for *greater* intimacy with the physical world rather than less. This intimacy is based on heart-to-heart connections and the desire to reconnect with an inner natural rhythm.

> *Intuition is the outcome of the fusion of a purified heart and illumined intelligence.*
>
> SWAMI RAMDAS

Jung also warned that an overdeveloped intuitive can get mesmerized by visions, using them to promote personal ego rather than the common good. This ego-centric behavior leads to people's fear that through trusting intuition they could become a "crack pot" or be influenced by a Jim Jones–type cultist. If you accept for the moment that intuition connects you with all things, you realize that everyone's role in life is equally important. We'll all benefit from you pursuing your unique life path. When you live from that authentic source, you have an internal fire and presence greater than any egotistical behavior can provide. You recognize yourself and, in turn, are recognized. Intuition welcomes you with assistance, synchronicities, and creativity.

Although Jung's professional writings are vague on his precise meaning of intuition,[6] his autobiography, *Memories, Dreams, Reflections,* is replete with intuitive experiences. Jung describes visits from visionary guides, synchronistic events, and telepathic experiences. These stories of his personal experiences combined with this scholarship and work with clients suggest why Jung understood the challenges inherent to the intuitive journey so well. While the ideas that people might "lose their minds" or follow "weirdos" if they use intuition are not new, Jung's model goes one step beyond because it provides a map for avoiding the pitfalls. The key word is *balance.* If the intuitive enjoys physical reality while integrating the thinking (judging) and feeling (evaluating) functions, he or she will operate with clear, detached judgment and moral imperatives. All four functions are balanced and then, according to Jung, he or she "can render exceptional service as the initiator or promoter of new enterprises."[7]

If you find yourself wondering whether you are becoming "weird,"

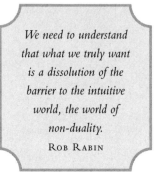

We need to understand that what we truly want is a dissolution of the barrier to the intuitive world, the world of non-duality.

ROB RABIN

check Jung's four functions for balance, paying particularly attention to the sensate function. Ask yourself, "Am I respecting physical reality enough and exercising thinking and feeling about what's happening?" Take confidence in your developing abilities: remember that Jung's model teaches us that (1) intuition is a prime way in which many individuals process the world; (2) the intuitive style often has an underdeveloped sensate or body-based style (the shadow function); and (3) balanced intuitives can bring great things into the world.

Exercise: The Psychologically Centered Model: Carl G. Jung's Four Functions

1. Label the next section of your journal "Intuitive Function." List the ways in which intuition has helped you in the past.

2. On a scale of 1 to 10, where ten is a lot and 1 is a little, rate how sensate you are (you experience knowledge coming through your body without thought).

3. Then, using the same scale, how intuitive are you? Are the numbers balanced?

4. Practice integration by going for a walk and letting your conscious intuition guide you.

4. WHAT IS THE DIFFERENCE BETWEEN PSYCHIC AND INTUITIVE EVENTS?

Last Monday night I had a dream that my former husband had been diagnosed with a serious illness. When he surprised me with a call on Tuesday, I told him about my dream. He lis-

tened quietly while I recalled my
dream but said nothing. Yesterday,
a week later, he called to tell me
that, although he didn't tell me
the full story Tuesday, he wanted
me to know that a few days before his call he had been diagnosed as HIV positive. My dream
was accurate.

> *If the doors of perception
> were cleansed, everything
> would appear to man
> as it is—Infinite.*
>
> WILLIAM BLAKE

This true story comes from Mary, one of my students. What is your opinion of it? Did Mary have a psychic or an intuitive experience? The working answer to this question rests in Mary's understanding and use of her experience. If it was strictly a psychic experience, Mary would remain an observer of the event, reporting it as a phenomena, a curiosity, or an oddity. In the philosopher Martin Buber's terms, the experience would remain an "it" to study, control, explain, or simply observe. But since Mary processed this experience from a broader intuitive perspective, the psychic components of her experience are set in the context of the inner communion and reinforce the lasting connection she has with her former husband.

Intuition activates a deep encounter with what Buber described as a "thou" experience and often catalyzes transformation in all of the participants involved. Put briefly, psychic experiences are frequently seen as special or apart from ordinary experience, while, if the very same experience (1) is processed as part of the continuum of direct knowing; (2) serves the growth of the wise self; and (3) propels one into more creative and inclusive behavior, intuition is at work. To explore why this is so, let's look at the third way of understanding intuition: The Religious Model: The Ancient Chakra System.

While the modern world begins its exploration of intuition through science and psychology, the ancient systems found in Eastern traditions have long recognized the existence of subtle realms, intuition, and psychic phenomena. The physical and psychological components of people, according to these philosophies, are only part of human makeup. A fully developed human being is actualized on many subtle levels beyond these and understands that the body also circulates "qi," a powerful finer energy that has been the foundation of acupuncture for thousands of years. Most systems depict seven or more levels of human awareness through which finer energies gather and flow. Taken together, these levels are the foun-

FOUR WAYS OF UNDERSTANDING INTUITION

The Religious-Centered Model: The Chakra System

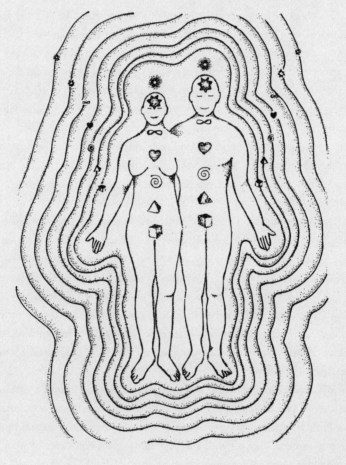

dation for the chakra system, a collection of seven "wheels" of awareness which surround and co-habitate your body.[8]

Name (Symbol)	Location Along Back	Values
1. Root Chakra (Cube)	Base of torso	Survival
2. Sacral Center (Pyramid)	Just above pubic bone	Sexuality Reproduction Sensuality
3. **Solar Plexus (Spiral)**	Just below belly button	Emotions Vitality Power
4. Heart Chakra (Heart)	Center of chest	Compassion Love Empathy
5. Throat Chakra (Infinity)	Lower throat area	Creativity Actualization
6. **Eye (Radiant Star)**	Center of head Just above eyes	Intuition Illumination
7. Crown Chakra (Sun Burst)	Top of head	Oneness Universality Pure Essence

Each of these levels, as you may have guessed, is indicative of a state of consciousness or awareness. Higher states of awareness are the result of ethical and spiritual unfoldment, and, according to these traditions, these states often produce psychic and intuitive experiences. Although intuitive information can be found at every level, the two levels associated the most with these experiences—Solar Plexus Chakra (emotions) and the Third Eye (wisdom)—highlight a working difference between psychic and intuitive experiences.

Modern anecdotal reports, as well as the research of parapsychologist

> *All these wheels are perpetually rotating, and into the hub or open mouth of each a force from the higher world is always flowing. . . . Without this inrush of energy the physical body could not exist.*
>
> LEADBEATER

Sybo Scouten and others and the lore of ordinary people, support the ancient idea that strong emotions, a third chakra phenomenon, play a role in conveying non-rational knowledge. Therefore, it is not surprising that spontaneous psychic experiences occur most often between people with emotional bonds (as in Mary's story), during highly charged emotional events such as danger, death, victory, etc., and in an atmosphere of emotional tension. These occurrences are often so dramatic that people often react in one of two ways: either forgetting the experiences quickly because they don't have a model for integrating them into their lives, or getting hooked on the experiences themselves. The latter is such a problem that, in Eastern traditions, students are warned not to give emotionally laden, psychic experiences too much importance even if they are precisely accurate. Students are to view these experiences as a *by-product* of development and not the purpose for it. This warning is similar to Jung's concern that the intuitive may get lost in inner ephemeral or imaginary life.

There is cause for concern. While working at JFK University, I saw how psychic experiences, without a psychological and/or spiritual context, can literally throw a few individuals off balance and become preoccupations, if not obsessions. For example, some people became mesmerized by their experience(s), reliving it over and over either in their minds or by compulsively telling people about it. Others thought that psychic experiences implied that they were special or chosen by God; a few people believed the experiences were connected to the devil. People who had a precognition about something bad which later happened often felt they were responsible for the event or could have stopped it. Those individuals who had very strong reactions in these directions needed clinical care. Most people simply had a lot of questions and were afraid they'd be seen as crazy if they told others of their experience(s).

Cynthia Seigel, my fellow professor, and I created some guide questions for people to ask themselves to make sure they were keeping these experiences in perspective. They are:

1. Is your social life alive and well?

2. Are you functioning effectively in the world?

3. Are your eating and sleeping habits normal?

4. Do you have friends to discuss your experiences with?

5. Are you working with your experiences or are they "working you"?

6. Are you being pulled by polarities, e.g., feeling blessed versus being cursed, or super powerful (causing things to happen to others or self) versus feeling powerless?

7. Are you worried you are "going crazy"?

The first four questions, which we hoped people could answer "yes," help assess if you are staying balanced. If people answered "no" to these questions and/or responded "yes" to the last three, we recommended they seek therapeutic care. Seeking help when you need it is a sign of health. Remember that intuitive and psychic development need to go hand-in-hand with psychological and character growth. Without this growth, you will not be able to take full advantage of your wisdom.

Before we go on, take note of this important point: psychic experiences can be the *limits* of someone's understanding, while intuitive experiences *include* psychic components. To see why, look at the seven chakras on page 25 and imagine them as awareness skills nestled inside each other. Starting from the inside, each level is bounded by its edge and includes the previous levels. For example, when just the Root chakra is awake, survival will be your focus. When your awareness extends to the Sacral chakra, the values of sexuality and sensuality will be *added* to survival. It continues on like that, so that when a person's awareness has reached the Solar Plexus chakra, psychic information tends to be used directly or indirectly for vi-

> Intuition training does
> not create a new set
> of abilities; instead,
> it identifies and
> reduces interferences . . .
> HELEN PALMER

tality, power, and control, as well as the values of the previous levels—sexuality, sensuality, and survival. Emotions rule the day, which is why many psychics, who are still working to develop above this chakra, can be known for manipulating their clients emotionally, faking their work, or creating emotional dependency.

In contrast, when you look at the diagram, you'll notice that by the time awareness reaches the Third Eye, the values of creativity, love, compassion, and empathy have already been added to all the others. The Third Eye—the dwelling place of intuition, illumination, wisdom, inspiration, transpersonal awareness, and "brightness upon brightness"—adds wisdom to the already potent mix. Here is the place where you turn your personal will over to divine will and the guidance of your soul, because the Third Eye sees the divine potential in everything. It is not that a person at this intuitive level does not have psychic experiences, but rather that he or she will automatically process psychic experiences in the context of love and wisdom.

In short, the Religious Model suggests the following working differences between psychic[9] and intuitive experiences: (1) psychic experiences are often based on emotional content or emotional connections and may be used without regard to higher values while (2) intuitive experiences are placed in the context of higher values and serve the good of the whole, not just the individual. They do not generate or promote manipulation, competition, and egotism. Wisdom is inherent to their existence. This is not to imply that you will not confront challenges to the wise use of your intuition but to establish unequivocally the appropriate intention and context for its development.[10]

Therefore, as I've suggested, the answer to whether to label Mary's dream of her former husband's diagnosis psychic or intuitive rests in your understanding of how Mary responds to her dream. You'd want to know if the experience went "in one ear and out the other" or if it caused her to reflect, enjoy, and enhance her relationships with her soul, her former

partner, and others. You'd also want to
know what intentions for her life have
arisen out of it, if any. The answers to
these questions would help you classify
Mary's experience.

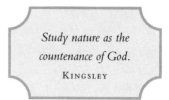

*Study nature as the
countenance of God.*
KINGSLEY

In summary, the Religious Model
also tells us that (1) human beings are comprised of more than physical
and psychological components; (2) seven (or more) subtle levels of existence are anchored in the body; (3) two of these levels are known for
non-rational knowledge; and (4) the power of this knowledge can distract
people from the task of spiritual unfoldment. The last one provides you
with a map for self-reflection on your journey. You want to avoid detours
into power, egotism, and manipulation.

Exercise: The Religious Model:
Seven Levels of Awareness

1. Label the next section in your journal "The Religious Model" and do
   the following:

2. Identify the wisest thing you have ever heard or seen. For example,
   a coach or teacher handling a difficult situation well, a spiritual
   story which demonstrates wisdom, a moment when you felt particularly wise. Using charades, act it out with friends. (If you are alone,
   you can do this by yourself.) When the game is over, name why the
   thing you picked was *wise* rather than just good.

3. You have smart emotions. Name a time when your emotions *were*
   correct, but your logic didn't believe it.

4. On a piece of paper, draw a ladder with seven rungs. Starting from
   the bottom, label each rung with a different level of awareness as
   found in the chakra system. Hang the picture where you can see it
   and imagine yourself climbing the ladder, developing your knowledge and wisdom as you go.

5. In the Big Picture,
What Purpose Does Intuition Serve?

Several years ago, a friend who used to be involved in psychical research and I had a heated discussion on the value of research on these topics. Glad to be out of the field, Julia suddenly shouted, "Who cares? Who cares if this experience is psychic or not?" I laughed hard because, although I am devoted to my field, I knew what she meant. Indeed, who does care? Why is intuition important? Even if the business executive gets a sudden flash of what to do, the parent recognizes what to reinforce in his or her child, the mystic brings us an image of Oneness, or the athlete makes a fabulous play, what does it all mean in the Big Picture?

Thus far, we've explored three important answers to this question— intuition helps develop whole brain thinking; it brings your four Jungian functions into balance; and it provides access to wisdom. While the first two reasons are derived from relatively modern systems (science and psychology,) the third, the chakra system, is an ancient teaching. Our fourth and final way of understanding intuition is also an ancient teaching: the Earth-centered philosophy of Indigenous people. It is here that we find an answer to our Big Picture question.

Earth-centered philosophies teach that intuitive knowledge of other people, things, plants, animals, etc., arises out of spirit-to-spirit communication and is not dependent on verbal or physical exchange. This soul-to-soul talk can happen because all events are occurring in the context of the Great Spirit, the source of the Big Picture. In short, intuitive wisdom is obtained by establishing a relationship with the soul of the whole and each of its parts. Your ability to participate consciously in this vast relationship web rests on one thing: evolving your spiritual presence.

The spiritual self is powerful; it facilitates and actualizes intuition. For example, medicine people connect intuitively with the spirits of the plants and herbs they harvest. This connection reveals how each plant may serve the health of their clients. Holy people take intuition a step further. They use intuitive power to help identify which of today's potential decisions and acts would be most beneficial to future life and which might be detrimental. Both uses of intuition can make an immense contribution to the Big Picture, healing and protecting life for future generations—human and otherwise.

> Dear God, Dear Stars,
> Dear Trees, Dear Sky,
> Dear Peoples. Dear
> Everything. Dear God.
> ALICE WALKER

The ability to achieve these things is based on constant intuitive communication with your own spirit and with the spirit in all life. Black Elk, a Holy Man of the Lakota (Sioux) tradition, expresses this core relationship with the Great Spirit as

> The first peace, which is the most important, is that which comes from within the souls of men when they realize their relationship, their oneness, with the universe and all its powers, and when they realize that at the center of the universe dwells *Wakan-Tanka* (the Great Spirit), and that this center is really everywhere, it is within each of us.[11]

Like Alice Walker's "Dear God, Dear stars, Dear trees, Dear sky, Dear peoples. Dear Everything. Dear God," Black Elk explains that this Big Picture includes everyone and everything, "the trees, the grasses, the rivers, the mountains, and all the four-legged animals, and the winged peoples." Relating to these things is not different from relating to the core of the self because the Great Spirit dwells in each of them as it dwells in each of us. From this perspective, information flows intuitively because *all* relationships are neither more nor less than spirit linking with spirit (see diagram on page 32). This is the reason why, in the American Indian tradition, all meetings, events, and ceremonies begin with a ceremonial greeting, honoring, and blessing phrase which means "All My Relations." Like the clear vision of the Third Eye, the divine in everything is first recognized, which in turn establishes the foundation for authentic relationships, harmony, balance, and the Good Red Road.[12]

In his book *Fools Crow: Wisdom and Power,* a Sioux Holy Man named Fools Crow describes making himself a "hollow bone" so that the Great

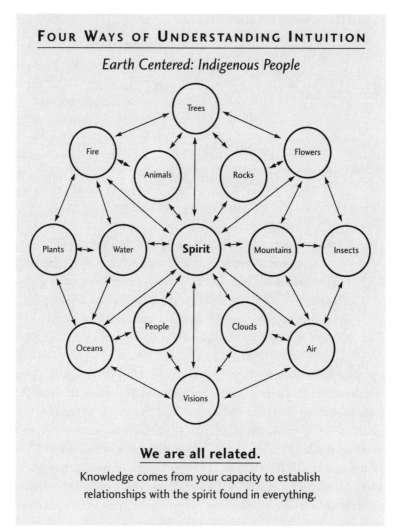

FOUR WAYS OF UNDERSTANDING INTUITION

Earth Centered: Indigenous People

We are all related.

Knowledge comes from your capacity to establish
relationships with the spirit found in everything.

Spirit, *Tunkashila* (Grandparent) and the Helpers can pour themselves
through in order to heal and help all human beings. Making oneself a
hollow bone activates the core relationship between one's spirit self
and the Great Spirit and provides access to inner knowledge. Although
Fools Crow recognized that "medicine and holy people work the hardest

to become clean," he believed that "everyone can become a bone to serve others."[13] The Lakota word for such human beings is translated "he or she who goes far beyond knowing."

Obviously, such people are intuitive. They teach us that pure intuition or knowledge can be obtained only by first purifying our spirits and connect-

> By whatsoever path you come to Me, I shall welcome you, for the paths men take from every side are Mine.
>
> LORD KRISHNA

ing at profound levels with other spirits. The cultivation of the power implicit in such relationships requires not only intense dedication and sacrifice but also profound respect for their right use. My Lakota father, Harry F. Byrd (I was adopted in 1987), frequently advises all of us to "not play around" with sacred prayers, ceremonies, and knowledge, but to unite head and heart with sincerity. As the Eastern traditions suggest, your task goes beyond knowledge and power to the development of the character and spiritual presence which are wise enough to contain them.

The ancient Earth-centered Model, exemplified by Native American traditions, emphasizes reverence for the Earth and Her teachings in their natural state. To the uneducated eye, people wearing eagle feathers, bear claws, or buffalo robes may look primitive, superstitious, or like people just dressed in costumes when, in fact, it is an honor to wear such sacred items. These individuals are striving, or have already earned the right, to unite intuitively with the wisdom found in the spirit of these animals. Although most of us have not been raised in the context of such a philosophy, your intuitive development will provide you an opportunity to establish some deeper connections with nature.

For example, one of my students kept having random, frequent, and seemingly intuitive encounters with skunks. She decided to explore what her relative, the skunk, was trying to teach her. The next time she encountered a skunk, instead of shying away, she sat very still, entered her inner self, and asked her relative what the lesson was. Deep within, something spoke to her saying, "It is time for you to learn how to protect yourself in a relatively harmless way." My student instantly recognized the

> A sacred relationship with you [all the Powers] is all that will be asked by this young man, that his generations to come will increase and live in a holy manner.
>
> BLACK ELK

importance of this lesson and thanked her skunk relative for its many appearances during the previous months. She immediately placed a picture of a cute skunk in her room, practiced with applying this lesson by drawing stronger boundaries around her home and family, and speaking up for herself more. She gave thanks for a new way of understanding her relationship with nature and, interestingly, her frequent encounters with skunks stopped as her ability to protect herself grew.

Although we explore this theme more thoroughly in Chapter Twelve, if you discover a tree, a spot in nature, or an animal which calls to your spirit before you get to that part of the book, work with it. Explore your intuitive connection by visiting your relative often and carefully observing everything during the encounter. Always ask yourself, "What am I learning?" "What am I offering?" "How am I thanking my spirit friend?" and "How does this relationship fit into the Big Picture of my life and all life?"

Earth-centered teachings emphasize that human beings are only one part of the web of life and are not the only creatures on Earth to seek transcendence. Other creatures have their ways of honoring the Creator of life, so uniting intuitively with animal and other nature spirits is another avenue to the Creator's wisdom. For example, Indigenous peoples believe that the spirit of the buffalo teaches two things: (1) profound kindness and an understanding of how to live harmoniously as a group and (2) how to face into a storm because, unlike cows who form a circle with their heads in the center and their rumps outward, buffalos greet a storm face first. To Native people, intuitively aligning oneself with the buffalo spirit is saying, "I want to practice kindness in community and learn to face difficulties head on."

From a Big Picture perspective, the belief that we are deeply connected with our animal, plant, and mineral relatives shifts our attitude toward them. For example, besides being a great physical loss, the slaughter of buffalo in the nineteenth century can be interpreted as eliminating one human opportunity to intuitively discover collective kindness and the capacity to face problems directly. Sadly, our modern world fosters the destruction of rain forests, the elimination of species, and the encroachment on, if not elimination of, Indigenous ways of wisdom. But when we have the Big Picture perspective that everything is spirit based and a participant in intuitive communication, we want to work in concert with all life so that today's decisions are wise in light of tomorrow's realities.

Key understandings of intuition from the Earth-centered Model are (1) we are all spirit, therefore related; (2) knowledge about each other is available through this spiritual connection; (3) this knowledge enhances our ability to heal and help others and ourselves; (4) we are all birthed from Mother Earth, and as part of her it is important to connect with Her and Her creatures; and (5) if we don't gain awareness, we may destroy the things that are designed to teach us what we want to learn.

Exercise: The Earth-centered Model: Indigenous Wisdom or The Wisdom of Indigenous People

1. Label the next section in your journal "The Earth-centered Model" and then record your responses to the following: Create a prayer for the nature that surrounds or the house plants which live in your home. Utter it.

2. Ask yourself, "Which animal in nature attracts me the most?" Assume the animal you selected has something unknown to teach you, something that you want to learn. Research your animal (if you can't observe it in the wild) even if you think you know everything. Look over what you have gathered. What is one quality which surprises you, and how does it contribute to your learning?

3. Take time to go to a beautiful place in nature. Breathe very slowly. Find a tree, stone, or spot. Sit still and commune with your chosen object. Do nothing but commune.

USING THE MODELS

I hope this chapter has answered your most pressing questions about intuition. In addition to learning that you can improve on your intuitive abilities, you now know you can:

1. Keep your logic from putting down your intuition by strengthening your right-brain skills until they are in balance with the left (the Science-centered Model).

2. Understand that intuition isn't weird by holding it in light of Jung's four natural psychological functions—intuiting, sensing, thinking, and feeling—and keeping these functions in balance (the Psychologically Centered Model).

3. Discriminate between what is psychic and what is intuitive by differentiating between emotionally based and wisdom-based experiences (the Religious Model).

4. Apprehend the purpose of intuition in the Big Picture by developing your relationship with your own spirit, which empowers you to intuitively connect spirit-to-spirit with all life (the Earth-centered Model).

One of these models will likely be most natural and comfortable for you to use as a framework for understanding intuition. Make that model the foundation for your intuitive development, and throughout this book return to it whenever you have questions. For example, if the Science-centered Model was the most comfortable for you, and if you are working with developing your intuitive body, you'd want to review your exploration from the perspective of enhancing your right-brain capacities. On the other hand, if your favorite model was Earth-centered, you'd do the same activities from the perspective of strengthening your spiritual ability to connect with other spirits. In the end, it doesn't matter which model you find most effective. They all lead to the same end: demystifying intuition while honoring its capacity to evolve your full physical, creative, psychological, and spiritual presence.

The journey you are about to embark on is worthy of life-long learning. Having accepted your soul's invitations to explore this new territory, you will always find something new to discover, something grand to dream about, and something simple to relish. And, like all good journeys, it is wise to prepare yourself before departing. This is the subject of the next chapter, "Preparation for Your Journey."

CHAPTER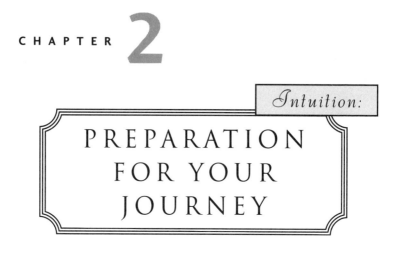

Intuition:

PREPARATION FOR YOUR JOURNEY

ECOLOGICAL INTUITION

I ntuition is ecological; it uses natural, clean, and respectful methods to communicate. Not being wasteful, it conveys layers of meaning with a few broad strokes and often delivers its powerful message in a few seconds. Because intuition is sustainable—its messages endure without creating harm—it has been part of the communication process in many cultures for centuries. Its methods have not changed in millennia.

Sometimes intuition uses words—the most conventional form of symbols—to communicate. For example, Colleen Mauro, now the editor of *Intuition Magazine,*[1] heard the words *"Call the Center for Applied Intuition"* clearly in her head when she was searching for a next step. Giacomo Puccini, author of the opera *Madame Butterfly,* claimed the work was dictated to him word-for-word by God.

Other times intuition uses non-verbal symbols or images to communicate.[2] A famous example of this comes from the Bible. Joseph, while imprisoned, was called to the Pharaoh's side to interpret a symbolic dream, one with seven fat cows and kernels of grain and seven very skinny ones. Joseph's interpretation of the intuitive dream—seven years of prosperity followed by seven years of famine—eventually elevated him to

second in command in Egypt, and re-
stored him to his family. Author Nancy
Rosanoff turned to her intuition when
her family dog's love of chasing the
neighbor's livestock was putting him in
danger. Her intuition kept giving her a
picture of a cow bell. Try as she might

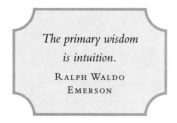

*The primary wisdom
is intuition.*
RALPH WALDO
EMERSON

it didn't make any sense. Her dog wasn't a cow and the livestock tended
to be chickens. Yet, the bell belonged in her country scene. Finally, she
realized that her intuition was not just giving her a symbolic answer (a bell
tolling death-knells for her pet); the answer was also literal. She bought
her dog a bell and hung it around his neck so that he couldn't catch anything. Intuition had "rung a safety bell" and averted the danger.

Whether or not intuition is using verbal or non-verbal cues, it is
never verbose. It always takes the shortest, easiest route to its target even
when the naked eye might judge its path to be irrelevant or meandering.
With practice, you'll learn to trust your intuition's verbal and non-verbal
intuitive messages and break any habits you have of dismissing them, becoming impatient with your InQ, or sabotaging your journey into expanded awareness.

Each of the following ten invitational chapters contains exercises designed to give you that practice. You'll be invited to practice developing
your intuitive body, experiment with non-linear time, cultivate your silence, and explore how intuition works in intimate settings. Although you
do not have to do all of the exercises in this book, *do not skip Your Guiding Image* and *Your Intuition To Do List* exercises. The former begins each
chapter; the latter ends each chapter. Together, these exercises establish
both a guiding non-verbal image for the entire chapter and an activity you
can do to apply the principles you've learned. Once you learn to establish
the images and words of intuition, your intuition uses them like shorthand, flashing a picture here and a word there. This saves you time and
energy. It is fascinating to watch how intuition efficiently and sometimes
humorously uses the potency of words and non-verbal images to convey
its message. To explore these two methods of communication, let's begin

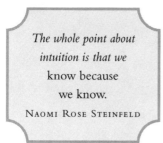

The whole point about
intuition is that we
know because
we know.

NAOMI ROSE STEINFELD

with words, the most common method of communication.

VERBAL INTUITION: WORDS

It was a lazy, sunlit afternoon and my mind drifted along on the cadence of my colleagues' voices rather than on the specific intuition topic our work group was supposed to be exploring. Suddenly business consultant Madeline Hughes pierced my trance, saying, "Someone told me once that using the sentence 'I don't know what to do' was a denial of spirit. I have retired this sentence from my vocabulary. I *do* know what to do somewhere inside. We all do."

She had hit the nail right on the head. The truth is, like Madeline, most of us spend time saying to ourselves and to others, "I don't know what to do," when we face changing employment conditions, unsatisfactory relationships, boredom, or other challenges. We expect our overworked logic to tell us what to do, when to do, how to do, and why to do. When logic fails us, rarely, if ever, do we retire the words "I don't know what to do" and enlist intuition's ability to access a deeper "I do know what to do" reality. Words can help us do that.

On the first night of my graduate school classes at JFK University in Orinda, California, I would usually hand out index cards and ask my students to write down the first word or phrase which came to mind, no matter how absurd it seemed. I encouraged the students to trust that their intuition knew what it was doing and that the meaning of the word they wrote would become apparent some time in the future. After they dated their cards and put them in white envelopes, I collected the envelopes and put them away. A month or more later—long enough so that most students had forgotten all about the word that was written on their first index card—I instructed them to write on another index card their instant response to the word "mission." I told them that I wanted their intuition, which already knew what was presently most important, to identify a word related to a good mission for their semester (it didn't have to be school related). When they were finished with this second index card, I handed out the envelopes with the original index cards and asked students to assess how the word(s) on their first card were related to the mission message they had just written. When they finished their personal evaluation, we discussed why they thought their intuition linked these two cards together.

> *The term intuition does not denote something contrary to reason, but something outside of the province of reason.*
>
> C. G. JUNG

During one of these discussions, a student told this story. She'd come to class completely preoccupied with a confrontation she'd just had with her eighteen-year-old daughter. She was angry and irritated, and therefore was somewhat surprised when she quickly responded to my directions by writing the word "freedom" three separate times and encircling each one with a heart. After contemplating the word for a few minutes, she began to associate it with her daughter. Her surprise turned to shock when I handed out the envelope containing her original index cards. The message on my student's original card read, "Discover a deer that is wounded. I see a brown leg that is broken and bleeding." She told the rest of the class, "At the time that I wrote this on the first card, I took it literally. I couldn't imagine finding a wounded wild animal. But when I reread those words tonight, I got the shivers all over. We have always referred to my daughter as a deer because of her large soft eyes." She went on to say how unhappy and rebellious her daughter's teenage years had been. The image of a wounded deer with the broken leg made her realize how much pain her daughter was experiencing. When she looked at the connection between the wounded deer and the word "freedom" encircled by a heart, she realized that her intuition was describing her present mission clearly. It was time to recognize her daughter's condition, help her in whatever way was appropriate, and *lovingly* set her free to be an adult.

This is a good example of intuition at work. It played with a nickname (deer) and provided an image which captured the deep currents of a present problem (the deer is wounded) so successfully that this parent was unable to identify what the phrase meant (she wondered if she'd meet

> *Intuition always has our best interest at heart.*
> CHRISTINA BALDWIN

a wild deer in the woods). The mother, who might have resisted seeing how wounded her daughter was, had no trouble seeing that the deer was going through the world broken and bleeding. She fully accepted this imaginary story with no judgment attached. This opened her to help her daughter, who synchronistically she argued with before the second index card class (the need for the mission was made apparent before the guidance was given,) and freed her own clear, loving path as a parent in this situation.

The reasons for three rather than one heart remain to be seen. Perhaps this mother would need to launch her daughter in three different ways, at three different times, or involve three different family members. Although you may not always understand everything intuition is telling you, this example demonstrates how a few words written on some index cards can suggest a whole healing story and display intuition's ecological nature.

PUTTING WORDS TO WORK

Your Intuition To Do List exercises get intuition working for you. In these exercises, you'll complete sentences by spontaneously listing things that you already know to do. For example, you'll complete the sentence, "Because my soul or best self wants to prepare me for expanded awareness, I already know to . . ." by rapidly listing the first five to ten activities which come to your mind. You can list anything with this one proviso: *keep them simple and do-able.* In the case of this example (expanded awareness), you might list:

- Stretch my mind with unusual ideas.

- Read inspirational stories.

- Play basketball.

- Listen to my favorite music.

- Plan a fabulous vacation.

- Set aside my preconceived ideas.

- Go for walks.

It's always with excitement that I wake up in the morning wondering what my intuitor will toss up to me like gifts from the sea.

JONAS SALK

Notice that this list contains both external and internal activities. Both are relevant and do-able. The activities themselves do not have to be intuitive, or, at the other extreme, they do not have to make logical sense. If you believe your lists are primarily coming from your cognitive mind, don't worry about it. It's O.K.

Your next task is to look over the list you've generated and, using a criteria I'll provide, highlight one particular activity. If you'd created the list above, for example, I might ask you to highlight the activity which appears most *expansive* for you, and then suggest you DO the activity you highlighted. It is essential to DO what you chose because action moves intuition from the ephemeral world of potential to the world of power and presence. When something is present, you can evaluate the power of its impact. Fortunately, you can't lose by following intuition's advice because, even if the impact of your choice seems minimal, your actions exercise your intuition's muscles and invest in the learning process.

In the beginning, many people find that their familiarity with language tends to keep them from letting intuition burst through. It may take several chapters of To Do Lists before you experience your intuition flowing freely. Don't be discouraged. Remember: although verbal language is rule based and logical, words themselves are symbols. Intuition always knows how to work with symbols, so once you've expanded beyond the edges of your familiarity, verbal language is a rich communication medium for intuition.

It is time for you to practice with your first Intuition To Do List ex-

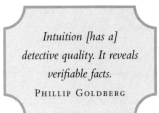

Intuition [has a] detective quality. It reveals verifiable facts.
PHILLIP GOLDBERG

ercise. It covers a lot of territory; you'll complete sentences on everything from healing to dreaming.

Exercise:
Your Intuition To Do List

1. Turn to the *third* page of your Intuition Journal (you'll be using the first page for Your Image Vocabulary) and label it "Chapter Two: My Intuition To Do List."

2. Sit quietly for a few seconds and internally ask your intuition to guide your responses. Do not make this request elaborate. Imagine you're simply asking a friend for assistance.

3. Write the incomplete sentence provided below in your journal.

4. Read through the following list of phrases and rapidly complete those sentences whose words come easily. Skip any phrases which take a long time. Write the sentences which come easily in your journal as you go (they will be listed first). This provides a record of your most automatic response. Your intuition is unique; therefore, the order of your list will be.

5. When you finish your first pass through the sentences and have written them all down, begin again at the beginning, completing the sentences you skipped as best you can. If nothing comes to you for a sentence or two, leave them blank. Don't force anything.

Example: *Sentence Completion:*

"Because I accept my soul is guiding my intuitive development, I already know to . . .

- believe . . . *more fully in my dreams.*

Sentence Completion:

"Because I accept my soul is guiding my intuitive development I already know to . . .

> *Intuitions are the reward of ancient gropings.*
> STEPHEN MACKENNA

- act on . . .

- feel more passion about . . .

- heal my relationship with . . .

- believe more in . . .

- complete . . .

- create . . .

- have fun doing . . .

- invest in . . .

- relax about . . .

- be more intimate with . . .

- plan for . . .

- give to . . .

- explore . . .

- develop community with . . .

- pursue my dream of . . .

6. When you've completed your sentences, look them over and high-light the choice that *attracts* you the most right now.

7. Choose a date, time, and place to make this choice an actual activity and then, upon its completion, record what you did, any reactions to it, and what it means to you in your Intuition Journal.

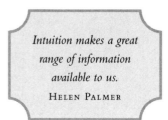

Intuition makes a great range of information available to us.
HELEN PALMER

Now that you've seen how intuition puts words to work, and you've applied it in one exercise, let's explore how intuition communicates with non-verbal images.

NON-VERBAL INTUITION: IMAGES

Frank, a participant in one of my workshops, was discouraged about his marriage. He and his wife were barely communicating, and life had become superficial and flat. Divorce was dominating his thoughts, so he decided to focus on this topic during one of our healing exercises. Everyone was directed to go into the depths of himself or herself and enter a chamber of silence to the best of his or her ability. Because our souls already know our needs, participants were advised not to "ask" their souls for help. All they needed to do was enjoy sitting in silence for ten minutes and pay attention to any vivid sensations they experienced.

As Frank was returning his attention to the room, a quick, sharp inner image of his wife and he sitting in front of a fire burst into his consciousness. He acted on this inner invitation immediately and built a fire in their fireplace that evening. When his wife came in, he suggested they send out for food and sit in front of the fireplace. At first she was cautious but eventually warmed up, and for the first time in years they began a deep dialogue about their problems, the purpose of their life together, and what they truly wanted. They tentatively explored returning the "fire of love" to their marriage rather than let it slowly "go up in smoke." Of course, this one intuitive experience did not imply that all of this couple's difficulties were healed. Rather, an opportunity for authentic presence, a bridge to their deeper selves, was co-created.

This story is typical of ecologically sound, non-verbal intuition. The single image of fire, a wonderful addition to Frank's image vocabulary, operated on many levels. For example, it operated inside Frank; nothing would have happened if Frank hadn't acted, but enough of an internal "fire" had been lit to renew hope. The word "fire" also operated externally; he built a fire in the fireplace. In addition, the image had depth to it, conveying traditional "positive" meanings such as passion, heat, warmth, light, and protection as well as the more "negative" meanings such as purification, change, and destruction. It was important for

> *Symbols . . . are not merely means of communicating truth, they are embodiments of reality itself.*
>
> IRA PROGOFF

Frank to hold the full spectrum of possibilities in his mind as he talked with his wife about their future.

As you build your image vocabulary, know that, contrary to the promises many books on intuition suggest, intuition is not a panacea or pill we acquire to solve all of life's dilemmas. It is, however, a potent ally for the acquisition of wisdom. In this case, Frank wanted wisdom to cast light on the parts of his relationship that needed healing, passion, and destruction in order for the whole to go forward successfully. Frank's decision to act on his intuition was courageous because it revealed his willingness to learn from the vocabulary of his deepest resource. When Frank placed the fire image in his Intuition Journal, he took the first step in developing a definition of what his own unique intuition meant by fire images. Eventually, he would have no question of its meaning or validity.

Images are unique because, although they have many interpretations, they can be "left alone" to do the work. Sometimes the results are so astounding that a single image appears to be a beacon which calls you toward your future. An example of this comes from an exercise I use in my workshops called "A Logo for Your Future Life."

> *The new then came to them out of obscure possibilities; they accepted it and developed further by means of it.*
>
> C. G. Jung

Logos are very powerful images. Most people recognize these images instantly. When these images were first introduced, words or products accompanied the presentation. After a time, the words or products were no longer necessary; the images themselves began to convey facts and evoke attitudes about the companies they represented. For example, in one intuition training group, people identified the apple symbol with friendliness and humor, the RCA dog with basic family values, and the United Way logo with humanitarian efforts. But while logos can be effective communication tools, they don't last forever because companies, like people, change. When a company's change is profound enough, it creates a new logo to reflect who the company has become.

Look at the difference between AT&T's old logo on the left, and the new one on the right.

The old logo tells us that AT&T rang our bell and called us. The old bell was placed inside an enclosed circle while the new logo is itself a circle—an open one which tells us that AT&T is no longer contained. It is open and unlimited. The shadow reminds some people of the sun falling on the Earth, and for these reasons the company can be associated with the entire Earth. How amazing: a company's major philosophical and corporate changes can all be conveyed without a single word. A "Logo for Your Future Life" exercise on page 50 utilizes this concept of the changing logo.

Following my directions, my daughter Chris created this image below by first drawing a logo which represented her present life on the left-hand side of a 11½ x 8 piece of paper, and then a second logo, which represented her desired future, on the right. When both logos were finished, I had her draw a large arrow, which pointed to the future, between the present and future symbols. Finally, she drew a symbol which represented the transition between her present and future self un-

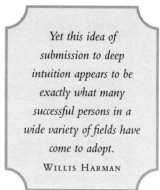

Yet this idea of submission to deep intuition appears to be exactly what many successful persons in a wide variety of fields have come to adopt.

WILLIS HARMAN

derneath the arrow, and, for fun, I asked her to write a date by which the future logo would be active.

Let's look at the specifics of Chris's example which she drew on August 17, 1996. She had been struggling with an unsatisfactory employment situation for three years. She desperately wanted a transfer, but her present boss didn't want to lose her. The logo on the left shows that the

> The soul is capable of
> knowing all things in
> her highest power.
>
> MEISTER ECKHART

life Chris wanted, symbolized by the plant, could only be looked at through a window. Notice how the plant appears to have no roots. It is an in-the-sky type of dream, disconnected and ungrounded. In contrast, her future logo depicted the same plant now rooted, potted, and growing. The plant came "inside" as the window had completely disappeared. With this image, her intuition had hinted that her desired future was quite accessible. Her transition symbol was depicted as wavy lines which started as choppy turbulence and became calm. Chris interpreted this to indicate a gradual transition which would have a rough beginning but would ultimately go smoothly. Notice the happy face sun which shines between the transition and the future, the word "relieved," and her projected date of 2/15/97.

After many stops and starts, Chris's desired transfer was obtained on 1/1/97, six weeks ahead of the 2/15/97 schedule her intuition had predicted in August 1996. It is interesting to note that the fifth wave down (two before things begin to smooth out) has been drawn through several times. In real life, Chris received a transfer which permitted her to move before Christmas, but then it was "scratched out" and she had to wait until after the holiday.

Following this experience, plants, particularly trees and this looks like a small one, became a major part of Chris's image vocabulary. You, too, can create a logo for your future and watch how intuition helps you unfold its meaning.

Exercise: A Logo for Your Future Life

1. Turn the *third* page of your journal sideways and write the date and the title of this exercise at the top.

2. Draw a logo for your present life on the left-hand side of the page. Your symbol can be as simple or detailed as you like. Relax and don't focus too hard. Your symbol is for you only. It can't be wrong or not good enough.

3. Ponder on a future you'd like your intuition to help you attain. Focus on something which is possible. Then draw a symbol which represents it on the right-hand side of the same page. Do not add written words to your picture.

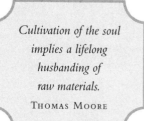

Cultivation of the soul implies a lifelong husbanding of raw materials.
THOMAS MOORE

4. When both sides are completed, sketch a large arrow, which points to the future, between the present and future symbols. Underneath the arrow, draw a symbol which represents the transition between your present and future self.

5. Above the right-hand logo, write a date in the future when you think this logo will be relevant.

6. Pin the sheet of paper somewhere that you will see it. Then put it out of your conscious mind.

I tell my students, "Even if the date you've written on your future logo comes and goes without your goal being obtained, know now that something important about your logo will be illuminated for you by the time your intuition training course is complete." I can say this with confidence because over the years I've watched hundreds of students experience the effect of images. This is why you'll work with them in each chapter.

YOUR IMAGE VOCABULARY

Intuitive images can have wide-ranging impact. For example, the inventor Elias Howe once had a dream in which he noticed something odd about the spears some warriors were carrying past him. The tip of each spear had a hole drilled in at the end. Eureka! This dream image told Howe to "put the eye of a sewing machine needle at its tip," and thus the

> A person is neither a thing nor a process, but an opening or clearing through which the absolute can manifest.
>
> KEN WILBER

machine which would clothe the world was born. Dozing chemist Fredrich August von Keule watched in fascination as a visionary snake with its tail in its mouth flashed before him, revealing to him the nature of the Benzine ring. As a result, the study of organic chemistry leaped forward. These imaginary spears and snakes altered the world for millions of people.

The power to alter your personal world or a larger world is inherent to intuitive images. You can tap that power by being proactive with images. You don't have to wait until your intuition presents an informational image to you; you can use images to communicate to your intuition. To do this you will be creating what I call an Image Vocabulary. This vocabulary, which you will be creating with magazine images, is like shorthand between you and your intuition. It sends powerful messages. For example, Verna, curious about intuition, decided to join a year-long intuition training program I was conducting. She had no particular objective and was shocked by the life-size image of herself she envisioned and drew during the first session. Power radiated from the figure, which was crowned by a huge headdress of snakes.

"What does it mean to you, Verna?" I asked, because symbols are interpreted best by the person using them.

"Knowledge," she answered without a moment's hesitation.

Many months passed. Verna, whose personal life had gone through substantial change, sat down in one of our class sessions surrounded by magazines, scissors, poster board, and glue. Her assignment was to create a collage which represented her next step in life. Appropriately, she found a picture of a woman's face crowned by snakes and pasted it on the bottom part of a piece of poster board.[3] Above that, Verna pasted a picture of a lovely woman holding aloft a heart and circle. The woman appeared to be rising out of the snake headdress, much as Athena rose out of Zeus's head. Smaller images of women praying, emerging out of a cyberspace-type grid, and riding a winged Pegasus surrounded the figure. Key words accompanying the towering column were: mind, heart, brain, wide open, and goddess.

Verna then told the class that years earlier, fascinated by the meaning of knowledge, she had spent hours doing library research, meditating on knowledge, and even developing a book manuscript. Because she believed there was no financial payoff, she had abandoned this passion in order to run a business and take care of her husband. But during our exercise, these images had called to her from the well of her abandoned passion, and she could no longer ignore her destiny. It comforted her to realize the images represented an intuitive dialogue between herself and her soul. Encouraged by this communication, she opened, trusted, and dedicated herself. Within two years, her first business book, *The Knowledge Evolution,* was published. Verna's intuition, a central player in the whole affair, had helped her actualize a hidden dream.

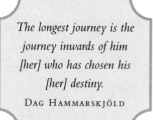

The longest journey is the journey inwards of him [her] who has chosen his [her] destiny.

DAG HAMMARSKJÖLD

To begin creating your Image Vocabulary, surround yourself as Verna did with a wide variety of magazines. If you are doing this exercise in a group context, you can pool the magazines together so everyone can select from any of them. You'll also need a 9 x 12 manila envelope to hold your images, some glue or paste, and a pair of scissors. Many people enjoy playing music in the background. Now, put your mind on hold and cut out thirty or more images from the pages of the magazines. Think about the long-term appeal of these images, asking yourself, "Will I still want this image ten weeks from now?" Base your choices on the following three categories: passion, purpose, and power.

Categories:

1. Passion: These are images you love. They capture your imagination; they make you smile; they offer inspiration; or they simply attract you for unknown reasons.

2. Purpose: These images evoke a sense of accomplishment in you. They may remind you of something you want to do; they may provide a sense of direction; or they may capture action.

3. Power: These images depict power. Power images can come from nature, the accomplishments of humanity, or abstract ideas. The important point is that the images empower you. Imagine yourself harnessing this power to achieve your passion and purpose.

You don't have to balance the three categories, 10-10-10, but make sure you have some representation from each of them. As you select your images, write the word they are associated with (passion, purpose, or power) on the back. When you have at least thirty images, lay them out in front of you, pick your favorite twenty, and put those pictures in the manila envelope. Label the envelope "My Image Vocabulary" and keep it with your Intuition Journal. Eventually, without looking in your envelope, you will select a total of eleven images—one for each of the ten invitations and one for your overall work with intuition.

Your soul, knowing the purpose of your journey, guides you safely from one stage of development to the next like an inner North Star. It has an overall perspective and can, therefore, suggest directions for intuitive growth, healing, and accomplishment. The image you select now will represent this overall guiding perspective. It is like the cover of a book which attracts your attention and hints at what's inside.

Exercise: Your Overall Guiding Image for This Book

1. Turn to the *first* page of your Intuition Journal.

2. Without looking inside, reach into your Image Vocabulary envelope and pull out one of the twenty magazine clippings you placed within it. This is your guiding image.

3. Paste or tape your image onto the *first* page of your Intuition Journal.

4. Date the *second* page, and then write down the answers to these questions about your chosen image:

   A. *What do I love about this image? (Answer this regardless of what category the image comes from.)*
   B. *What purpose for my intuitive journey does this image suggest?*
   C. *How is it a source of strength or power for my development?*
   D. *What needs for healing does it reveal?*
   E. *How does it stimulate my potential accomplishments?*
   F. *If this image represents my soul talking to me about my intuitive journey, what is it saying?*
   G. *If this image represents me talking to my soul about my journey, what am I saying?*
   H. *Look at the label on the back of your image. What category does it represent (passion, purpose, or power)?*
   I. *Why is this category important to me at this time?*
   J. *Is there anything else I'd like to note about this image?*

There are no right or wrong answers to these questions. They are designed to stimulate interactions with your image. Remember, images are as much a message to your intuition from you as they are the reverse. Intuition spoke to Frank with a fire image, while Frank's willingness to follow intuitive guidance communicated to his intuition, "I got the message." Likewise, Verna's spontaneous drawing of a snake headdress was a clear intuitive message, while her conscious, deliberate selection and placement of the snake headdress at the base of her collage signaled to her intuition, "I am ready to go forward."

Thus, the dialogue between intuition and self proceeds. It is important to acknowledge this two-way conversation throughout this work and throughout your life. Those who do not do so are forced to wait passively for intuition's magic instead of utilizing proactive conversations with intuition to unleash the genie within and reveal an exquisite strategic planner: the soul. As I'm fond of saying, "Images are the strategic plans of the individual or collective soul." They appear to establish an infrastructure for spiritual evolution and, although they lack the linearity of logically developed and verbalized strategic plans, they provide guidelines and stimulation for progress. Don't skip building your non-verbal vocabulary and its subsequent strategic plans; do your non-verbal Guiding Image exercises in addition to your verbal Intuition To Do List exercises.

Congratulations! You've just finished your preparations and are ready to begin the first invitation, "Just Say 'Yes.'" A favorite cartoon I use in my workshops suggests the intent behind this chapter: it depicts a startled man standing in the middle of his living room. He had obviously been sitting in an overstuffed chair reading the newspaper when a strange sight made him jump up and stare at a nearby wall. Sticking through the wall is an arm with a telephone in its hand and the caption reads, "I have a collect call for anyone in this dimension."

This is your situation. Intuition is calling you to a more meaningful life on an inner dimensional phone line. All you need do to answer its call is Just Say "Yes."

CHAPTER **3**

Invitation One:

JUST SAY "YES"

Turn on Your Intuition

You have an inviting soul. It does not demand that you turn on your intuition; it simply invites you to turn it on, to Just Say "Yes." This step is often overlooked. Many years ago when I began teaching intuition, I overlooked this step myself. Students and I would plunge directly into exercises and applications without ever stopping to make a formal commitment. We were like a ship without a deep keel or rudder: although our enthusiasm was genuine, our work together skimmed the surface of intuition's ocean. To dig deep, to mine intuition for its creativity, guidance, peace, and knowledge in every situation, it is wise to answer your inner call and consciously declare your intentions.

An example of doing so comes from the life of Dag Hammarskjöld, a highly respected figure in Swedish politics, a financially comfortable man, and a sought-after social companion. Hammarskjold had attained everything he wanted, but he inexplicably began to experience great inner restlessness. At first he treated these sensations through normal recourse, such as exercise, diet, sleep, etc. When they didn't go away, he sought medical help. That changed nothing. Next, he began psychological care. In spite of everything he did, the nagging restlessness and bur-

> The real valuable thing
> is intuition.
> ALBERT EINSTEIN

geoning depression did not go away. One night, when he was alone in his apartment, he abandoned himself to those pressures. In a flash, he recognized that something was calling him. He did not know what it was, why he was being called, or where he was being called to; he only felt the pressure of the call. Hammarskjold spontaneously turned on his intuition, crying out "Yes" to this other dimension caller. Over and over he chanted "Yes, Yes, Yes" into the quiet emptiness of his apartment.[1] His life subsequently took an unexpected turn, and Dag Hammarskjöld began his famous work at the United Nations.

This story captures the principles of saying "Yes" to intuition: (1) give up the need to know what, why, when, and where of a situation; (2) open your heart to the mysterious; (3) trust inner wisdom; and (4) respond to subsequent opportunities. Two things are important to note. The first is that after Hammarskjöld said "Yes," he had to stay open to subsequent opportunities *and* he had to affirm his "Yes" each time doubts assailed him. The second is that Hammarskjöld took these actions after he established a healing context for his experiences by caring for himself, obtaining allopathic opinions, and seeking psychological perspectives. Once his intellect had satisfied itself of the mystery, Hammarskjold invited his intuition in to heal and help.

This story teaches another important point—authentic intuition is not fainthearted, and it survives the time it takes you to check out other potential explanations. Once you have done so, you are free to turn on your intuition by selecting the image which represents two levels of your commitment: the "Yes" and the vow.

Exercise: Your Guiding Image for "Just Say 'Yes'"

1. Create a new section of your Intuition Journal and label it "Chapter Three: Just Say 'Yes.'"

2. Reach into your Image Vocabulary envelope and, without looking, pull out your guiding image for this chapter.

3. Paste this image on the first page of this chapter section.

4. Note which category it comes from on the bottom of this page.

> *To say "Yes" to life is at one and the same time to say "Yes" to oneself.*
> HARMON BRO

5. Jot down a few reasons why this is a good image for your "Yes" to your intuition.

6. When you've finished, look at the image and, silently or out loud, say "Yes" to your intuition. If you'd like, you can chant it over and over.

A "Yes" to intuition automatically implies a "Yes" to a bigger vista. A famous sixteenth-century wood cut, *The Vision of Ezekiel,* depicts our situation well. Ezekiel is seen crawling on his hands and knees from the world of material reality through the starry heavens into an infinite universe. We are like Ezekiel, and intuition is the starry night which mediates our passage to the infinite vistas of our souls. Sometimes those vistas surprise us as they did Tom with his routine job before success. Other times the vistas have more to do with inner peace than they do with outer activity. In any case, like Hammarskjöld, we are often invited to say "Yes" before we know fully what our souls have in mind.

Although most people are willing to say "Yes" to exploring intuition, when it comes to their vow many face the first challenge to developing intuition: hesitation. They protest saying things like, "I don't even know what I'm vowing to" or "I don't take vows easily." People are right. Most vows occur in the context of established relationships or well-thought-out commitments, but this is not true for intuition. At our present levels of understanding, mystery is part of intuition's nature; therefore, a commitment requires the courage necessary to face, explore, and trust the unknown. Your ability to do so will serve you well in today's rapidly changing world.

Another reason for people's hesitation is that most of us have been conditioned to believe that vows require giving up something or becom-

> *All great men are gifted with intuition. They know without reasoning or analysis what they need to know.*
>
> ALEXIS CARREL

ing more selfless. In the case of intuition, however, your vow invites intuition to be present; it dose not require logic or something else to be completely absent. Intuition is an addition, not a subtraction process.

Over the years, I have learned that it is wise for all of us to address any conscious or unconscious hesitations we have. You can do this by holding two healing conversations with your soul. The first conversation focuses on self-love—your passion for yourself—because without it you won't trust yourself enough to experiment fully with intuition. The second conversation utilizes prayer to activate your purpose. Purpose gets your life on target and funnels your intuition.

HEALING CONVERSATIONS WITH THE SOUL

Conversation #1: Self-Love

"We're all running around with inner bullet wounds and holes," a Native American healer I know used to express. When you work in the intuitive world as he does, these things become visible, and you recognize how deeply we all need healing. For one thing, most of us do not know how much we are loved. Spiritual literature is very clear about this. Whether we are One with Allah, whether we're not meant to suffer, or whether God sent His only Son for us, does not matter. It all adds up to the same thing: we are the beloved.

Too often, we are unaware of this love. The best exercise I've ever found to help people reconnect with it is "A Love Letter from the Soul." Approach your love letter as a long overdue conversation with your soul. To prepare for your letter, create an outline based on (1) what you admire about yourself; (2) what you think the soul loves about you; and (3) what areas of yourself need healing. Your love letter from the soul, which I suggest covers at least both sides of an 8½ x 11 sheet of paper, is then com-

posed by weaving together loving statements from all three categories. It is
relatively easy to formulate the soul's
message from the first two categories
(e.g., I admire your spontaneous nature
and love your dedication), while the
third requires more compassion for the

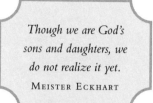

*Though we are God's
sons and daughters, we
do not realize it yet.*

MEISTER ECKHART

self. For example, a third category statement such as "I want to heal myself of self-criticism" becomes the soul saying, "I am gently sending you
loving self-regard every day." Or, "I'm afraid the people I love will leave
me" becomes "I, your faithful soul, will never abandon you. I am always
here."

Some people are so ready for this love letter that they can write two
or more pages without an outline. Others find it so difficult that I suggest
they base their outline on the lives of people they love or admire. If you
find yourself procrastinating, getting interrupted, or at a loss when you
are approaching this activity, recognize how important it is for you. Do
your best to both acknowledge your resistance and then *do* the task. You
won't regret it.

Exercise: A Love Letter from the Soul

1. Title the next page in your journal "Love Letter Outline" and create
   your outline as described above.

2. Write a love letter to yourself based on your outline and as if it were
   coming from your soul.

3. THIS STEP IS ESSENTIAL. After the letter is written, read it onto an
   audiotape cassette addressing yourself by name frequently. You can
   play favorite music in the background if you wish. *Listen to your love
   letter from your soul at least three times a week.*

4. Record responses to this exercise in your journal.

There are a variety of ways people record this letter. Some read the
letter over and over again onto their tape so they have a continuous letter

> You do not make yourself
> love. You allow love
> to enter.
>
> JAMES REDFIELD

to listen to, while others finish their tape with soothing music. People have listened to their tape during commutes to work, while falling asleep at night, during dressing, cooking, exercising, or working on the computer. The letter works whether it has your full or partial attention because we rarely get a chance to hear our own voices loving us.

Your love letter brings you into alignment with your soul's love and cracks open a window to your unique passion and purpose in life. Inner wounds can prevent people from opening this window even to themselves. They distract themselves by doing what is required or maintaining ambivalence toward opportunities for their uniqueness to express itself. The soul doesn't want this; you are meant to shine. Healthy self-love promotes your radiance and fuels an intuition highway.

In addition, as you are working with your intuition, remember this principle: *intuition travels on love.* In the beginning I didn't get this. Like everyone else, I assumed Samuel Coleridge, Elias Howe, chemist Keule, and many others simply had more intuition than everyone else. Now I know that it is not the amount of intuition they had which generated their success as much as it was the depth of their passion. Intuitive success is often a naked testimonial to the intense and private love affair people have with their life and its purpose. This love gets to the soul of things where intuition reveals hidden knowledge. Remember this next hint: when you want more intuition about something, pour your passion, courtship, and love into it. When you do so, you are acting like the soul, for this is how the soul loves you. It knows your purpose.

Conservation #2: Morning Prayer and Purpose

The second healing conversation is based on prayer and focuses on purpose. I define prayer here as an ongoing conversation between oneself and Life (a force, a power, God, or your concept of an animating principle) and purpose as your calling. Although most people identify purpose with an activity in the world, I believe it is also deeply linked with the development of character or inner capacities. Conversational prayer helps people identify all aspects of purpose because it bridges the gap between the conscious self's sense of what might be true callings and the soul which knows them. In his book, *Higher Creativity,* Willis Harman says:

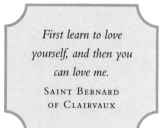

First learn to love yourself, and then you can love me.

SAINT BERNARD
OF CLAIRVAUX

> In institutionalized religions, prayer probably originated as a living exercise in affirmation, but degenerated to a ritual of supplication or penance directed toward some external being. Yet those whose devotion leads them to the true meaning beneath the outer form of their religion's prayers come to realize that it is not an external message system, but a dialogue between self and Self (Soul), a channel to the wisest of our inner personalities.

The requirement for this self-to-soul prayer is simple: just talk to the spark of life inside you. The resulting conversation is prayer. As author Neale Donald Walsch points out in the introduction to his book, *Conversations with God,* too often prayer is relegated to our childhood supplications of a parental God figure.[2] God as soul, friend, mentor, and daily companion waits in the wings of our maturation process. Eventually, we can convert activities such as thinking things over mentally, rehashing past images, or fantasizing about the future into conversations with the soul. For example, when a good friend and employer terminated his employment, Michael was left feeling wounded, adrift, and dispirited. He didn't know what to do next, and he rattled around his house talking to himself for weeks. All that talk, however, did not add up to one healing conversation with his soul. As Life would have it, my Lakota (Sioux) father, Harry F. Byrd, was visiting from Porcupine, South Dakota, at the time. Although Michael had only recently met *ate* (the Lakota word for father,

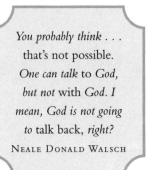

pronounced, *ah tay*), he decided to seek his wisdom and advice. True to the spirit of his beliefs, *ate* provided no answers but sent Michael further inside himself.

Get up early . . . before sunrise. Go to a high place and pray. Talk about your needs. Be open. Humble yourself. When you're finished and go home, don't forget what you have done. Trust, watch and you'll see. The answers will come.

Of course, Michael could not have known beforehand that *ate* is famous for saying, "A *sincere* [the word "sincere" is emphasized as he speaks] prayer is more powerful than an atomic bomb." In his opinion, one births life and the other destroys it. It certainly worked in Michael's case because, although he went up a hill on that morning lost, he came down confident of his direction, subsequently enrolled in school, and became a therapist. The point is that the answers to Michael's search lay within him, not in another human being. Morning prayer had tapped his inner wisdom and revealed a clear life path. Having seen the results of people's experience over the years, I always recommend this healing conversation to anyone who is struggling with an ill-defined sense of purpose or next step. I've found that even people who don't believe in a spiritual force by any name find it useful to rise before dawn, seek a high spot, and dialogue with their own spirit on the course of their life.

Exercise: Morning Prayer

1. Go to a high place before sunrise and have a conversation with your soul about your purpose (remember, your purpose doesn't have to be something you do).

2. Record what happened in your
journal.

Teach us to pray. [The only recorded request Jesus' disciples made of Him.]
THE BIBLE

These two healing conversations lay the foundation for your vow. They help eliminate the hesitations which can surface as people approach a deep commitment to intuition. You can also ask yourself the following three questions, which provide insight into the most common ways in which fear of intuition is masked.

The first is: *Am I waiting for a sign?* Waiting for a sign is a popular type of hesitation when intuition is urging you to make radical changes. For example, an executive I worked with had a lucrative and interesting job which, unfortunately, wasn't satisfying his lifelong desire to be an artist. Although his job was creative, it wasn't hands-on work. When faced with the option of cashing out some of his investments (which were considerable) in order to explore his inner longing, he hesitated. He was waiting for a sign that this was the "right" thing to do. He wanted to feel safe with such a big step. When I pressed him about what would have to happen to let him know he was "supposed" to leave, he suggested a few things such as making a lot of extra money in the stock market, finding a job as an artist (although he had no professional experience), or meeting the right people.

The truth is, safety in decision-making does not arrive from the outside. Whenever I find myself or my colleagues getting excited about the latest way intuition can be used to predict or nail down the future, I cringe. I think we are missing the point. The point is to become comfortable with your inner *knowing* and let that *knowing* interface with a vast network of fluid, interlacing probabilities. It is not about making something "out there" happen as much as letting "something in here" participate in evolving a life story you enjoy. In short, make a decision because your intuition is urging you to participate in a different story. With practice, you'll eventually learn to distinguish between waiting until everything, outside and inside, tells you you're ready, and waiting for an outside "sign" to tell you what to do.

> *Make up your mind to act decidedly and take the consequences. No good is ever done in this world by hesitation.*
>
> THOMAS HENRY HUXLEY

The second question to ask yourself is: *Am I being patient or passive?* Many years ago, when I was facing a big decision and waiting for "a sign" to guide me, a friend listened to me go back and forth for months and then finally asked, "Sharon, the question is, are you being patient or passive?" I knew instantly that I was being passive. I was afraid of what I knew to be true. I was scared to take a stand, to act. Also, at the time I didn't have the interior skills to own intuition as a centerpiece in my decision-making process. Subsequently, I have used this question both for myself and those with whom I work. Usually, a person knows instantly whether he or she is being *patient,* allowing things to unfold more before deciding, or *passive,* due to fear of deciding or taking a stand. Your answer to this question will help you distinguish between inner urging and outer signs.

The third question to ask is: *Am I afraid I'll look foolish if I follow my intuition?* Hesitation can be fueled by the fear of looking stupid, foolish, or flaky. The antidote to this fear is willingness. Willingness goes beyond merely allowing intuition to influence you; it takes you to enthusiasm for intuition. When you are an enthusiastic learner about intuition, fear of how others will judge you does not outweigh the potential gains of an intuitive life. You are willing to learn that your intuitive hunch about your business project was more wishful thinking than intuition. In fact, you look forward to distinguishing where the fine line between intuitive knowing and wishful dreaming is drawn. No person outside yourself can supply the answer to that inquiry.

Of course, sometimes intuition's suggestions operate very quickly and you have little or no time to evaluate whether or not you should respond. There is no time to even hesitate before the opportunity passes. Saying "Yes" and making a vow to your wise Self increases your chances of bypassing evaluation procedures, taking advantage of intuition's suggestions automatically, and never having to say, "I already knew to do that, but I didn't listen to myself."

MAKING YOUR VOW

Each person shapes their vow differently. For example, Karin Jansson, an artist, brought the picture below to a year-long study group I was facilitating. It symbolized her inner relationship with intuition and her contract to uphold her vow. Entitled *Integreation,* the piece suggested that Karin's intuition is both innocent (the deer) and powerful in its creativity (the strong hands of the musician).

> *Fear not. What is not real, never was and never will be. What is real, always was and cannot be destroyed.*
>
> BHAGAVAD-GITA

Although Karin was not certain if the group would receive her drawing as a legitimate vow, her courage in bringing this work and others to the group was rewarded. Years later she said:

> I gained so much from the intuition work. This was the first time I had a community, other than the general public or art school students, with whom I could share my deepest visions. Through their witness, the world of my artistic intuitions came alive.

> *For whereas the mind works in possibilities, the intuitions work in actualities, and what you intuitively desire, that is possible to you.*
>
> D. H. LAWRENCE

People have danced, drawn, sung, played, and read their vows. Your vow does not have to be fancy. For example, a different person in another group produced this simple vow:

I take thee, my best self, to be the
   true essence of me.
I will listen to you.
I will accept you.
I will love you.
I will honor you.
I will trust you.
For all of our life here on this physical plane as well as in the
   beyond, we will be friends, lovers, and companions
   through all our experiences. We will be together as one,
   one with the source of all things.

In yet another context, body worker Monica Hernandez created a beautiful vow which included these important points:

I vow to discover you and own you.
I vow to recognize you in my body.
I vow to wait for you knowing you are waiting for me.
I vow to not judge your signals.
I vow to look for you in times of doubt, confusion, and
   impatience.
I vow to look for you in times of joy, celebration, and peace.
I vow to let you lead me to the light, to the creator, to the
   source.

Some people have taken wedding vows and rewritten them from self to soul. Others have presented plays which include great mythical figures such as Father Sky and Mother Earth uniting. Of course, most of the vows I've observed have been delivered in a study group or conference context. You may be working alone. Alone or with others, your Intuition Journal will be a permanent witness for you.

Enlightenment was achieved with your first vow.
DOGEN

Exercise:
Your Vow to Intuition

1. Create and enact your vow.

2. In your journal, record the time, date, place, and details of your vow.

Commitments have impact. For one thing, your "Yes" and your vow shift the focus of your life from your physical appearance and personality (the first two ways of knowing, according to the sage Patanjali) to your purpose and soul. This shift has ramifications. New people, ones who nourish your purpose and soul as you do theirs, may enter your life. Or you may find yourself investing in making your present relationships more meaningful. Your career might shift, too, from one which satisfies your external appearance and personality to one which is also connected to your inner passion. Of course, the changes you experience could be only visible to yourself: a change in attitude, an increased practice of prayer, or inner peace. Regardless of what happens, you have now consciously invited intuition into your life. This act alone awakes more of your slumbering uniqueness or genius.

Final Exercise: Your Intuition To Do List

1. Complete the sentence: "Because I am accepting my soul's invitation to 'Just Say "Yes,"' I already know to . . ." List 5 to 10 things you know to do such as "call Aunt Donna," "write a poem about the music I heard last night," "invest in my car," "take a camping trip." When you've finished, read your list over, highlight the activity for which you have the most *enthusiasm*, and do it. Record everything in your journal.

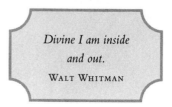

Divine I am inside and out.

WALT WHITMAN

2. Go back and look at your Guiding Image for this chapter. How does it symbolize your "Yes" to intuition or relate to your vow? What part of the Image hints at how to have conversations with a force greater than yourself, or pray for your intuitive development? Record in your journal.

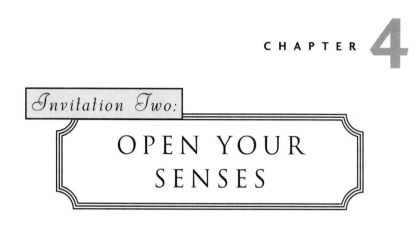

CHAPTER 4

Invitation Two:

OPEN YOUR SENSES

Body Changes

A sincere commitment to an intuitive life brings body changes. These may come about slowly; you don't want that second cup of coffee; you find yourself looking for healthier food at the grocery store; your tolerance for alcohol drops sharply. This gradual revolution eventually sends people on a conscious quest for the diets, exercises, rest, and recreational activities which serve their physical, emotional, mental, and spiritual well-being the best. The driving force behind this revolution is the development of an exquisite communication system for your soul: your intuitive body.

You may have met your intuitive body already. For example, your intuitive heart might have urged you to make an unplanned phone call just in time for someone else's needs, or perhaps you discovered a long-lost report when your intuitive hands opened the "wrong" filing drawer by accident, or maybe like successful designer Donna Karan, you've run your professional life "not by the numbers but on gut instinct."[1]

As these stories capture, the intuitive body is smart. It is part of your InQ (intuitive intelligence), and it expresses itself through your feet, belly, hands, heart, ears, voice, and your entire body. When you open your senses,

> Intuition isn't something mystical that God sends down to you. It's very physical; it's in your body.
>
> BARBARA MYMAN

your body and all of its parts start sending you information. You become aware of what Gary Zukav, author of *The Seat of the Soul,* calls your multisensory nature. As he suggests, your intuitive body is not limited to your five physical senses; your soul's sensory mechanism extends far beyond the limits of your skin.

Joan Senzel, a dedicated mother and Sunday school teacher at the local Methodist church, experienced a direct spiritual connection and the wisdom of her intuitive body this way. "Joan!" A clear, powerful commanding voice called her out of a deep sleep. She glanced around, but there was no one there. It was pitch black outside and the clock read 2 A.M. When Joan noticed her husband, Chuck, wasn't in bed next to her, she instantly knew what to do. The Holy Spirit had called to her and, although she wondered about her faith at other times, a direct connection took over.

In that spirit-directed state, it is not surprising that her hands threw off the blankets, her feet took her to the closet, and she began dressing as if there was nothing abnormal about her behavior. She thought about her four children who were sleeping soundly throughout the house. Although she had never before even considered leaving them alone in the middle of the night, she continued to dress serenely as if her body had an important appointment with Chuck that wasn't on her calendar.

Her hands calmly picked up her car keys, she quietly closed the door, and she steered her car silently down their wooded driveway. The narrow, winding beach road to town was absolutely empty, and only the sound of her car's engine pierced the silent night and her still mind. Joan didn't know where she was going or why, but she did know she needed to find Chuck.

As she turned a bend in the road, her car's headlights fell on the familiar sight of her husband's car, but this time it was crumbled by an impact with a solid, stone pillar. Joan found Chuck inside slumped over the wheel. Not sure whether he was asleep, unconscious or badly hurt, Joan shook him carefully. When Chuck came around, he told Joan that the last thing he remembered was having trouble staying awake at the wheel.

There was a large, bloody cut over his eye, but other than feeling exhausted, Chuck seemed O.K. They drove home together but in the morning, when Chuck was continuing to shiver, they visited an emergency room, where he was treated for shock and released. As for Joan, to this day she cherishes the

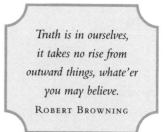

*Truth is in ourselves,
it takes no rise from
outward things, whate'er
you may believe.*
ROBERT BROWNING

mystical experience she had with the Holy Spirit that night and the loving connection with Chuck that the incident revealed. She remembers the faith that guided her actions that night. It was simple—her body's InQ knew what to do and her logical mind didn't argue.

Most people's minds would have talked them out of getting up and driving anywhere at 2 A.M. Joan's choice to trust in the Spirit's call freed her body to take action. In some ways, she had nothing to lose; if her drive hadn't amounted to anything, she could have chalked it up to a mistake. The point is, however, she did find something that not only helped her partner but revealed the depth of their mutual connection and love— a gift at any time.

Your intuitive body is a gift of your soul. To establish your guiding image for working with this gift, do the following exercise:

Exercise: Your Guiding Image for "Open Your Senses"

1. Label the next page of your Intuition Journal "Chapter Four: Open Your Senses."

2. Without looking, reach into your Image Vocabulary envelope and pull out your guiding illustration for this chapter.

3. Note which category it comes from on the bottom of the page you've labeled.

4. Paste your Guiding Image on this page.

Spiritual literature describes your intuitive body and its different attributes in a variety of ways. I discussed one way, the seven levels of

> My beliefs I test on my
> body, on my intuitional
> consciousness, and when
> I get a response there,
> then I accept.
>
> D. H. LAWRENCE

awareness (the chakras), in Chapter One. According to this perspective, your intuitive body registers information at increasingly subtle levels of awareness. As your awareness increases, so does the size of the world in which you're participating. The Sufi tradition also teaches that your body has seven subtle energy centers, called *latifa,* although their locale and purpose differ in some ways from those of the chakra system. Both systems agree, however, that intuitive wisdom is located primarily in the sixth subtle energy center in the forehead between the eyes.[2]

The subtle energy center associated with the greatest Light in the intuitive body is located at the top of your head. This is the reason why many traditions depict the bodies of saints and holy people with halos around their heads or streams of light flowing from their heads. Christianity teaches that while alive, Christ's body was transfigured in front of Peter, James, and John, and that after death His body was resurrected. According to the scriptures, His resurrected body was capable of walking through walls, appearing out of nowhere, and possessing the attributes of solid matter when touched.

The ability of the body to do these things and more is not new. Teachers in all traditions are said to appear to their followers in nonphysical bodies which radiate, educate, and inspire. The best research on the topic is found in Michael Murphy's book, *The Future of the Body.*[3] Citing evidence from a variety of sources, including psychosomatic medicine, spiritual healing, hypnosis, biofeedback training, and sports, Murphy concludes that the human body is changed through transformational practices which in turn foster what he calls metanormal experiences. Intuition is one aspect of your metanormal nature.

Although most of us relate to our bodies as if we are in metanormal kindergarten, it is my goal to introduce you to some aspects of your body's InQ. You deserve to know what it knows. The remainder of this chapter is dedicated to a seven-day fitness program for your intuitive body.

YOUR SEVEN-DAY INTUITIVE FITNESS PROGRAM

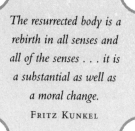

The resurrected body is a rebirth in all senses and all of the senses . . . it is a substantial as well as a moral change.

FRITZ KUNKEL

Today the intuitive body is known by many names: the radiant body, the soul-infused body, the essence body, the etheric body, or the energetic body. It doesn't matter what you call it. Choose a name from this list, another name you know, or make up a name, and then for the duration of your Intuitive Fitness Program use that name to refer to your body. It helps to name the type of expansion you are seeking. And never forget this body resides in your physical body; it is not separate from it.

Besides providing access to inner knowledge, the Intuitive Fitness Program is important because it combats what I call the "Out-to-Lunch" phenomenon that can accompany intuitive development. This phenomenon occurs because people mistakenly believe intuitive awareness is achieved by going into a trance, mentally ascending, emotionally leaving, or in any other way not "staying" inside their bodies during metanormal or intuitive experiences.

Your Intuitive Fitness Program covers these seven areas:

Day One: Your Intuitive Feet
Day Two: Your Intuitive Power
  Centers
Day Three: Your Intuitive Hands

Day Four: Your Intuitive Heart
Day Five: Your Intuitive Voice
Day Six: Your Intuitive Ears
Day Seven: Your Intuitive Eyes

Each area contains at least one explanatory story and an exercise. You may find that one or more of these areas is easier for you: if so, that area is part of your InQ's strong suit. Pay particular attention to your experiences with this area(s), recording and highlighting all of your experiences with it in your journal. Also, be aware that your development might be accompanied by tingling sensations at the top of your head, throbbing in

> We could realize a
> metasomatic existence,
> coming ashore like
> amphibians into a world
> beyond our first habitat.
>
> MICHAEL MURPHY

the subtle energy area of your forehead, the sensation of your heart area being stretched, or fiery feelings in your belly. These sensations are a natural part of development. If you find them unpleasant or interfering with your daily life, slow down, move to another exercise, or stop your work temporarily. Trust your body's messages.

The context for this work is increasing your soul embodiment. Therefore, every intuitive body exercise is preceded by a breath exercise. This is because breath work slows you down and relaxes you. When you are relaxed, you are more likely to recognize the information your intuitive body is conveying. In addition, the breath—considered the wind of the spirit, the Holy Spirit, the giver of life—is symbolic of spirit or soul. Metaphorically, attending to your breath is synonymous with acknowledging your embodied soul. Let's practice now with the Basic Breath exercise.

Exercise: The Basic Breath Exercise

1. Find a comfortable place to sit. It is advisable, but not absolutely required, for you to close your eyes.

2. Focus on your breath. Follow it as it comes in and goes out. If you have trouble concentrating, count one as you inhale and two as you exhale.

3. Do this for 10 to 20 minutes or until you are very calm.

4. Record your reactions to the Basic Breath exercise in your journal.

That's all there is to it. This exercise, or slight variations, will precede every intuitive fitness exercise. Done consistently, this simple act has the power to transform your life. Your body will enjoy it so much that eventually you will automatically relax as soon as you start breathing. A student of mine, Joyce, was just learning this technique the week of an important

job interview. She decided to do the
Basic Breath exercise during the entire
train ride to her appointment. Joyce
remarked, "I didn't even recognize
myself, I was so calm. I was myself
throughout the interview. The inter-

> *If life and soul are sacred,*
> *the human body is sacred.*
> WALT WHITMAN

viewer and I really enjoyed each other, and I wasn't surprised when I
landed the job." The Basic Breath exercise had taken Joyce out of her
mental machinations about the coming interview and placed her squarely
inside her relaxed and confident body. She knew what to do—be herself.

You, too, can have access to the true wealth which dwells within you.
Even if Joyce hadn't landed the job, she'd landed something more important: her best self. Your intuitive body is an expression of that self, so let's
begin your Seven-Day Intuitive Fitness Program now.

Day One: Your Intuitive Feet

Cartoonist Pat Brady's "Rose Is Rose" strip recently featured the title
character running barefoot over the grass. A dialogue box showed her feet
saying, "Did you tell your mom we can't see where we're going with
shoes on?" In the next panel, Rose answers, "She says toes shouldn't make
decisions about where to go!" The final panel depicts Rose sitting with
her feet in a luscious mud puddle while her toes' words, "Stop here in the
mud! Woo!" are surrounded by hearts and a smiling sun.

This cartoon captures our situation. All too often when our feet or
toes urge us to do something, we behave like Rose's mother and worry
about the mud or other obstacles in our way. We have a thousand reasons
why we shouldn't follow the spontaneous, sensory urges of our intuitive
feet or our feet InQ. If we chose to follow our intuitive guidance, we may
be pleasantly surprised. For example, during a happy childhood period,
Anne Drissel took piano lessons with a beloved teacher, Mrs. Harris. At
her teacher's house two sets of cameo pictures, the first of a pioneer boy
and girl and the second of a gypsy boy and girl, fascinated her, and she
spent time every week identifying with them. As an adult, whenever she

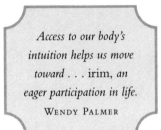

played the piano she would recall happy childhood memories and remember those two picture sets. She occasionally thought about trying to find something similar for herself but never followed through with her musing.

One day, when she was living thousands of miles away from her childhood home, a professional colleague suggested to Anne (who was then the director of a psychiatric hospital) that they take a break from days of steady work and go shopping for antiques. Ann confessed that she didn't like antiques, but, when her colleague asked if there was anything from her past she'd like to have as a reminder, she found herself immediately naming the cameo picture sets.

Entering a large antique store, Anne was welcomed by a hodgepodge of miscellaneous stalls, which her colleague greeted like a pro. Unlike her colleague, Anne wasn't sure what to do or where to go, but her InQ feet carried her to the back of the store where her eyes were drawn to the floor. There was her childhood gypsy girl cameo! She screeched in delight, grabbed it up, and headed off to tell her colleague. On the way to the other side of the store, her eyes fell upon the gypsy boy propped on a buffet. She burst into tears, but the story wasn't over.

> As I was paying for the gypsy children cameos and telling the cashier my story, I said that the only thing that could be better than this would be to find the matching pair of pioneer children. As I said that, my eyes gazed across to a stall area I had missed earlier and there, amidst a display of old linens, was a mint-condition set of pioneer children pictures!

Finding these two sets went deeper than the synchronicity of the moment. For Anne it signaled that (1) it was time to pursue more happiness, even if that meant moving back to her childhood home area; (2) she honored her own pioneer gypsy–like attributes; and (3) she had followed

the right path all along. Her intuitive
feet, which had carried her to the back
of the store that day, had initiated a
dream-come-true find and potential directions for her next steps.

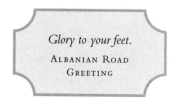

Glory to your feet.
ALBANIAN ROAD
GREETING

Your intuitive feet can do this for
you, too. It is good to let them do some spontaneous wandering from
time to time. You never know what that wandering might reveal.

Day One Exercise: Your Intuitive Feet

1. Do the Basic Breath exercise on p. 76 with this variation: as you
   breathe in and out, visualize the air you're breathing going all
   the way down to your feet on the inhale and all the way out from
   your feet on the exhale. Do this exercise until you are thoroughly
   relaxed.

2. When you are relaxed, get up and wander. You can wander around
   inside your office, your home, your yard, your town, or anywhere
   that attracts you. If you find yourself getting tense or distracted, do
   the Basic Breath exercise again.

3. Let your intuitive feet guide you until you stop. When you stop, notice your surroundings. Ask yourself, why did my feet bring me
   here? What is here for me to learn? What is my insight telling me?

4. Record your results in your journal.

5. (Optional) Like Ann, before you go for your walk, name what you'd
   be interested in finding, discovering, or learning.

Intuition loves to work with symbols, and your feet are symbolic of
the things you stand for while you're here on Earth. A person I once knew
used to express this truth as, "You vote with your feet," meaning that we
are constantly choosing (voting) where to be from moment to moment.
These decisions, one by one, add up to the sum total of how we spend
our lives. Setting your intuitive feet free to communicate to you allows

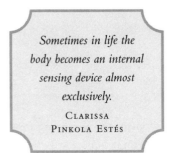

Sometimes in life the body becomes an internal sensing device almost exclusively.

CLARISSA
PINKOLA ESTÉS

them to cast a vote for what your intuition believes to be important.

One more thing about your feet before we move on to day two: walking with *all* your attention on each step while emptying your mind is an ancient way to meditate. This style of meditation, like most meditation, requires strong mental discipline, but it is a natural for outdoor enthusiasts.

Day Two: Your Intuitive Power Centers

You have two power centers in the lower cavity of your body. One is at the very base of your torso near your sexual center, I call it your lower power center, and the other is a few inches below your belly button and I call it your upper power center. When these two points are fully developed, you have strong self-confidence, a lot of energy, and the ability to take strong stands in life. In addition, they can provide good intuitive information about events, circumstances, or people in your life.

It was a lovely house in Yosemite, California, with a hot tub, a swimming pool, acres for walking, and plenty of big, comfortable bedrooms. Although the March equinox is not a particularly warm time of year in the California mountains, I had arranged for a weekend retreat to be attended by some of my Transformational Management and Leadership Board colleagues. One of my friends, Dr. Joan Kenley, author of *Voice Power*[4] and *Whose Body Is It Anyway?,* seemed inordinately focused on the weekend: her voice was particularly charged when she talked about it in the planning stage. Picking up on the tone of her voice, I finally asked her, "Why are you so charged up or excited about this weekend?"

She answered, "I don't know the details, but I've felt this way before certain life-changing events in the past." The fact that Joan had such a strong "belly hunch" that the equinox event was going to change her life significantly made me curious. I wanted to see how her intuitive information would emerge in real world events. What happened on the

Yosemite trip? She and her husband-
to-be fell madly in love, although neither of them had any romantic thoughts
about the other prior to that weekend!

It didn't surprise me that Joan knew
ahead of time that something important
was going to happen. As a highly successful body psychologist who taught
voice using techniques of deep physical
awareness, emotional connection, and

> *You feed your longing
> and desires and they do
> the work. My whole life
> has been following my
> intuition and strange
> beckonings.*
> DAVID WHYTE

spiritual consciousness, Joan respected her intuitive body more than most
people. She acknowledged that healthy, flowing sexual energy was necessary to lower body well-being and the sensation of rich physical aliveness.

Most of us are unaware that the lower body—the muscles, nerves,
and various sensitivities of the sexual organs, and the urinary and anal
areas—all work together with your lower intuitive power center located
here. This center is called the "Root" chakra in the ancient system you
studied in Chapter One. Although people resist working with this center
because of its association with sensuality, sexuality, reproduction, and
elimination, I encourage people to enlarge their perspective and tell them
to look at the torso as a vessel for the soul. From this point of view, your
lower power center is the vessel's bottom where activities come to rest.
This is why in disciplines such as aikido, tai chi, and karate the practitioner "sinks" his or her body into the lower body cavity. An imaginary
line like an anchor is drawn down the center of the body, through the
pelvis, between the feet, into the ground, and into the center of the
Earth.

Your anchored, lower intuitive power center doesn't come into play
when you are tense because one way it conveys excitement (excitement
in this area comes for many reasons other than sexuality, e.g., creativity,
leadership, passion for a purpose) is the warmth of powerful circulation.
When muscles are tense, circulation is limited. If you use the power center exercise on page 82 whenever you are nervous, upset, or fearful, it will
automatically relax you, enhance your ability to receive intuitive messages, and restore your alertness.

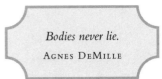

Bodies never lie.

AGNES DEMILLE

Your belly or upper power center works interactively with the sexual and power energies found in your lower power center. When I ask executives or others what sensations they notice when their intuitive power center is speaking, they say things like, "I feel my power" or "My gut gets warm and fiery." Both descriptions reflect that your intuitive power center is designed to be fiery and alive. This upper power point of your intuitive body is known as the *hara* in Japan, *tan tien* in China, and *kath* in the Middle East. When you are in balance, this energetic place provides confidence, a sense of profound connection, and safety in the world. This is the way your upper power center is intended to operate. When this part of your intuitive nature is solid, you know who you are and what you stand for. The body is positively ablaze with its own fire, a fire which doesn't burn destructively but fuels intention and forward motion. In fact, Japanese business people have a special name for its information. It is called *haragei,* which literally means "belly talk."[5] It is said that some Eastern yogis know how to use this internal belly fire to keep themselves warm in extremely cold temperatures. For most of us, this inner fire signals that we are deeply connected.

Before you build your connections by doing the second day's power centers exercise (it requires you to hold two images at once), do these simple warm-up exercises.

Warm-ups:

A. *Your Lower Power Center:* Sit on a chair and imagine that your torso is one large lung. Breathe in deeply as if your breath was going all the way to the bottom of your torso. Relax your groin muscles completely as you do so. Now, tighten your groin muscles (they pull up), imaging that they are forcing the air out of your nose or mouth as you do so. Repeat until you are very relaxed.

B. *Your Upper Power Center:* Imagine that your entire hip cavity is a cauldron or vessel and that hovering, suspended in the center of this cauldron approximately three or four fingers down from the belly button and in the center of the body, is a bright, blazing, fiery ball, a type of internal light or sun. Attempt to feel the fire within as a gentle warmth.

Day Two Exercise: Your Intuitive Power Centers

1. Do the Basic Breath exercise with this variation: as you breathe in and out, visualize the air you're breathing going all the way down into your torso on the inhale and all the way out from your torso on the exhale.

2. Stand, bend your knees slightly, and allow your body to "sink" into its lower cavity, awakening the energy of your power centers.

3. Then combine warm-ups (a) and (b) by breathing in and out all the way to your lower power center while you imagine a fiery ball at the upper power center.

4. Make sure all the muscles in your groin area are completely relaxed. Think of something you'd like to have help with or insight about and notice how your vessel responds.

5. Record anything of interest in your journal.

Day Three: Your Intuitive Hands

Fifteen of us wandered our Consciousness Studies classroom in complete silence. The milling about seemed to go on forever, and I was beginning to wonder if there was any purpose to our exercise. My mind wandered, so I was caught appropriately off guard when the professor announced quickly, "Stop walking, stand still, and let your body make a motion which is very important in your future."

As soon as she finished these words, my hands leaped up and began to type furiously. I was shocked. While I watched my fingers fly across imaginary keys, my logical mind tried to figure out what this typing was about. The only thing I could think of was a dissertation, but the thought

> One of the first things a student of aikido learns is to become conscious of his "one point." This is an energy or spirit-center located about two fingers below the navel.
>
> SADAHARU OH

confused me because I'd just decided *not* to pursue a Ph.D. in clinical psychology. I was stumped, but my hands were so insistent that I never forgot the image. Although it was ten more years before a phone call from a book publisher solved my mental puzzle, my hands' InQ had known a decade earlier that I was going to be an author.

Artists and musicians through the ages have described moments when they got out of the way of their hands and let them spontaneously dance across piano keys or a canvas. Healers also tell of their magic hands which know precisely where to touch someone. Parents and lovers demonstrate an intuitive ability to know just where, when, and how a loved one needs to be touched.

Words or gestures are not always necessary. The intuitive hand, which helps anchor creativity and love, is a strong avenue for expressive communication. Of course, there are no guarantees that you'll like the information it can deliver. For example, Vicki, a student of mine who had been out of town, told me that when she placed her hand on the back of her lover upon her return, she received an instant message of infidelity. Eventually her lover confessed to the accuracy of her impression. It took courage for Vicki to pursue her impression and, as a psychologist, to work through the idea that she was projecting her fears onto her lover. As painful as it was, her intuitive hand had sensed what was going on openly and accurately.

The fact that intuition can deal up such stark realities—the validity of which always needs to be investigated—seems to create in people an emergency sensory switch called "Numb Out Fast." Phrases such as "I don't want to see or hear it," "she is blind to the truth," "that's tasteless," or "his words were heartless" are commonly used to describe situations where sensory numbness might be employed. Likewise, when faced with the possibility that our intuitive senses might provide us with information we do not want to know, we automatically cripple, distort, or completely shut down our subtle, intuitive senses.[6] Therefore, as psychoneuroimmunological research might suggest, unsolved emotional conflicts can block your intuitive experience and repress your intuitive body as well as impact your health.

> *It is so many years before one can believe enough in what one feels even to know what the feeling is.*
> W. B. YEATS

To help you avoid blocking your intuition during your Intuitive Fitness Program and beyond, remember these three hints:

1. If you suspect you are repressing information your intuition is sending you about yourself, invite your intuition to tell you more directly and then *check* out the information with those who know, e.g., check out health information with a doctor, facts about a possible promotion with your boss, potential upsets your partner is feeling with your partner.

2. If you suspect you are repressing intuitive information about someone you know or love, unless it is very important, let it alone. If the information is important, say to the person, "My InQ makes me wonder if _____ (fill in the blank, e.g., you are secretly angry or disappointed with me, you are expecting a promotion but afraid to hope for it, you are worried). Is this true or is it just my projection or wishful thinking?"

3. Challenge yourself to trust the presence of truth absolutely. Dare to speak and act from your truth (this does not mean you think your truth is *the* truth). Take a long view and watch what happens over time.

Day Three Exercise: Your Intuitive Hands

1. Do the Basic Breath exercise with this variation: as you breathe in and out, visualize the air you're breathing going all the way down to your feet on the inhale and all the way out from your feet on the exhale.

2. Either alone or with others, put some music on and mill about a room.

3. After about 5 minutes, stop suddenly and ask your hands to make a gesture that is important to your future.

4. Record your results.

Options: Ask permission of someone to place your intuitive hands on them with the intention of healing and helping. Or, let your intuitive hands create a picture, a dance, or a poem without direction from your mind. Record what happens.

Day Four: Your Intuitive Heart

Author James Stephens expressed the actions of your intuitive heart best when he said, "What the heart knows today, the head will understand tomorrow." From a linear perspective, the heart appears to intuit the future better than the mind. Whenever you use expressions such as "I knew in my heart" or " my heart told me," you are talking about the wisdom of the heart.

For example, Thomas, a business client of mine, once stated, "I knew in my heart not to go forward with the plans, and I'm very thankful I listened." Or consider Laura who told me right after she met the man she was eventually going to marry, "Although we've just met, my heart tells me he'll be a very important person in my life." Betty, a successful CEO who was thinking of changing fields to environmental work, remarked after a workshop, "It doesn't make any logical sense, but my heart leaped at the chance to participate. I still don't know how or when I'll be working for sustainable development, but my heart knows I belong with these people and this work." People say these things because they are true; your intuitive heart (this phrase does not refer to the physical organ as much as it does the energy or force field in your chest area) has rich perceptual skills and is a powerful communicator.

Although our use of language suggests that we all recognize the ac-

tions of the intuitive heart, to date
Western science has not produced insights into the mechanisms behind the
intuitive heart as it has for the gut
(Goleman's *Emotional Intelligence*) and
frontal lobe (the research of Dr. Dimasio and his colleagues at the University

*The heart has its reasons
which reason
knows not of.*
PASCAL

of Iowa). Therefore, I must be content to just tell you that I know intuition travels on love but lack a physiological correlate which hints at how
this might work.

After years of work in my field, I've concluded that your heart is central to intuition because it:

1. returns magic to your life;

2. is a hub for intuitive communications;

3. fosters character development;

4. unites a group or community (as we'll see in Chapters Eleven
   and Twelve).

1. Your Intuitive Heart Returns Magic to Your Life

Shamanic literature suggests that you can judge how open and receptive
your heart is by the amount of magic—joy, gratefulness, synchronicity,
expansiveness, connection, love—you judge to be in your life. You have a
lot of magic when your heart is in its natural state—open—and little
when it is closed and shut off. This is why the falling-in-love period is so
magical for people and why it feels so awful when love dies. In the latter
case, people protect themselves from further hurt by closing their hearts
like the aperture of a camera.

The principles behind this open-and-shut reaction of your energetic,
intuitive heart lead to this shamanic axiom: your heart is the path back to
sensory and intuitive magic. Accordingly, when your life is without this
magic, your path is suffering from a closed heart. To get magic back in

> Merge with your intuitive love, this is to become the true agent of your encounter with Reality.
> EVELYN UNDERHILL

your life, you need to consult with, listen to, speak from, and cherish your own heart. Doing this regularly will turn your life around.

Although it is easy for me to prescribe how to return magic to your life, I recognize it isn't always easy to do. Many people have avoided or covered up their hearts for years. They fear that the vulnerability lurking there will reveal weakness, pain, or confusion. And there is another complication. As your intuitive abilities grow, so does your sensitivity. You feel more pain and know more joy, whether it's your own, someone else's, or the world's. For example, people report that watching the news can become hell as their intuitive empathy expands. Shamanic traditions teach us that, although we can take a break from the news, we should not run from the sensitive, vulnerable states we experience. In fact, shamans believe healing means going straight toward our vulnerability. It is deemed essential to remove all coverings linked to shame, so that freedom, openness, and space can occupy the heart. This allows the soul to expand, bringing multisensory, intuitive awareness with it. Never forget that the healthy intuitive heart is comprised of immense space and can hold within a huge amount of diverse things. When you feel yourself shutting down, breathe into the heart and imagine it getting bigger than the level of pain you are experiencing. There is always room for joy somewhere.

2. Your Intuitive Heart Is a Hub for Intuitive Communications

Besides a key to magic in your life, your heart is the Grand Central Station of intuitive communications. Messages go out; messages come in. Your intuitive heart radiates; your intuitive heart resonates. Pay close attention to the next two sections on radiance and resonance. Understanding them will help you avoid common problems people face when they develop intuitive heart skills.

Common Problem #1: When the intuitive heart begins to operate, people feel empathy for others and want to give from their hearts. Unfortunately,

many people respond to this desire by
doing what I call "putting your heart on
the end of a long stick." In short, they
metaphorically give their hearts away.
This creates a type of hole in their energetic chest, and they naturally seek to
fill it in one form or another.

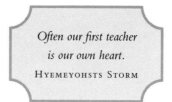

*Often our first teacher
is our own heart.*
HYEMEYOHSTS STORM

Solution #1: Your heart doesn't need to "go" anywhere. It stays in your
body; it *radiates.* Information, love, caring, concern, well-being, joy, and
many other positive emotions flow out of your radiant, intuitive heart.
People receive these. You don't have to be taught how to do this; you already know because it happens naturally when you see someone you love,
enter a cherished home, or greet a beloved pet. The next time it happens
spontaneously, pay attention to the sensations in your chest area. Once
you know how your radiant heart feels, you can practice developing
conscious application of its love. One thing further: pure radiance has no
emotional agenda. It is unconditional.

Common Problem #2: When the intuitive heart begins to operate, people
sense what others are feeling, such as sadness, anger, joy, curiosity, or depression. Sometimes the sensations of others can be so strong that they
swamp your developing sensitivities. For example, you might engage in
casual conversation with someone but notice by the end of it you've become very angry or depressed. Before the encounter, you were not angry
or depressed; afterward you were. Something in the conversation may
have triggered your anger or depression, but, if not, you may have intuitively picked up on what your conversation partner was feeling but didn't
want to talk about. It appears that your intuitive heart has absorbed your
partner's vibration like osmosis. (For more information, see Chapter
Eight, "Shift Space.")

Solution #2: This will not happen to you if you understand and use the
principle of *resonance.* Your intuitive heart doesn't have to be swamped or
overly identified with another person's state. Resonance has to do with
vibration, rhythm, or frequency. Your heart is on one frequency; other

> *What happens in your innermost being is worthy of your whole love.*
> RAINER MARIA RILKE

people's are on another. With practice, it is possible for you to resonante momentarily with another person's vibration long enough to share and learn something, but short enough to maintain strong contact with your own frequency. For example, when you listen to the radio between stations, sometimes you can hear them both, but as soon as you want to, you can turn the dial back to your station of choice. Remember this analogy and use it by knowing your own intuitive heart station well. I often tell students to imagine that they are resonating with another only on the surface of their hearts or skins, not at the depths. They are to reserve the depths of their hearts for themselves and their evolving soul natures.

3. Your Intuitive Heart Fosters Character Development

The third reason the heart is so important to intuition is that it fosters character development. I talked about this in Chapter One when I told the story of the man who collected $150 more than was required from his client and then subsequently dented his fender to the precise tune of $150. There is an ethical sound barrier to intuitive development which resides in the heart. While people can use psychic information exclusively for their own benefit, opening the intuitive heart makes it uncomfortable to do so. This is because when your heart is open you know what another is feeling. You can't hurt your neighbor without knowing his or her pain. If you do contribute in some way to another's pain, your intuitive heart protests. You hear a distant nudge, persistent whisper, or loud inner call to a higher ethical dimension. Deep inside, you know there is a better way and can view things from multiple perspectives. Your heart is big enough to encircle even those with whom you vehemently disagree. This heart tolerance sets the stage for the fourth reason the heart is so important to intuition: finding and belonging to your community, your tribe. I'll explain more about this in Chapters Eleven and Twelve.

Welcome to your magical, communicating, ethical intuitive heart. If you keep this information in mind and practice with these ideas, your intuitive heart will stay fit and healthy. And, like the eye, it will provide you with a window to your connected soul.

> *Education has for its objective the formation of character.*
>
> HERBERT SPENCER

Day Four Exercise:
Your Intuitive Heart

After you've finished with your Basic Breath exercise, do A or B (below).

1. Do the Basic Breath exercise with this variation: as you breathe in and out, visualize the air going into your intuitive heart like a zephyr (a soft breeze). If you feel your heart is blocked or shut down, send your zephyr breath to the area underneath your heart. Do *not* try to remove the block or shut down feeling. Simply support the heart with your soft breath. If tears begin to well up, let them follow a natural course.

2. Continue the breath until you are relaxed and feeling in touch with your heart nature. When you reach this state, you are ready to do the exercises.

A. Heart Magic

1. Take out your journal and list all the ways magic (joy, gratefulness, synchronicity, connection, love) is in your life. On a scale of 1 to 100, what number would you assign to the amount of magic in your life? Is the number where you want it to be?

2. If the number is lower than you want, ask yourself how and why your heart is shut down. Write about it in your journal.

3. In your journal, formally ask your intuitive heart to help you heal and to reopen. Date your entry.

B. Radiance and Resonance

4. Go out to a spot in nature and practice radiance and resonance. Do not take your journal with you. Don't be distracted by needing to record your sensations at the time of your encounter. You'll remember everything that is important.

5. Imagine that your heart is opening like the eye of a lens, and allow love to radiate outward. Remove your attention from this exercise when you feel done.

6. Experience the ideas, feelings, or vibrations which are in your heart in the moment. Know them well. When you are ready, allow your heart to "pick up" or resonate to a frequency that is in the nature surrounding you. Discern the difference between those vibrations and your own. Let go of everything that is not yourself.

7. Go home and record what you remember of the experience in your journal.

Day Five: Your Intuitive Voice

Judy was exhausted. She'd quit her old job a year and a half earlier to travel, but by the time she returned to her home state a recession had hit and jobs were difficult to find. After months at a menial temporary job, she sank down on her couch one night, turned on the TV and tried to relax but couldn't get her employment situation out of her head. The company where she was temping asked her to consider making her temporary job permanent. She weighed her situation: she needed the money, but the work was tedious and the hours were long. Her musings lead her to mentally ask herself, "Do you want this job, Judy?" and she was shocked when a thundering voice came out of her mouth and boomed an emphatic "NO!"

She turned down the opportunity at the temp agency and was thrilled when her risk was rewarded the following week. A previous em-

ployer, whom she hadn't heard from in
years, tracked her down from another
state and offered her a lucrative consulting job. She accepted immediately.

This story exemplifies the actions
of the intuitive voice, a voice which can
express insights that surprise its speaker.
I believe these types of thoughts are

> *For the human body is
> not a finished, arrested
> form; it is ever in the
> process of becoming.*
> ROMANO GUARDINI

from the speaker's soul and are often uplifting for more than the speaker.
Your intuitive voice is not what is known in psychic/intuitive circles as
channeling, a time when someone's voice is expressing thoughts which
appear not to be that of the person speaking. Your intuitive voice is something you recognize as your own but are surprised by its power, insight,
and authority.[7] There is no sensation, as there often is in channeling, of
the self disappearing or letting another entity express through your vocal
chords.

Spiritual literature has talked about the importance of the voice for
centuries. The Christian apostle John, in describing Jesus Christ, wrote
that "the Word was made flesh and dwelt among us." According to Hindu
beliefs, the world came into existence at the utterance of the first sound.
The Lakota creation story holds that the Great Spirit Eeah, the giant, became lonely and wanted a companion. Realizing that he had to shed his
blue blood in order for his companion to be birthed, he uttered, "So be
it." That first sound created the breath of life.

All of these teachings imply not only that words matter, but that they
can actually *create* matter. In addition to creation, wisdom, and guidance
in crisis, the intuitive or knowledge voice has been linked with destruction and healing. The single cry of Joshua's army knocked down the walls
of Jericho while the mere sound of a parent's voice soothes the infant.
This does not imply that every sound we utter creates, destroys, or heals.
It does imply, however, that the intuitive voice is powerful and ought to
be developed and used with responsibility and respect.

One positive use of the intuitive voice is "soul-speak." People recognize when the soul is talking because they are warmed by the communi-

> *Voices—I think they must go deeper into us than other things. I have often fancied heaven might be made of voices.*
> GEORGE ELIOT

cation and they sense the wisdom in it. I had this experience with such a voice many years ago. At a conference sponsored by the Spiritual Frontiers Fellowship, I decided to have lunch with a friend (we'll call her Betty), who some might have considered slightly overweight. We were chatting away about the conference when a third person we knew joined us. Thoughtlessly, our mutual friend began to gossip negatively about overweight people. To my amazement, Betty turned to the gossiping party and, without a hint of judgment, spoke powerfully on behalf of those who struggle with weight problems. Her words attacked no one; they simply explained the situation. As she spoke, I watched beautiful purple clouds pour out of her mouth. Both her listeners were speechless and awestruck. Twenty-four years later, the purple I saw that day (I don't normally see colors around people) is still the most beautiful purple I have ever seen. When I think of it, I remember how impressive wisdom and truth can be, no matter who delivers them or why.

Day Five Exercise: Your Intuitive Voice

1. Do the Basic Breath exercise with this variation: as you breathe in and out, relax your throat completely.

2. Pick an area of your life about which you'd like to hear the advice or insight of your intuitive voice.

3. Using your imagination, *before* saying anything and without knowing what you are going to say, picture clouds of truth (they can be your favorite color) pouring out of your mouth for 3 minutes.

4. Mentally or aloud, ask yourself a question about your chosen topic.

5. Say the first thing that comes to you. Does it seem truthful? How is it related to your area of concern? Is it helpful?

6. Write what you said and your
   reactions in your journal.

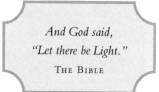

And God said,
"Let there be Light."
THE BIBLE

Day Six: Your Intuitive Ears

The intuitive voice is closely connected to our ability to hear. The story of a voice which "calls" someone to a higher life is classic in spiritual literature: the apostle Paul was called by the resurrected Jesus on the road to Damascus; Mohammed heard a voice in the cavern of Mount Hara; and God called out to Abraham to stop his sacrifice of his son Isaac. Intuition sometimes issues one of these sacred calls, or it might behave more like the trumpets of angels, the flute of Kokopeli, or the thunder of Zeus and herald that something important is about to happen. In every case, people are listening with their intuitive ears for intuition's messages.

Marlene Sider once quit an unsatisfactory job with confidence that she could find something better.[8] But months went by with no offers, and her savings were almost gone. Insecure and at a loss for what to do, Marlene began to hear her "little voice" urge, "Try out for the TV game show *Wheel of Fortune*." Since she barely had enough money in the bank to cover traveling for auditions and the show itself, she tried to ignore what she heard. When her intuition continued to nag her, she finally relinquished and went after success vigorously. She studied, tried to identify the best dates for her, and did all her interviews on one day—her birthday. After being chosen, she performed very well during the game, and, when the bonus round began, her intuitive ears heard the correct answer. She went home $30,000 richer.

Not all experiences with the intuitive ear are about grand callings or dramatic events like winning a game show. One of my students, Thomasine, said she had listened to her inner disk jockey for years. Her DJ appeared to select inner tunes which offered educational commentary on her life, analysis of her situation and feelings, and potential guidance for the future. The songs reduced her resistance to her inner wisdom and often provided comic relief. Another of my students was depressed and

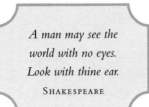

A man may see the world with no eyes. Look with thine ear.

SHAKESPEARE

was wondering how to go forward with her work. When she heard her inner DJ play "Whistle While You Work," she decided she needed to bring more joy to her work station. Yet another student recalled rather humorously that one time when she was debating whether to throw a wild dance party or host a quiet evening with a small group of friends, she found herself humming the tune of Irene Cara's "What a Feeling" over and over. She took her DJ's advice and went with the wild dance party.

Day Six Exercise: Your Intuitive Ears

1. Do the Basic Breath exercise with this variation: as you breathe in and out, relax the area all around your ears. Then visualize your ear drums moving very subtly when your intuitive voice sends them a message.

2. Do exercise A or B. (A) Close your eyes and listen to the sounds which are all around you. Heighten them. Now turn those sounds down by losing interest in them. You already know them. Now listen for an unexpected intuitive message. If nothing comes, act "as if" you'd heard the message you wished you had received. Record your experience in your journal. (B) Make a list of potential DJ tunes and circle the ones you think are most relevant now. For example, you might intuitively hear "On the Road Again" when you are thinking of a trip, "Get Up, Stand Up" when you hesitate to pursue your dreams, or "We Are the World" when you are working on diversity issues. Make it a habit to listen for your DJ, record his or her choices in your journal, and why you think them relevant.

Day Seven: Your Intuitive Eyes

One day, in the spring of 1993, Peter Einstein stood in the shower and let the water stream over his body as he reviewed his wife Pat's intuition exercise. He'd done the first step, creating a clear question, "What is the best environment for presenting a large-scale intuition event that would attract lots of attention to intuition in general and Pat's training techniques in particular?"

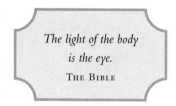

The light of the body is the eye.
THE BIBLE

He was now in the second phase, "the shower-induced flow state," and not thinking about anything except shampooing his hair. As hot water rinsed off the suds, he received this vivid, visual intuitive image: "As if seen through the lens of a hand-held video camera, I 'saw' a group of ecstatically happy people on what I somehow knew was the top deck of a cruise ship."

Although his intuitive eye had revealed little more than a blue sky, happy people, and the glimpse of a cruise ship, Peter *knew* to put together top intuition experts, invite the public, and create a cruise for intuition development. Years later Peter and Pat are still conducting their successful Inner Voyage cruises to the Caribbean, Alaska, and Hawaii.[9] The cruises are highly recommended in travel guides, advertised in major magazines, and have been the subject of TV and radio show commentary. In this case, the InQ of Peter's eye served up a single image (like Frank's fire image in Chapter Two), which went on to guide his life path and offer an opportunity for thousands of people to learn and play together.

Albert Einstein identified the workings of his inner eye as the mechanism for his thoughts:

> The physical elements which seem to serve as elements in [my] thought are certain signs and more or less clear images which can be "voluntarily" reproduced and combined. . . . Conventional words or other signs have to be sought for laboriously only in a secondary stage.

Nikola Tesla, inventor of the fluorescent light and the AC generator, once said that his inner visions of machinery were so detailed that he could mentally run a new piece of machinery for weeks, test it for wear, and then physically make the necessary adjustments to its design. This

> I am learning to see . . .
> everything penetrates
> more deeply within me,
> and no longer stops at the
> place, where until now, it
> always used to finish.
> RAINER MARIA
> RILKE

inner "fast forward" of Tesla's and Einstein's abilities to reproduce and combine specific elements of a problem were powerful techniques that contributed to the work of these scientific geniuses.

This type of vivid, inner image is also found among mystics and teachers. The movie *Kundun,* which chronicles the life and development of the present Dalai Lama, depicts his precognitive daytime visions and his nighttime dreams. His images were all quick, accurate pictures of a future situation. Apparently, images such as these do not need to last for more than a split second in order to make an impression. Mystics have described being lifted into the vaults of Heaven, surrounded by angels, graced with visions, and inspired creatively. Saint Teresa of Avila described "knowledge of the grandeur of God, because the more we see this grandeur the greater is our understanding." Walt Whitman described the sight of God's light as "light rare untellable, lighting the very light, beyond all signs, descriptions, languages." In such words, the mystic records the sights of the intuitive eye. Blake went even further, comparing his physical eye to a window which is used to see the "real" thing. "I question not my corporeal eye than I would question a window concerning a sight. I look through it and not with it."

In many sacred traditions, the eye is considered the window of the soul. Metaphorically, the eye teaches important spiritual principles because its perceptual skills arise out of the void, the dark place, the pupil. Stated differently, the soul works through emptiness and, therefore, the eye demonstrates this simple paradox: it is the place of emptiness which gives birth to our enlightenment. Most of us are afraid of this emptiness. Distrustful that the emptiness will birth something we don't want, or too impatient, we rush to fill emptiness with anything. It is too difficult to wait for the soul or intuition to fill that space for us. In contrast, seeing with the intuitive eyes of the soul requires us to consecrate this black emptiness and label it, too, as sacred space.

Day Seven Exercise:
Your Intuitive Eyes

1. Do the Basic Breath exercise with this variation: with your eyes open or closed, visualize the air coming in your eyes on the inhale and out your eyes on the exhale.

> *The living body is a work of art. Its beauty resides in its internal teleology.*
>
> T. DOBZHANSKY

2. Do exercise A or B. (A) In a darkened room, close your eyes and imagine your empty pupils. There is nothing striking your retina. When inner thoughts or images come, return your attention to your empty retina. After at least 5 minutes or as long as you want to take, ask your intuition to open your inner, intuitive eyes and give you a quick vivid image. It doesn't matter if it is meaningful or not. Record this image and any reactions you have to it in your journal, and look for its significance in the future. (B) Use Pat Einstein's shower exercise to seek a guiding inner image. Ask for specific guidance or insight about something before you get in the shower, and then let go of all thoughts as you let the hot water flow over your body and bring a shower of images.

YOUR INTUITIVE BODY

Congratulations! You've completed the Intuitive Fitness Program. Was any part of the program most effective for you? Is there a part you want to develop more? Your sensitivity to and awareness of intuition have now been enhanced, and, in addition, being more sensitive to all types of body messages, you'll be less likely to ignore your body's requests for rest, better food, exercise, and fun. The benefits of enhanced sensitivity are not limited to intuiting better; postmodern medicine suggests that a pragmatic by-product of your increased sensitivity is better health.

Physician David Michael Levin points out that today's patients must realize that their body is "a body of meaningful experience, a body of sig-nificant intelligence, and is inherently informed about itself." According to Levin, the body *changes* in reaction to the patient's sensitivity and awareness of itself. This awareness ranges from your responses to basic needs to what nurtures your body's contentment, provides it meaning, and gives shape to its joy. You are now more likely to know what is needed to maintain your health and when things aren't quite right. In short, the Intuitive Fitness Program can be part of preventive medicine and a prescription for optimal health.

The program takes things a step further and encourages you to view your body as a living temple for your soul. Spiritual literature ascribes shimmering colors, radiant halos, perfect symmetry, and diamond-like precision to the fully developed body. All of us can, at times, be described as radiant, symmetrical, shimmering, and colorful. This happens naturally when your senses are open and you are at peace with knowing *all* that you know. You've put out the welcome mat and invited your soul to come home.

Final Exercise: Your Intuition To Do List

1. Complete the sentence "Because I am accepting my soul's invita-tion to 'Open My Senses,' I already know to . . ." List 5 to 10 things you know to do such as "breathe into my body power center every morning for a week," "wander around town this week," "practice with my intuitive, healing hands with my children." When you've fin-ished, read your list over, highlight the simplest activity which *uses your favorite Body InQ (heart, hand, eye, etc.)*, and do it. Record everything in your journal.

2. Go back and look at your Guiding Image for this chapter. How has it symbolized your experience with the Intuitive Fitness Program? Does any part of the illustration hint at what area of your intuitive body would be most effective? Record in your journal.

CHAPTER 5

Invitation Three:

CULTIVATE SILENCE

SILENCE: REST FOR YOUR INTUITIVE BODY

No matter what stage of intuitive skills you have reached, as your abilities increase you will experience a leap in the amount of information passing consciously or unconsciously through your system. My students often wonder why they are elated, very hungry, and pleasantly tired after a good intuitive workout. This is why: expanding awareness takes energy. Strengthening your intuitive life is similar to building your cardiovascular and muscular strength and endurance.[1] Both require effort and, as a result, both require rest.

Silence is rest for your intuitive body; therefore, cultivating silence is part of your Intuitive Fitness Program. This silence is not just a matter of silencing your voice; it requires you to also still (1) your body; (2) your emotions; and (3) your thoughts. Mystical traditions refer to this experience as entering the garden of silence, a place where your soul lives without interference. Imagine yourself walking into a beautiful garden on a gorgeous day, sitting down on a comfortable chair, and completely letting go of all distractions, thoughts, evaluations, plans, or need to interact. The garden is filled with the pageantry of colored blossoms, the sounds of insects, the brush of breezes, the sight of butterflies, and the smell of the

Then when all things were wrapped in deepest silence, to me was uttered the hidden Word.

MEISTER ECKHART

Earth. Abundant life is all around you, yet you have nothing to do and nowhere to go. Silence reigns within you.

This deep silence allows space for your soul to come forward. It provides rest for your intuitive body, and a supportive environment for your developing InQ skills. The beauty of this deep silence is that once you've cultivated its presence within you, you can rest your intuitive body whenever you want to and wherever you are: at work, at play, at social events, and in the midst of turmoil.

Take a moment now to select your Guiding Image for cultivating silence.

Your Guiding Image for "Cultivate Silence"

1. Label the next page of your Intuition Journal "Chapter Five: Cultivate Silence."

2. Without looking, reach into your Image Vocabulary envelope and pull out your guiding illustration for this chapter.

3. Note which category it comes from on the bottom of the page you've labeled.

4. Paste the image on the page.

In addition to rest, silence fosters two very important things: the ability to listen to your intuition and the ability to send clear intuitive messages. When you can hear your intuition, you know what to do; when your intuitive communication is clear to others, they can evaluate how to respond to you.

LISTENING FOR INTUITION

> *Silence is the garden of meditation.*
>
> MAXIMS OF ALI

Silence is a listening post for intuitive knowledge, including the knowledge of when to do nothing. Silence, therefore, has a direct impact on your ability to live a more efficient, productive, and stress-free life. Another potential outcome of cultivating silence is tapping the intuition necessary for creative breakthroughs.

In 1926, the psychologist G. Wallas, recognizing how vital silence was to the creative process, named the second step of his four-step creativity model "incubation." This term refers to the moment in the creative process when you let go of all conscious thinking or working toward a creative goal and, instead, send it into the womb of your silence. There it incubates or gestates. Eventually, intuition delivers an illumination or an Ah Ha! flash, the third step in the creative process. This is because intuition and creativity are so entwined that one does not succeed without the other. Intuition without creativity lies dormant as unlived potential; creativity without intuition lacks the spirit necessary to make a lasting difference. The hinge pin between the two is silence.

Silence also helps you intuit what is needed for peak performances. As the research of Michael Murphy, Rhea White, Charles Garfield, and others reveals, people often have to let go of striving and enter a confident stillness in order to succeed. Examples include the following: golfer Jack Nicklaus attributes 50 percent of his success to first visualizing his future success and then letting go of the image; race car driver Jackie Stewart talks about first creating a mental plan for his race and then recognizing that he needs "to put aside all these thoughts lest I lock myself into a plan that might interfere with my driving"; and author Howard Slusher says in *Man, Sport and Existence* that "one quickly hears the roar of the crowd, the crack of the bat, and the thundering of racing feet. But if one listens a little harder and little longer, one comes to hear silence. There is silence within the performer. . . ."[2] In short, when athletes silence their worry and/or effort, a deeper part of themselves can arise.

> But amidst attainment devote a time to silence of the spirit. Then shall I approach thy inner being.
>
> R. L. POTTER

That part, which has nothing to do with the conscious mind, is masterful. Thus, in addition to creativity, silence can birth the intuition necessary for peak performance.

Silence is also an important ingredient in spontaneous interpersonal psychic or intuitive communication between people. The anecdotal research of parapsychologists indicates that many "real" life intuitive experiences occur when at least one of the parties is in an altered, more silent state such as dreaming, day dreaming, driving, or taking a shower. But silence's gifts are not limited to creativity, peak performance, or powerful inner communications.

Gandhi looked to silence, saying, "Silence is a great help to a seeker after truth." Christ suggested people withdraw from the world, enter silence, and then pray. Buddha withdrew and meditated under a tree before He obtained enlightenment. Native American traditions suggest that people clarify their vision by withdrawing into prayer under the watchful guidance of a Medicine person. Thus silence rests your intuitive body, and, in that state of repose, you can intuit creative acts, peak performances, inner communications, truth, effective prayer, clear vision, and what is necessary for enlightenment.

Exercise: Listening for Intuition

1. Write in your journal one experience you have had with intuition and silence, e.g., a creative act after incubation, a peak performance or finding a solution after letting go, a telepathic experience or a spiritual insight during a retreat from daily life. It doesn't matter if you had sought silence consciously or not.

2. Of the four types of experiences I just named, which one would you like to experience the most, and what question about your life would you like it to address? Record and date your answer in your journal.

SENDING CLEAR
INTUITIVE MESSAGES

Silence is a good inner highway for intuition, but traffic doesn't flow in just one direction, toward you. You also—often without your conscious aware-

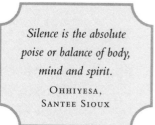

Silence is the absolute poise or balance of body, mind and spirit.

OHHIYESA,
SANTEE SIOUX

ness—send out strong intuitive messages to others. The latter requires a secret ingredient: the ability to enter and reside in deep silence. Today's fast-paced world provides little training for this type of silence or the confidence in life it fosters. Nonetheless, the ability to send clear intuitive messages out from yourself and into the world can lead to rich rewards.

The following story is a good example of what I mean. Things were a mess when Helen returned to Canada after six months of working at an exhausting pace in the Far East. She was in danger of losing her relatively new house because a serious roof leak had occurred while she was away. Relationships with her estranged husband had deteriorated to the point that if she didn't lose the house to damage, she might lose it to him. Her health was also deteriorating, and she was flat broke; no money, no health insurance, no lawyer. What was she to do?

Helen decided to do the only thing that seemed natural. She went home to her dry bedroom and slept. She slept for weeks. She spent the few hours she was awake staring at her walls before she'd fall asleep again. She had no energy to worry. Finally, another type of rest began to enter her body. Silence filled and fed the nooks and crannies of her mind. Her soul oozed peace. There was nothing to plan, no need for strategy, no "how to's" and "what if's," or even a call of destiny. All was silent.

Then in the silence, her phone rang. A friend, who was managing a legal case Helen was involved in, called to say that the case was coming up and the court might decide in her favor. If so, she'd receive a nice sum of money. She didn't have to *do* anything; he'd handle the whole affair. To Helen's amazement, they won the court case and she was awarded enough

> Under all speech that is
> good for anything there
> lies a silence that is better.
>
> THOMAS CARLYLE

money to repair her house and restore her life. She summarized the whole affair, saying, "Although I was doing nothing—sleeping and staring at walls, suddenly my needs were abundantly met. I only hope I never work as hard as I did in the Far East again and that for the remainder of my life I remember what true silence is."

In this case, Helen's silence fostered a mysterious, intuitive dialogue with the world, and events which had been set in motion years ago came forward at her moment of need. This principle of sending an intuitive call out into the world and getting a response is described in *The I Ching* hexagram called "Inner Truth." The text reads: "A crane calling in the shade. Its young answers it. I have a good goblet [the crane says]. I will share it with you." The crane, symbolic of spirit and related to intuition, calls to us from the shade or, in my metaphor, silence. It doesn't have to show itself. Those that belong to it recognize its call and receive its gift. Usually we are too busy, too excited, or too distracted to be silent enough to hear our crane calling. When Helen slowed down and was silent enough to get in touch with her inner crane, the latter emitted an intuitive call for help. Her forgotten legal case, long pushed to the back of her mind, and her friend were the response.

Cathy provides us a more consciously directed example of the power inherent in deep silence. Having worked for years to get a second book published, Cathy was fed up with "efforting" to make things happen. When she got a phone call requesting an outline of her book for a speaker's bureau, she automatically said, "Yes," but the minute she got off the phone, she knew it was inappropriate for her to push hard to get it done. Out of her depths, something flashed, "I am NOT going to throw another ounce of my energy into the black hole of effort. It'll have to arise out of my peace or it won't happen." She immediately sent the project into silence, relaxed, and enjoyed her son's presence during his school break. To Cathy's amazement, the speaker's bureau called her again a week later. They'd managed to get a copy of her book and had created an outline designed for their audiences. Of course, she'd have final approval. Was she interested in seeing what they had planned? Yes. Yes, she was interested, and now burdensome advance work was unnecessary for her.

As is always the case, there are two sides to Cathy's "crane" story. The first is that she had mastered her proclivity to always be doing something. This mastery[3] invoked her inner silence; then her silence evoked a solution which was more masterful than the one she had anticipated. It is important to realize Cathy hadn't entered silence to manipulate the speaker's bureau. She had acted on the faith that slowing down and taking care of herself and her family would work to everyone's advantage somehow. She had no idea that the speaker's bureau would be so resourceful. The second side of the story is that the staff of the speaker's bureau learned more about Cathy's work than they ever would have if she had authored the required outline. This is intuition at work: it fosters inner dialogue in a plugged-in, hooked-up, and communicating world. It's so wise and masterful that everyone gains. Cathy empowered and trusted her silence, her son received her attention during his visit, the speaker bureau's staff challenged themselves to learn and create, and the pubic had the benefit of information which was especially designed for them.

Sitting quietly, doing nothing, Spring comes and the grass grows by itself.
ZEN POEM, JAPANESE

The silence found in Helen's and Cathy's stories goes beyond being silent in order to have a psychic "hit." Instead, it implies a type of silence that produces a deep echo, a sounding of what is needed into the emptiness. One does *not* develop such powerful intimacy with silence in order to gain control, manipulate, or get what you want from the world. The silence I am speaking of doesn't arise from ego gratification but from the spacious freedom of the soul; it is the essence of connection.

Exercise: Sending Clear Intuitive Messages

1. Think of a time when you stopped yourself or when circumstances stopped you from maintaining your normal routines. For example,

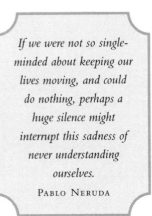

If we were not so single-minded about keeping our lives moving, and could do nothing, perhaps a huge silence might interrupt this sadness of never understanding ourselves.

PABLO NERUDA

you took a silent walk instead of running errands, you had breakfast in bed, you went away alone for the weekend.

2. Describe how you responded to this slow down, this visit with internal silence. Did anything happen or get done that surprised you?

3. If an opportunity to attain this deep silence occurred in your life now, how would you respond today?

4. Helen's intuition called for financial help. Cathy's intuition called for professional help. What help do you wish your intuition would call for now, and why? Record your answer in your journal.

INTUITION, WISDOM, AND SILENCE

We've explored how silence allows you to listen to your intuition and emit a strong intuitive call. In addition to this, silence offers you one more advantage: it births your wisdom. A wise person does more than merely know something; he or she makes elegant use of the knowledge obtained. Wise ones practice right timing, right setting, right words, and right silence. Their wisdom creates a natural synergy; everything works together for the good of all. The wiser you are, the greater your influence. For example, people such as Gandhi, Einstein, Jung, Martin Luther King, Mother Teresa, and Black Elk all had their particular brand of wisdom and impacted generations of people. Each of them reported intuitive callings, chose to serve human evolution, and demonstrated intuitive insights far beyond the norm. The light of their souls guided them and illuminated something about life for all of us.

You have the light of wisdom in you, too. Western mythic traditions suggest two ways for you to manifest your wisdom. Most of you have been trained in the first way, which I call the Athena method of obtaining wisdom. Athena is the Greek goddess of wisdom, who sprung fully developed from her father Zeus's head. From this perspective, wisdom arrives from masculine intellect. (All men and women

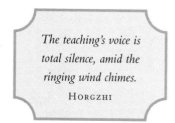

The teaching's voice is total silence, amid the ringing wind chimes.
HORGZHI

have inner masculine and feminine sides. Sexual gender is irrelevant.) The search for this type of wisdom leads us to study more, read, practice debating, and hone our intellectual skills.

There is also a second, lesser known Western myth about the acquisition of wisdom: that of the Roman goddess Sophia. This myth is more closely aligned with intuition and offers another perspective on how your wisdom is acquired. Sophia, whose name is synonymous with illumination or light, is the daughter of Sige, the Roman goddess of silence. The myth of Sophia teaches us that our wisdom is born from Sige's womb, the womb of silence. Sige is usually depicted as a hooded figure with her finger blocking her lips, the universal sign for "don't speak, remain

SIGE

silent." Her gesture warns us not to tell too much; it encourages us to master silence; and it beseeches us not to divulge our inner knowledge to those who are not ready. In each case, silence is a disciplined choice, not a repression of what you want to say.

Sige reminds us that wisdom's presence is not just a product of masculine intellect[4] but is also born from the womb, a dark place inside the silent feminine. Often this dark place is cloaked (notice Sige's shawl), for it contains the hidden creative power of the Universe. The unprepared are warned that, unless they want to risk death from a direct encounter with illumination, they must not peek behind the coverings.[5] Therefore, in

> The cost of liberty is
> less than the price
> of repression.
> WILLIAM E. B. DU BOIS

many traditions, female figures like Sige are veiled or covered not only for their sake but also for the sake of the seeker. Sophia, wisdom itself, however, is available to all. By implication, once you have gone through the educational experiences necessary for obtaining deep silence, your intuition's wisdom is available for yourself and others.

Unfortunately, in today's world all too often Sige's "shhh" has implied the silencing or repression of intuition rather than the authentic silence which fosters it. People repress sharing intuitive experiences with others for fear of misunderstanding or ridicule. They may repress their desire to study intuition because intuition is not proven scientifically and is judged unreliable (usually *before* the judgmental person has done a thorough intuition workout). Or, worse yet, people may repress their own intuitive information: data that tell you that your body is struggling with health issues, your work is not fulfilling, or your partner has become bored with the relationship. According to Gavan de Becker, author of *The Gift of Fear,* most of us have been so trained to ignore intuitive signals that we can jeopardize our very lives by disregarding signals that suggest we are in danger.

The following exercise is designed to help you harvest the wisdom that authentic silence promises to birth.

Exercise: Forgiveness

1. Bring your journal and find a comfortable place to sit.

2. Working at a pace which is natural for you, complete in your journal either of the following sentences by listing appropriate answers as quickly as you think of them. If you wish, do some from both sentence options.

   Sentence: Option #1: "*I forgive myself fully for any way that I repressed my intuition about . . . (list 5 to 10 things you've rejected or repressed intuitive information about, e.g., my addictions, my child's difficulties), and I ask my soul to begin my healing today."*

> *In every pardon there is love.*
> WELSH PROVERB

Sentence: Option #2: *I forgive myself fully for all the ways I repress my intuition, such as . . . (list your favorite ways of repressing your intuition, e.g., putting it down with my logic, thinking my intuition is stupid), and I ask my soul to begin my healing today."*

3. When you've finished, read your list over. If you find any items that challenge your ability to forgive, remind yourself that *forgiveness* means "to give be*fore* you are ready."[6] Read those items over again until you can forgive completely. Don't forget that forgiveness doesn't mean that you have to stop knowing the truth of the situation as you experience it; forgiveness implies freeing all parties of the psychological burdens associated with pain.

CULTIVATING SILENCE: MEDITATION

With your understanding of the gifts of silence in place and an exercise to begin healing any tendency you may have to repress your intuition, you are ready to explore cultivating your deep silence skills.

Meditation is the most powerful tool for cultivating silence. Nothing else is its equal. Some of my students have worried about this; they're convinced they cannot meditate. Regardless of what you think meditation is, I assure you that you've already developed some meditation skills and are probably using them in a variety of settings. Remember, the choice of how to meditate and when to meditate is always yours.

Meditation is an act of attention. Even if you experience scattered-attention skills, your soul knows what to do. At one time or another, for example, you've probably found yourself focusing on something beautiful in nature, a great sports game, a piece of music, the sight of your child's face, the sound of your beloved's voice, or a roaring waterfall. Many

> *Wisdom is also developed through spiritual practice, for in silence you learn what can never be taught.*
>
> FRANCES VAUGHAN

people say the world "disappears" during these moments. This is because their consciousness has entered another dimension. If you have ever had one of these experiences, you are already acquainted with meditation skills. The only distinction between meditation and these moments is conscious awareness or intention. When you meditate, you focus your attention with the *intention* of welcoming silence and filling yourself up with the dimensions of your soul. It doesn't matter what you focus on. It could be your cat.

I am going to take you on a step-by-step journey into what I call the InQ Attention Style. Pay careful attention to the diagrams, and come back to them as often as necessary. Although the journey is long and a little bit complicated, *stick with it*. It contains keys to meditation for the rest of your life and will answer many questions you might have about meditation. Remember: meditation is your greatest tool for manifesting intuition, wisdom, creativity, peace of mind and heart. In addition, as research has shown, it may help you maintain lower stress levels. By the end of your journey, you should be able to:

1. understand how meditation works;

2. know at what point InQ attention skills go beyond right-brain processing;

3. recognize when and how your attention can get distracted, which in turn postpones or short-circuits the meditative process;

4. tell when the deep silence of the soul begins to arise. This will help you identify the precise state of meditation, which births intuition and wisdom.

Meditation and the InQ Attention Style

Most of us think attention is a logical process. For example, if you are sitting at your desk with a pile of tasks to accomplish, you probably prioritize them and then focus your attention on task #1 until it's done, then task #2 until it's done, then task #3, etc.

This exemplifies the left-brain attention style. Remember this fact about left-brain attention style: the power to get things done is invested in attending to one thing at a time. This is because its attention model is based on the belief that reality is comprised of separate, discrete events.

In contrast to this belief, the InQ Attention Style builds on right-brain skills such as wholistic processing and spatial recognition and rests on a unified field perspective. In other words, it is assumed that task #1 is directly or indirectly related to tasks #2, #3, and #4, or they wouldn't be on your desk at the same time. The relationships among the tasks can be superficial (they happened to be on your desk at the same time), very deep (there are many meaningful ties among them), or anything in between. From this unified field perspective, meditation on any one object implies that everything you relate to it, and more, will come up in your meditative practice. Do not be disturbed if this happens. It doesn't mean you are not meditating right. Greet each thing, notice how many rela-

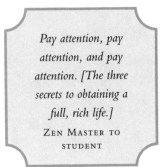

Pay attention, pay attention, and pay attention. [The three secrets to obtaining a full, rich life.]

Zen Master to student

tionships there are, and return your attention to task #1.[7]

In other words, when you achieve inner silence through focusing on task #1, you will automatically be linked to all the other tasks on your desk. Although it feels strange, if not chaotic, to have everything in your attention field all at once, I promise you that order and priorities will emerge organically out of the sea of possibilities. When you do finish task #1, the most appropriate next task arises naturally. As long as the daily focusing technique is employed, your tasks will all be completed with a wise sense of timing. There is no doubt of this.

A balanced person knows how to match the most appropriate attention style (left-brain, right-brain attention style, or the InQ Attention Style) to the tasks at hand. For example, Bill uses the left-brain attention style when he has lots of small, straight-forward tasks to accomplish,

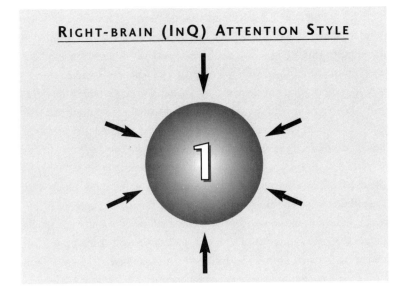

RIGHT-BRAIN (InQ) ATTENTION STYLE

the right-brain attention style to access a creative order for completing his tasks, and the InQ Attention Style when he wants to access his intuition and go for the wisest possible outcome.

> *If we truly pay attention, our Essence [soul] takes over and directs our attention and responses in . . . a resourceful way.*
>
> MICHAEL RAY AND ROCHELLE MYERS

THE InQ ATTENTION STYLE: THREE STEPS

With this background in place, you are now ready to begin your three-step journey to silence, intuition, and wisdom. Each step contains a brief explanation and an exercise. To understand the differences between the left-brain attention style and where you are going, all the exercises assume that:

- you are confronted with a pile of tasks on your desk;

- you've decided to experiment with using intuition to organize your tasks and facilitate your wisdom;

- you are going to use a simple meditative process to access the silence which will help you.

You can either sit at a desk or imagine that you are doing so. The point is you have a pile of tasks to do. How do you know where to start?

Step #1: Choose Something You Like

Start by choosing something you'd like to do from the pile. It should be something that attracts you, makes you smile, piques your curiosity, or evokes your passion. Whatever it is, you care about it. Once you identify your chosen task, focus all your attention on it. For example, Rob decided to focus on the car he needed to buy. He gave all his attention to a picture of the particular car he wanted.

> *Only through the divine can one hurry without haste and reach the goal without walking.*
>
> WILHELM/BAYNES

Exercise: Step #1: The InQ Attention Style

1. Look over your pile of tasks and choose the one that you like the most, even if your conscious mind thinks it is frivolous or the least important.

2. If there isn't a single task in your pile that you like, choose something on your desk or computer desktop that you do like.

3. In your mind, label this object #1.

4. Sitting calmly, do the Basic Breath exercise on page 76 until you're relaxed.

5. Focus all your attention on the object for a full 2 minutes. If you find it difficult to do, ask yourself questions about your object such as: Why does my soul like this task for me now? How does it contribute to my aliveness? What does it remind me of? If it is still difficult, make sure your body is silent, then check your emotions and your mind. Silence them, too. Return your attention to your object.

6. Record the name of your object and what it was like to focus on it for a full 2 minutes.

You can't fool yourself in step #1. Your intuition knows if you are choosing something you think you ought to choose rather than something you enjoy. Stick with an object that really attracts you.

Step #2: Hold the Fort: Welcome Chaos and Changes

The InQ Attention Style begins to emerge in step #2. In step #2, objects other than your chosen task begin to enter your attention field (see the diagram; the numbers 2 and 3 represent these new objects). The objects which you believe—consciously or unconsciously—are related to your chosen task come into your field of attention. Don't think that you are failing when this starts to happen. This lack of order or chaos is natural.

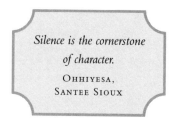

Silence is the cornerstone of character.
OHHIYESA,
SANTEE SIOUX

Be careful about these objects because they can distract your focus. For example, Rob's mind wandered from his desired car and jumped to where he should buy the car, how he can get a loan, and the status of his bank account. If he didn't keep his main attention on the car itself or return his attention to it, he'd miss his journey to silence. By the way, once Rob is experienced with focusing his attention in step #2 and accepts how natural it is that other things enter his consciousness, he will be able to focus his attention on the car while simultaneously holding any related objects in the periphery of his consciousness.

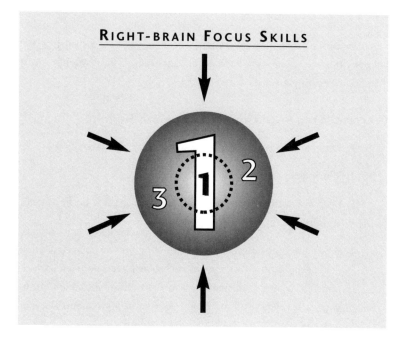

RIGHT-BRAIN FOCUS SKILLS

> *There is no time to stop, even for a moment, to try and hold on.*
>
> JOSEPH GOLDSTEIN

Look back at the diagram on page 117. There is another important point for you to know. Notice that your task #1 is subtly starting to change, going from the big 1 to a smaller 1 inside a dotted circle. Don't panic. This is the beginning of your InQ Attention Style; what you think is important or what you like the best starts to assume a different relationship with the whole. For example, while Rob is focusing on his car, a feeling of inner peace begins to enter him, and the car no longer assumes the importance he has been giving it. If he acts like most of us, Rob will begin to panic. "Hey, wait! I really want to buy this car," he says to himself and he tries to hold on to the image. The more Rob struggles to hold #1, as he has understood it, the more chameleon it appears. If Rob becomes locked into his original task, the chances of his intuition serving up the best car there is are decreased.

Actually Rob is being courted by his inner silence, but you couldn't convince him of that. Task #1, which has been used as a focusing device because he likes it, begins to fade as his inner nature starts to enter. As it does so, everything assumes different proportions.

Exercise: Step #2: The InQ Attention Style

1. Resume the Basic Breath exercise until you are relaxed again.

2. Return your attention fully to your original task.

3. Keep your attention on your task as other objects begin to enter your field of focus.

4. When the other objects start distracting you or your meditation field seems a bit chaotic, greet each object, acknowledge its relationship to your task mentally, and then return your attention to your task. If you need to, remind yourself how much you like your task and why.

5. After 15 to 20 minutes of doing this, you may become aware of a still, peaceful sensation emerging within you. It can come as a feeling of warmth, a cathartic sigh, a sense of wide openness, or love.

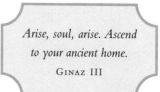

Arise, soul, arise. Ascend to your ancient home.
GINAZ III

6. As this happens, your task often begins to change, to assume a different relationship with the whole field. To the best of your ability, hold both the new sensations and your task in your attention.

7. After 5 to 10 minutes of doing this, take a deep breath, get out your journal, and record your reactions to this process. What, if any, other objects entered your mind? How were they related to your task? How hard was it for you to stay focused? Did your task begin to change in any way? Did sensations of greater calmness enter you? If so, how did you react?

If you didn't find your task changing or any sensations of calmness entering you, don't give up. Regular practice is more important than instant achievement. Never forget: you are the sole object of your soul's meditation. In many ways, your soul is both calling you to meditation and is seeking to meditate through you.

Steps 1 and 2 of the InQ Attention Style have been built in part on the right-brain attention style which emphasizes wholistic images. In step #3, the InQ style even lets go of wholistic vision in order to invite something deeper to enter.

Step #3: The Gift of Deep Silence

Ultimately, the gift of deep silence is contact with your soul and subsequent intuitive knowledge. Think of meditation as a process which clears your inner space, at least temporarily, so that the soul can more fully occupy your body, mind, and emotions. People adept at meditation are able

> *So what I advise my students to do when they encounter silence is: absolutely nothing. Bathe in it. Surrender to it. Let it work on you.*
> LARRY ROSENBERG

to maintain more soul contact throughout their day.

To get to the silence, you must learn when to completely let go of your attention on your task. If you let go too soon, your attention will springboard to other objects. If this happens, return your attention to your task because you do *not* let go in order to place your attention on another task (numbers 1, 2, 3, 4, 5, and 6 in the diagram below). You let go to allow deep silence to enter. Let silence fill you completely; identify yourself as silence. This is the state which is so restful for your intuitive body.

In this silence, Jackie Stewart's body knew how to drive a particular race; Mozart heard an entire symphony; and the still voice of what's right for you can arise. In the example of Rob and his car, when he leaves his meditative silence and goes back to his daily life, his built-in intuitive con-

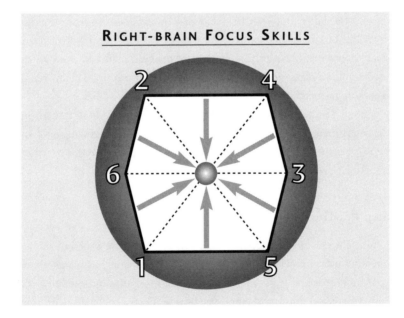

RIGHT-BRAIN FOCUS SKILLS

nections lead him to purchase the right car and reveal a good way to finance his entire project. Or perhaps after meditation Bob may intuit that this is not the best time for him to purchase a car. He peacefully puts the project aside until later.

> *The mind of the sage in repose becomes the mirror of the universe, the speculum of all creation.*
> CHUANG TZU

Exercise: Step #3: InQ Attention Style

1. Do the Basic Breath exercise until you are relaxed.

2. Focus on your task again, greeting any other things which arise and returning your attention to your task.

3. When calmness begins to arise in your body or when your task begins to change shape, importance, or intensity, gently turn your attention back to your task *without* insisting it remains the same.

4. Try to hold your attention simultaneously on the feelings arising in your body and the changing properties of your task.

5. When it feels right to you, let go of all the attention you have on your task and stay with the sensations of peace, calmness, and silence which are entering your body. Let them completely enter you. Stay in the silence, providing rest for your intuitive body and fostering your intuition. Do not do anything, including looking for intuitive answers.

6. After approximately 15 minutes of silence or when you feel done, take a deep breath and return your attention to where you are sitting.

7. Look at the pile of tasks on your desk and do the one you originally picked. If your intuition insists on another one, do that one instead. When you finish your first task, do the next one which seems natural. Quit doing tasks when you lose focus or feel tired.

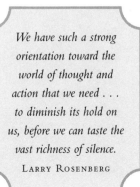

We have such a strong orientation toward the world of thought and action that we need . . . to diminish its hold on us, before we can taste the vast richness of silence.

LARRY ROSENBERG

8. Repeat the entire process again until all the tasks which your intuition deems important are done.

9. Record your experiences in your journal.

Option: Do the entire exercise, but apply it to the garden visualization which appears on page 101.

CULTIVATING SILENCE: NATURE

Some people can only meditate successfully in nature. For them, it is not enough to imagine nature or a garden; they need to be in it. Nature teaches us to let go and trust what appears to be nothingness, much as you must do when you decide to trust silence and your intuition. An old tale demonstrates this truth beautifully.

Once upon a time, a great river rushed with all its power into the desert, but its roaring presence only evaporated into the desert sands. The harder the river rushed, the more it disappeared. In its struggle, the river heard the voice of the wind saying, "Let go and trust me." The angry river rejected the wind. "I can't trust you. I am a mighty river and very determined. I can't even see you." The river continued to struggle; the wind continued to whisper, "Let go and trust me." Finally, the exhausted river gave up and, not knowing what else to do, turned itself over to the wind. Then the wind swooped down and gently picked the river up into the sky, where it disappeared into the air. The wind carried the river across the desert, and let it go against the mountain ranges on the other side. The river's waters fell to the Earth. Soon the might river flowed again for all to see and enjoy. When the river trusted, it learned that the best and only course for its re-emergence abided in what appeared to be nothing.

Exercise: Trusting the Wind

1. Take your journal and go out to a high spot where the wind is likely to be blowing. Sit down where you'll be comfortable. Date a page in your journal and write down what you'd like to

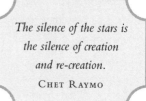

The silence of the stars is the silence of creation and re-creation.
CHET RAYMO

entrust to the wind and silence. Examples include a character trait you want to develop, a project you are working on, a relationship you want to strengthen. When you've finished, close your eyes.

2. When you feel the wind come, imagine it is picking you up and taking you to a silent place. Let silence fill you. As the wind whips around and caresses you, experience that you are being cradled by silence within and without. Trust.

3. After 15 to 20 minutes of this experience, take a deep breath, bring your attention back to where you are sitting, and open your eyes.

4. Record three pages of reactions in your journal. Write spontaneously about whatever you entrusted to the wind.

Larry Ramirez, an Apache friend of mine, once said, "I am glad I raised my kids in the mountains. They have their own kind of silence now and will take it with them wherever they go." For Larry and his family, it is mountains which foster the kind of silence we are after. As Larry's statement suggests, mountains, trees, and rocks, called the "standing still ones" by some Native American tribes, can help you obtain inner silence: a place where things happen without effort.

Exercise: Your Own Kind of Silence

1. Take your journal to a favorite spot and identify a tree, rock, or mountain that attracts you. Sit next to it or on it.

2. Using your imagination, have an intuitive interview with your chosen standing still one. Ask these questions or design some of your own.

   • How does it feel to be a standing still one?

   • What do you think of silence?

   • How do you experience it?

   • What wisdom can I gain from it?

   • What intuitive insight would you like to share with me?

   • What insights would you like to hear from me?

3. Write down everything you learn in your journal.

4. Identify and highlight one thing which would help you create your own kind of silence.

5. Record how you'll put this type of silence into practice tomorrow.

6. The next night, review your day and see if, how, and when you put your own kind of silence to work.

7. Visit your standing still teacher the following day, thank it, and discuss what happened. Record in your journal.

Although nature is far from silent, the rhythms of its noise—the rustle of trees, the chirping of birds, the scurrying of little animals—are a welcome break from the constant noise of modern life. Just visiting nature breaks the rhythm, style, and type of sounds which are normally part of most people's auditory environment. A new rhythm makes more room for silence.

If you can't get to nature, you can do something else to tap nature's silence. Playfully pretend that you are a plant or an animal. Try lounging around like a cat, taking in sunshine like a plant, or hibernating like a bear. Your goal is similar to your interaction with trees, rocks, or mountains.

While you're playing, find silence inside the animal's or object's behavior and try to bring that silence into your body. From our human perspective, plants and animals don't appear to ask why or try to understand things; they accept things as they are. This is what makes them unique catalysts of silence.

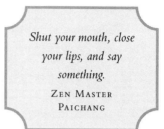

Shut your mouth, close your lips, and say something.

ZEN MASTER
PAICHANG

SILENCE AND POWER

Because I believe that silence equals power, I've used the phrase "the power of silence" throughout this chapter. Sige, a powerful teacher of mysterious silence, gives birth to wisdom. The intuition which fosters powerful human encounters with creativity, peak performance, telepathic connections, and profound insights is recognized by experts to arise out of silence. In silence, you hear intuition's voice. In silence, your intuition issues powerful calls to others. Finally, meditation or focused attention, which is the best skill for attaining silence, is power. In fact, your life is the sum total of what has held your attention. Most of us make the mistake, however, of thinking that it is the object of our attention—our jobs, partners, families, avocations—which brings success. Our focus is on the wrong things. When you realize that your focused attention activates the presence of your soul, you welcome silence and invite your soul to illuminate your life through the powerful light of intuition. You make silence your friend.

Final Exercise: Your Intuition To Do List

1. Complete the sentence, "Because I am accepting my soul's invitation to 'Cultivate Silence,' I already know to . . ." List 5 to 10 things you know to do such as "lounge around once a day like a cat," "read about Sophia on the Internet," "go to the local rose garden and

meditate." When you've finished, read over your list. Highlight the simplest activity which appears most *wise* to you and do it. Record everything in your journal.

2. Go back and look at your Guiding Image for this chapter. How does it capture the essence of silence? Does it contain a hint about the best way for you to obtain silence? Identify the most interesting thing you learned about intuition and silence in this chapter. How does your illustration relate to it? Record in your journal.

CHAPTER 6

Invitation Four:

NURTURE JOY

JOY, FOOD FOR YOUR INTUITIVE BODY

The ability to laugh at situations we encounter on the spiritual path is essential to the health of the intuitive body. Joy is food for your intuitive body, supplying it with energy, restoring its balance, and fueling its connections. The joy I am referring to arises from your soul and activates wide open and receptive inner states. Intuition thrives in this environment. Having a great sense of humor, your soul employs clowns, comics on the television, spoof movies, daily cartoons, satirists, or friends who are "good for a laugh" to keep the flames of your inner joy alive during difficult times. Your soul wants you to meet your cosmic comic, the part of you that has a big enough view of your life to keep things balanced. In all his or her different forms (clowns, tricksters, satirists, comedians), your cosmic comic helps you take your life more lightly. Lightness is good for your intuitive body, and an abundance of joy is its feast.

This chapter is about that feast. The areas we'll cover are: heart laughter, curing spiritual addictions, the need for a sense of humor, five things you can do to increase the joy in your life, how joy operates, and courting bliss. Fun and a transformed reality are your rewards.

Laughter can change reality. Norman Cousins's experience taught us

> A sense of humor can be
> a great help—particularly
> a sense of humor
> about oneself.
>
> DWIGHT D.
> EISENHOWER

that decades ago when he healed himself of terminal disease by continuously playing humorous videos, such as "Candid Camera," on his hospital monitor. I believe he proved this point: if we listened to our bodies' desire to laugh more, we'd all be in better health.

While Cousins suggests that laughter can heal life, Deepak Chopra, M.D., author of *Ageless Body, Timeless Mind,* believes that joy and laughter can extend life; a person can "laugh himself or herself young." According to Chopra, joy is a strategy for defeating entropy, the idea that everything including us and the Universe is on a downward spiral toward death. He quotes this Old Testament verse to demonstrate the link made over two thousand years ago between long life and joy:

Gladness of heart is life to a man,
Joy is what gives him length of days.

Barbara L. Schultz, a colleague, takes Chopra's idea a bit further. Her intuition has helped "youth" her body for many years. Believing that much of what we think of as aging is a state of mind, Barbara tunes into her body frequently and responds to the intuitive information she receives about her body's physical and energetic needs.[1] She has learned to trust the information she receives and believes that, as a result, she has been able to maintain the fitness and appearance of a woman years younger than she is.

The mere act of trusting the deepest part of yourself says, "My soul is on my side, on the side of my full life regardless of my chronological age." Of course, some would say this is wishful thinking and motivated by an avoidance of death. The truth is that some types of deaths—deaths of ideas, beliefs, or personal identity—are such a common occurrence on the spiritual path that it's a good idea to have laughter and your cosmic comic close at hand.

To establish your guiding illustration for this chapter, do this exercise
now. As you choose, remember that
laughter is great medicine in your intuitive world.

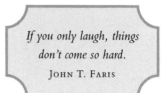

*If you only laugh, things
don't come so hard.*

JOHN T. FARIS

Your Guiding Image for "Nurture Joy"

- Create a section of your Intuition Journal and label it "Chapter
  Five: Nurture Joy."

- Reach into your Image Vocabulary envelope and, without looking, pull out your guiding illustration for this chapter.

- Label the category your illustration comes from on the bottom
  of the page you've just established.

- Paste your illustration on this page.

Unfortunately, people can see a direct link between silence (rest) and
the intuitive body, but often they have a hard time making the connection
between joy (food) and the intuitive body. There is a simple cure for this:
the next time you experience wonderful laughter, notice how wide open
your body and spirit feel immediately afterward. This is the plane of existence we are after.

HEART LAUGHTER

I had attended quite a number of gatherings of Native Americans before
I noticed subtle behavior patterns which were distinctly different from
those of the culture in which I had been raised. Laughter was the first to
catch my eye. According to my observations, every social gathering began
with honoring the elders, greeting each other, and then settling down
into inevitable waves of laughter. It didn't matter what generated the
laughter—a good story, jokes, or collective memories. Only when a gen-

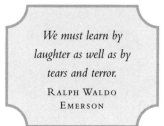

eral state of openness, relaxation, joy, and connection was in the room did people begin to talk about important matters.

I was amazed at the results. Meetings appeared to have a natural intuitive flow to them, tasks seemed to fall out easily at moments when discussion about them seemed a long way off, and all the people were really present whether they spoke or not. But this wasn't what intrigued me most. The most interesting thing was the constant river of synchronicities, telepathic communications, and exact right timing. I began to believe that laughter was a proficient weaver of intuitive communication and community. This laughter came from the heart and touched hearts; it was heart laughter.

The need for deep heart laughter exists in individuals as well as in tribes or organizations. In one of the most haunting pieces of prose I've ever read, Mary, a student of mine, expressed a spontaneous understanding of this universal human need for heart laughter. Her assignment for our study group was to write a short script, a type of personal myth, which did these three things:

1. identified an attribute she was working on;

2. helped her integrate the intuitive lessons of this attribute;

3. represented transformation.

Writing the myth normally required advance thought and planning because each person read their myth to the group, and then the entire group enacted their interpretation of the myth or the myth itself. Mary did it differently; she employed her intuition exclusively. Her myth told this story:

> Once there were Angels who lived inside a Mountain. They were born in the rivers which flowed deep in Her center.

The Mountain had been silent for millions of years, covered by the Sky, which was also silent.

> Everything was still.
> There was no laughter.

Inside the Mountain, the Angels sailed the course of the Rivers. In their hearts they could hear the thoughts of the Mountain, and they knew that She

> *We call "happiness" a certain set of circumstances that makes joy possible. But we call joy that state of mind and emotions that needs nothing to feel happy.*
> ANDRÉ GIDE

wanted to breathe into the Sky and create Laughter. So, the Angels looked for the heart of the Mountain by diving into the Rivers where they dissolved until only their hearts were left. And their hearts were the heart of the Mountain. Then they inhaled, drawing in the Earth with their breath. Then they exhaled, and the Heart opened freeing the Spirit of Laughter.

Mary "channeled" this myth, which came out of her in one stream without any forethought. When she was done writing it, she didn't question its perfection. She changed nothing. When I asked for the title, she answered, "It has no title."

Mary's tale of the longing Mountain speaks to the vacancy of life without heart laughter. It is up to each of us on our intuitive journey to nurture joy, to cultivate a relationship with our cosmic comic, to exercise our heart laughter, and to welcome the winks of our trickster. When you do so, you align yourself with the thoughts of Norman Cousins and Deepak Chopra. You also learn to shift space and change reality a bit by building intuitive connections, enhancing your health, and "youthing" yourself.

To assess how your heart laughter is doing, do exercises A and B. Record your activities and thoughts in your journal.

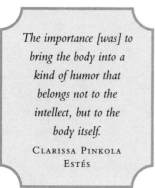

The importance [was] to bring the body into a kind of humor that belongs not to the intellect, but to the body itself.

CLARISSA PINKOLA ESTÉS

Exercise A: Your Laughter Questionnaire

Answer the following questions to the best of your ability.

1. Did you have an opportunity to laugh today?

2. When was the last time you laughed until your sides ached?

3. Does your work fill you with joy?

4. Do you look forward to your day when you wake up in the morning?

5. Does it make you smile just to think of some of your life companions?

5. On a scale of 1 to 100, what number would you ascribe to the amount of laughter in your life now? (95 means a lot; 10 means very little)

Exercise B: Heart Laughter

1. Write a letter to your cosmic comic. Discuss the amount of heart laughter in your life and, assuming you want more, ask your cosmic comic to help you increase the amount and the quality of your heart laughter experiences.

2. What is one thing you wish you could laugh about now, but you don't feel like laughing? What's so serious about it?

Heart laughter is difficult to develop if you are taking your growth—including the growth of your intuitive abilities—too seriously. Subtle addictions emerge if you tip the scales too much in favor of either all fun or all work.

CURING SPIRITUAL ADDICTIONS

Penny Yrigoyen is a cartoonist whose work often concerns spiritual and inner development topics. One of my favorite pieces of her work depicts a perplexed-looking dog sitting on the grass with six ridiculing cats all around him in his aura. The cats are jumping on his head, taunting him, sticking their tongues out, and generally making his life miserable. The caption reads "Dog with a bad case of astral cats."

> *There ain't no answer. There ain't going to be any answer. There never has been an answer. That's the answer.*
>
> GERTRUDE STEIN

After years of involvement with intuition and what is sometimes termed the New Age, I'm convinced that the collective aura holds these two common emotional or astral addictions: *spiritual highs* and *responsibility prisons.*[2] A spiritual high encompasses surface joy which produces spiritual "fads" as people flit from one spiritual path to another. These people are in search of the mystical orgasms which usually accompany new discoveries about God and the soul. Waves of well-being, cellular delight throughout the whole body, and a sensation of joy are part of the early stages of spiritual awakening. To add icing to the cake, people experience multiple synchronicities, plenty of intuition, and everything goes their way. Naturally, some people find this period addictive, and, in order to maintain the high, they continually seek out new and unusual spiritual experiences. It's not the spirituality they seek as much as the high which accompanies the opening. True joy is independent of these highs and arises from a different place inside you.

At the other end of the spectrum, people can make the pursuit of soul so serious that it becomes a responsibility prison. Fun and joy are foregone in favor of "spiritualoholism." This is often a subtle manifestation of the Messiah complex. Workers get convinced that their task is essential right now for the salvation of something—people, animals, towns, planets. For example, dedicated environmentalists can be overwhelmed by a feeling that our planet, who has taken care of Herself for fifteen billion

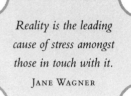

Reality is the leading cause of stress amongst those in touch with it.

JANE WAGNER

years, must be saved or transformed this week. I do not deny that we are, as a species, at a critical juncture in our relationship with the Earth, but acting *with* Her from our hearts and minds is a lot different than acting *on* Her or on each other out of our fear. Lasting change has never come about through fear; only love generates changes that endure. Unfortunately, regardless of who is doing them or why, many actions which come from responsibility prisons have their roots in fear or hurt. Yet, the minute your actions are motivated by love, the doors of your responsibility prisons spring open and you are set free.

Ridding yourself of these addictions is vital because they drain you. Your unconscious tries to use your intuitive talents to serve your addiction. In other words, if you were addicted to spiritual highs, your unconscious might lobby for your intuitive powers to find where your next high was coming from. If you were addicted to responsibility prisons, your unconscious might want your intuition to locate support for your cause and justifications for your behavior. In short, your unconscious behaves like the astral cats around our cartoon dog; it badgers you for attention. When you end these addictions, you get a surge of intuitive power because your unconscious is no longer trying to siphon off your skills in the direction of your addiction.[3]

A profound acceptance of intuition and the laughter it brings cures people of addictions to spiritual highs and responsibility prisons. In the case of spiritual highs, intuition continually connects you with your soul. The resulting sense of peace is all-pervasive: restoring confidence, providing a lifetime of uplifted feelings, and making deep exploration of your relationship with God enticing. Gradually, surface exploration of spirituality, including the initial highs, becomes less attractive than mining your depths for lasting wisdom and joy. The latter two bring more detachment; you take things more lightly. In the case of responsibility prisons, soul peace provides a profound sense of trust. Fears are recognized and can no longer generate tension in life over anything, spiritual responsibility included. You trust the process of life—its timing, its purpose, and its humor. You let go of urgency and the belief that you have to "save" anyone or anything. When you do this, joy and laughter return and can even become criteria for selecting tasks.

One filled with joy preaches without preaching.
MOTHER TERESA

Examine these two spiritual addictions now. Be honest with yourself.

Exercise: Addictions

1. Have you ever had a period in your life when you participated in spiritual highs or responsibility prisons? If so, when, where, and why? If not, have you ever seen the behavior?

2. What is the best, most realistic scenario you can imagine for an end to these addictions? For example, "I get such a quick, powerful glimpse of myself acting like a person in a responsibility prison that I laugh and in the future say 'no' to my seriousness." Or, "My next spiritual opening with a new tradition won't be as much fun as I expected, and I'll begin to see deep virtues in the traditions I've neglected."

3. Do you find anything about either of those two behaviors humorous? If so, what? How do you personally believe joy helps people with their intuitive process?

4. Record in your journal.

FIVE WAYS TO ADD LAUGHTER AND JOY TO YOUR LIFE

Happiness is a skill set. If you want to keep your intuitive body fit, you'll find authentic methods for honing your happiness skills. The following five methods are helpful, although some will attract you more than oth-

> . . . and since there is no
> joy without God, but all
> joy is in God, and God
> himself is wholly joy,
> it follows that the
> first speaker said first
> and before anything
> else "God."
>
> DANTE

ers, and some will be better catalysts for your intuition. You can identify which techniques are best for you by keeping a record of everything in your journal.

Method #1: The Trickster— A Helpmate

The trickster is one of the most famous satirists, comedians, and jokesters used by the soul to help you stay light. Ordinary rules do not apply to the trickster. He can do everything backwards, make lewd jokes, satirize that which is most sacrosanct, and make a huge mess of everything. He exists in you, and in each of us, just waiting to pop our false bubbles. Psychologist June Singer describes the trickster in the following way:

> He symbolizes that aspect of our own nature which is always nearby, reading to bring us down when we get inflated, or to humanize us when we become pompous.

In short, the trickster is a built-in jokester who won't tolerate a holier-than-thou attitude and who blasts us out of self-righteousness with his shenanigans. His activities restore a sense of proportion to our lives. In the development of intuition the trickster is often the one who reveals to you that you've been fooling yourself, that what you thought was intuition was just projection or wishful thinking. For example, a client of mine—we'll call him Tom—tells this story. He worked for a very wealthy man, whose support was being cultivated by a group of playwrights. Tom liked the playwrights and was flattered when they took an interest in a screenplay he'd written a few years earlier.

When the playwrights, whom Tom assumed had reviewed his play, invited him to a private business lunch, his "intuition" led him to think they wanted to talk about his play. Excited, Tom's imagination already had his name in lights and the curtain going up on his play's first act. Taking what seemed to be a cue from the playwrights, Tom began to wax poetic about his work over lunch.

Suddenly, Tom was struck with flatulence. He smelled horrible and, having been trained to look for the trickster in such situations, began wondering if he was "just full of it." As the smell contin-

> *The comic spirit masquerades in all things we say and do. We are each a clown and do not need to put on a white face.*
>
> JAMES HILLMAN

ued, he embarrassingly backed off discussing his play and started to probe for what the playwrights themselves thought. Before the lunch was over, Tom wasn't sure if they had even read his play and knew that what they wanted was his business advice on how best to approach his wealthy employer with their own projects. Disappointed but realistic, Tom later had to laugh at himself, and, while he appreciated being saved from making a bigger fool of himself, he wished the trickster had used less offensive tactics. The trickster, however, makes no promises to be nice and polite. Tom realized that his craving for artistic success, instead of business success, made him vulnerable to the situation and promised himself he'd take responsibility for doing something with his play and other creative projects.

If, like Tom, we are able to laugh and see how we've been fooling ourselves with a projection or wishful thought, the trickster waves goodbye, winking his eye as he goes. If we can't laugh at ourselves, anger, frustration, and powerlessness tend to take over. Refusing to examine the root of our delusions in order to heal, we rage against intuition and against life itself, accusing them of having played tricks on us.

Exercise: The Trickster

1. In your journal, write about a time when you discovered that what you believed was intuition was only wishful thinking or projections. What did you think about it at the time? What does the incident teach you now? Can you laugh about it now?

*An inexhaustible good
nature is one of the most
precious gifts of heaven.*
WASHINGTON IRVING

2. Think about comedies you've seen at the movies or on television, or comic stories you've heard or read. Identify ones with a trickster element. Write about one of them in your journal, describing what the trickster did, how the characters responded, and what possible lessons they could have learned.

Method #2: Consult Your Cosmic Comic

I met a second holy humorist, Anne Duram Robinson, at an Intuition Network Conference in San Diego. Eighty-three years old at the time, Anne was, and still is, an active business consultant for intuition and creativity. She introduced me to another humorous character, the cosmic comic (Anne calls this character the Court Jester of Consciousness). Anne advised the audience to which she spoke to consult with their cosmic comic whenever they were stuck for ideas. She explained what she meant by telling this story.

> When a large health organization called me to do a thirty-minute presentation on change and humor, I wasn't sure what to do. The company, like many others, had gone through a lot of down-sizing, and the remaining employees were discouraged and needed ways to handle the changes. The leadership was wise enough to prioritize helping people through these rough waters and had invited all levels of personnel to attend my session. Since I am *not* an expert in change management, I racked my aging brain for an effective and helpful approach.
>
> I went inside and asked my cosmic comic (Court Jester of Consciousness), a wise comedian, what to do. It kept nudging me, "Play with *paradigms,* Play with *paradigms,*" but I didn't

like the idea. When my other
ideas seemed flat, I finally surren-
dered to my cosmic comic's suggestion and drew a large curtain
with a young feminine head peek-
ing over the top and a masculine

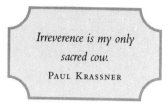

*Irreverence is my only
sacred cow.*

PAUL KRASSNER

head peering around the side on a poster board. The title read:
"How to Change Your Paradigms in Front of Everybody—
with Only Humor for a Curtain."

Anne then led the group through the steps of change, the gradations
of paradigm shifts, and on to "Paradigm Prestidigitation: A Sleight-of-
Hand Way to Fake It Until You Can Make It." Anne soon had the people
rolling on the floor with laughter (she did at the Intuition Conference,
too), and then she had them break into small groups to create limericks or
fun-poking cartoons about their situation. When the cartoons and limericks were ready, they presented them to each other with impressive results.
All of this was accomplished in thirty minutes, leading Anne to summa-
rize, "Once again I was rescued by my cosmic comic."

Anne's story reminds us that we can intuitively ask our inner cosmic
comic for help even when we are confronted with serious situations
(people losing their jobs). The laughter that your cosmic comic generates energizes and balances depressed spirits, allowing illumination to
enter.

Exercise: Consult Your Cosmic Comic

1. Identify a situation you find serious now, but believe your cosmic
   comic might help you achieve a more humorous perspective on.
   Record the situation in your journal.

2. Sit quietly. Go inside yourself and ask your cosmic comic to help
   you create cartoons, limericks, or puns about this situation which
   make you smile or laugh. Record them all no matter how absurd
   they seem.

Since everything is perfect . . . in being what it is, having nothing to do with good or bad, . . . one may well burst out in laughter.

LONG CHEN PA

3. Close your journal and return to normal life for 6 to 8 hours. When the hours have passed, open your journal. Star any of your cartoons or puns which make you laugh or smile, which remind you of a recent humorous insight, or which simply feed a good feeling inside you. Record any notes in your journal.

4. Thank your cosmic comic.

Method #3: A Morning Laughter Workout

In 1993, one of my teachers was on board the first Inner Journey cruise to the Caribbean. Peter and Pat Einstein, the organizers, had wisely decided to include a few open microphone evenings because the list of guests was as impressive as the list of presenters. Leila from New York City, a unique elder who always wore a black, small-brimmed fedora which framed her lovely face, took the microphone. Without much introduction she said:

"I'm going to introduce you to my favorite exercises. I warn you that if you live alone and do these exercises when you have overnight guests, they're likely to shake their heads and wonder to themselves, '*What could be going on?*' As for myself, I never tell them my secret unless they have the nerve to ask," she said with a twinkle.

"I always begin my day with a laugh," she told us. "Since it's the first sound I want to make and to hear, I always laugh before I get out of bed in the morning. If I don't do it, I might not get it in my schedule all day. I've developed a 'laughter workout' which I'd love to share with you."

Leila then led the room as we all practiced imitating four different styles of familiar-sounding fake laughter. Soon, as you might expect, genuine heart laughter took over, since our forced laughter sounded so funny. Leila then refined her coaching techniques, advising us to either repeat one of the ways of laughing over and over or cycle through all the types until we were genuinely laughing again.

I was deeply touched by Leila's laughter workout and have offered it since to help people set the stage for their intuitive day. It is a particularly good technique to use if you scored low on the Laughter Questionnaire on page 132.

> *I, God, am your playmate! I will lead the child in you in wonderful ways, for I have chosen you.*
>
> METCHILD OF MAGDEBURG

Exercise: Leila's Morning Laughter Workout

1. Take your journal and a pen and find a comfortable place to sit (sitting up in bed is fine).

2. Start your day by choosing one of the following styles of laughter and repeating it over and over until you are laughing naturally. Or, run through the four different styles sequentially over and over again until you are genuinely laughing.

   • The first is "Hee! Hee! Hee! Hee! Hee!"

   • The second is "Hi! Hi! Hi! Hi! Hi!"

   • The third is "Ha! Ha! Ha! Ha! Ha!"

   • The fourth is "Ho! Ho! Ho! Ho! Ho!"

3. Laugh until you are feeling good.

4. Write 2 to 3 pages in your journal in response to "I'd really feel great and laugh a lot if my intuition guided me to . . ." For example, a movie which helped you laugh at your life in a healthy way, an unexpected comic evening with your family, or an encounter with the canned laughter of radio and television.

5. Repeat exercise every morning for at least 5 days in a row.

> I asked for all things,
> that I might enjoy life.
> I was given all life, that
> I might enjoy all things.
>
> ANONYMOUS

Method #4: Situation Comedy and Synchronicities

Sometimes humor is deeply embedded in a situation. For example, one day when Paula was thinking about her sister Evelyn's new home in Oregon, a place where she wished she had the courage to move, coincidence after coincidence occurred. First, the phone rang. It was a misdial; the caller was trying to reach Oregon but reached New Mexico instead. Paula didn't pay too much attention to it, although she did note the Oregon reference and smiled to herself. An hour later, a friend she hadn't heard from in years called. She was in Oregon now. Her husband had been transferred. When she went to get her mail, there was the brochure for yurts she'd sent for weeks earlier. The company's home base was Oregon. When Paula turned on her TV and was greeted unexpectedly by a special on the Oregon Trail, she burst into laughter and said directly to the Universe, "All right. All right. I get it. Oregon is a good place for me!"

Paula was having a series of what Carl Jung called synchronicities, meaningful coincidences which are not related by our normal understanding of cause and effect. Paula knew that her inner yearning was somehow sending a clear intuitive message out, and she was receiving a response.[4] She decided to spend the Christmas holiday with her sister and to seriously explore the possibility of moving to Oregon at that time.

Synchronicities occur in a variety of contexts, not just those where important decisions are being reached. Sometimes their greatest gift is sheer laughter. I remember one time when an intuition study group was reviewing Pablo Neruda's poem "The Sea and Bells," in which Neruda pleads for silence. Living so close to the sea, we found the metaphors of the title particularly poignant, although we were missing bells. During the silence following the poem's end, one of my students, Karlotta, nonchalantly reached deep underneath the couch to retrieve a wayward pen and, to her surprise, returned with a bell I'd been missing for weeks. She promptly rang it, sparking peals of laughter.

You, too, can enjoy humorous synchronicities in your life.

Exercise: Situation Comedy and Synchronicities

Record synchronicities in your journal, watching for groups or strings of happenings which might humorously "bang you over the head" to announce the depth of a new direction, provide insight, or simply give you a good laugh.

> *When the source of immortal joy is opened within us, it flows and saturates every fiber of our being . . . and makes our life at once a waveless peace and ceaseless thrill of ecstasy.*
> SWAMI RAMDAS

Method #5: Tap into Humor

The fifth way to increase laughter and feed your intuitive body is to tap into the spiritual humor which is readily available. Rent video comedies which juxtapose spirituality and humor, such as *Oh, God, Golden Child,* or *Ghosts.* Cartoons and comic strips are another good resource for laughter. Clip out cartoons whose messages have something to do with intuition or psychic phenomena. For example, a favorite Gary Larson cartoon, which a student brought in, depicts two cave men gazing into a crystal ball. The one who is reading the crystal ball says, "I see your little petrified skull . . . labeled and resting on a shelf somewhere." My student labeled this cartoon "Prehistoric Intuition." You can also read books that are either humorous themselves or teach about spiritual humor. A good one in the latter category is *Crazy Wisdom* by Wes "Scoop" Nisker.

Exercise: Tap into Humor

Label the next 5 to 10 pages in your journal "Humor," and then do any or all of the following:

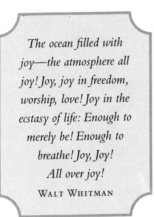

The ocean filled with joy—the atmosphere all joy! Joy, joy in freedom, worship, love! Joy in the ecstasy of life: Enough to merely be! Enough to breathe! Joy, Joy! All over joy!

WALT WHITMAN

- Collect cartoons with relevant themes—intuition, spiritual issues, synchronicities. Paste them in this section, labeling them as my student did, if you'd like.

- Rent video comedies with spiritual themes, watch them, and then write a short review of them in your journal.

- Add jokes, book reviews, and funny stories to your section as you encounter them.

- Read over your humor section whenever you need a good laugh.

When you're accustomed to looking for it, your soul's sense of humor can be found in countless ways. A friend clowns around about something you're inwardly focused on without knowing how poignant her behavior is. You see the antics of the trickster. You find solutions to problems that are so simple you have to laugh. Comical synchronicities surround you. You find yourself laughing with others for odd reasons. The point is to have fun while you acquire the power of intuitive wealth and experiment with happiness as a skill set.

YOUR SOUL'S JOY

In their book *Creativity in Business,* Michael Ray and Rochelle Myers discuss how essence, our soul nature, is an inner resource for reaching higher personal potential.[5] Two of the attributes they ascribe to essence are intuition and joy, so that when intuition gets activated "you get a hint of your own creativity or potential [and] you always feel this bright, shimmering quality of joy." I believe this "hint" is a direct glimpse into your shimmering soul, which allows you, at least momentarily, to know yourself as a living soul. The wonderful feeling accompanying these moments is the natural joyousness of the soul. Many spiritual traditions teach that soul's joy nourishes the self in spite of life's slings and arrows. Eastern mysticism goes further, calling the ups and downs of visible life *lila,* meaning the "sport" of God

To be happy in the being and the knowing, well that is beyond happiness, that is bliss.

HENRY MILLER

or "the musical manifestation of His creative joy."[6] Krishna, a Hindu god, tells his student Arjuna to go beyond identifying with the good and the bad, saying, "Rise above earthly opposites and do your duty."[7] Christ says to His disciples, "My peace I give unto you. Let not your heart be troubled."

A story which captures this concept is told by singer Chante Pierce. Chante and *ate* (my Lakota father) were driving down the road together on the Pine Ridge Indian Reservation in South Dakota. Chante was behind the wheel when suddenly a prairie dog darted out on to the road. Chante tried to avoid him, but instantly she heard the tell-tale thud of her wheels going over his body. Her heart sank. Then *ate* suddenly exclaimed, "He's all right! I looked back and guess what? He jumped up, did a dance, and scurried off the road."

Chante shot an incredulous look at *ate.* "What? He can't be all right."

Ate just kept talking, telling a cartoon-like story of the resurrected prairie dog who danced off the road. Soon he had Chante laughing and enjoying life again as they continued on their journey. *Ate* is well known for the strong pronouncement that "E-e-e-e-verything is going to be ALL RIGHT." This is not the "all right" of nothing tragic occurring. The *all right* he is referring to is deeper than that and resides in his bones, as it can in yours and mine. It carries the underlying meaning of "I love life" or "just being alive is joyful." When tragedy strikes, this deep resource of loving life allows an individual to bounce back again and lay claim to joy in life.

To help you cultivate this deep resource, you'll meditate on joy. Remember, you can't fail in meditation. In fact, this idea is antithetical to the

> *That which is Bliss is verily the Self. Bliss and the Self are not distinct and separate but are one and identical. And* That *alone is real.*
>
> SRI RAMANA MAHARSHI

intent of meditation. Meditation is a gift; it should never be used to beat yourself over the head for any reason. As a visit with your spirit, soul, or essence (choose a word with which you're comfortable), you can think of meditation as a date with a great friend, going to a favorite spot in nature, or doing something you love. The Dalai Lama has said, "Spirituality is a good feeling in the heart. That's it." Remember this goal. You seek to nurture your joy and invest your heart with a good feeling.

Exercise: Meditation for Joy

1. Get your journal and find a comfortable spot to sit.

2. Identify an area of your life which lacks joy, e.g., some area about which you are worried, fearful, angry, or disappointed. Write it in your journal.

3. Identify a memory or an imaginary event which fills your body with joy. Write the memory or event in your journal, and record how your body feels when it is filled with joy.

4. Now turn your attention to your breath, following your inhale and exhale until you are relaxed.

5. When you're relaxed, focus more deeply on your breath. Visualize yourself breathing in joy (feel it come into and flood your body). Hold your joyful breath for a moment, imagining it penetrating your concern.

6. As you exhale, visualize your area of concern leaving your body on your exhalation. Imagine that your concern now has flecks of golden light in it.

7. Continue inhaling joy: bathe your concerns with joy, and exhale your concerns for 15 minutes.[8]

8. End your meditation by inhaling and exhaling joy and joy alone for another 5 minutes.

9. Look back at the concerns you identified in steps 2 and 3. Record what has happened during the meditation and your hoped-for outcome.

Like the sun, joy is self-fueling: the more joy you share with others, the more returns to you. Joy is integral to spiritual awakening and to its subsequent character development. Teaching about joy and its authentic role in the voice, Joan Kenley, author of *Voice Power,* points out that although you expect to feel joy when deeply touched by something wonderful, you may be surprised by how much joy you will feel when you uncover what she calls your "finer energies"—the body-felt energies of compassion, courage, will, beauty, and intuition. In short, profound joy accompanies every step of your spiritual self-discovery and can awaken within you the greater joy of bliss.

BLISSED IN

Sometimes on the spiritual path, the ego can feel exactly like the mathematician in a Herman cartoon who says, staring at his calculation in shock, "I've just proved I don't exist." *What!* My intuition is just wishful thinking? *What?* My teacher is deeply flawed? *What!* My plans are irrelevant? *What!* My children find my beliefs weird? When these feelings arise, many people try to run away to a blissed-out state, which is characterized by not attending to the requirements of daily life. In this state, people let their personal affairs go; they pursue grand, unattainable dreams; and, in the extreme, they lose contact with Earth reality. In contrast, the promotion of a blissed-*in* state began some years ago when author Joseph Campbell urged us to "follow our bliss." Campbell's words turned the normal

> *The devotee, whose happiness is within himself, and whose light (of knowledge) also is within himself, becoming one with the Brahman, obtains the Brahmic Bliss [nirvana].*
>
> RICHARD MAURICE BUCKE

sense of duty inside out and implied that it is your spiritual duty to choose one activity over another according to which one evokes the most bliss.

It is your job, therefore, to become a bliss evaluator and to start right where you are in your life. Following the bliss criteria can change the world, much like laughter, and can produce human beings who strive to actualize and integrate spiritual ecstasies while being fully conscious in the here and now. Like the famous Star Trek phrase, "Beam me up, Scotty," these seekers say, "Bliss me in, Cosmic Comic. I want to feed my intuitive body, come home to myself, and open my eyes to joy."

In this state, the disintegration and death of various ego identities is known to be the cosmic dance of your own soul as it works through the shadows of astral addictions and seeks the radiance of pure inner joy. As a blissed-in being, you may surprise yourself by arriving at a place past your goal and not remember working hard to get there. When your cosmic comic winks at your surprise, don't forget to thank your intuitive body.

Exercise: Bliss-In

1. Record in your journal how your life would be different if you actualized a more blissed-in state than the one you are presently aware of, or

2. Write a letter to bliss-in your journal. Include how much you enjoy the feeling of bliss.

Final Exercise: Your Intuition To Do List

1. Complete the sentence, "Because I am accepting my soul's invitation to "Nurture Joy," I already know to . . ." List 5 to 10 things you

know to do, such as "call David. He always makes me laugh," "rent my favorite comedy," "do the Laughter Workout on Monday and Thursday mornings." When you've finished, read your list over, highlight the simplest activity which *makes you really laugh,* and do it. Record everything in your journal.

2. Go back and look at your Guiding Image for this chapter. How does it capture the principles of humor or joy? If you identified a hint for how to cultivate joy at the beginning of the chapter, was it helpful? Record in your journal.

CHAPTER 7

SET TIME FREE

TIME IMMEMORIAL

It's very common for psychic and intuitive experiences to go hand-in-hand with odd experiences with time. This makes sense; the soul is not bound by accepted laws of time-space. These odd experiences can be associated with precognitions (knowledge of the future), postcognitions (unexplained knowledge of the past), or simultaneous time (accurately describing something in the present which is occurring at a distance). As world-wide anecdotal reports of psychic and intuitive experiences indicate, our Western view of time marching out in a straight line from past to present to future is only one way of experiencing, understanding, and organizing time.[1]

This chapter is dedicated to an exploration of this odd or non-linear time. It includes other world views of time and exercises focused on guiding your experimentation with non-linear time. These experiments are designed to prepare you for some of the different types of experiences you may encounter as your intuitive skills grow. The exercises, which I playfully call Time Travel experiments, are based on the concept of subjective, or personal, time.

The vehicle you will use for your Time Travel experiments is your intuitive body and its imaginative inner world. You've learned that this body can take you places without thought (intuitive feet), provide you information without the use of rational processes (intuitive hands, ears, eyes, etc.), and peer into the future (intuitive eyes). Behind each of these experiences lies a different understanding of time or space or time-

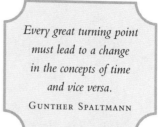

Every great turning point must lead to a change in the concepts of time and vice versa.

GUNTHER SPALTMANN

space. For example, seeing the future appears to be a time phenomenon, while getting information of your lover's infidelity by simply touching his or her back could either be time (you traveled backward through time and saw the event) or space (you telepathically connected with the memory banks of your lover). We know that time and space are so deeply intertwined that they are not separate identities. This is why scientists refer to a time-space continuum. For the sake of our exploration, however, I've separated them into two different chapters—"Set Time Free" and "Shift Space." As you explore the background information and experiments in both these chapters, keep your mind open and curious. For it is here, in the place of time-space, that you may encounter the greatest wink of your cosmic comic.

The following time story is a favorite of mine because it raises fascinating questions about how intuition, personality, and physical events can interact. Afternoon tea is a ritual in England and more sacred even than morning coffee in the U.S.A. This story revolves around two friends, a British gentleman and his female companion, who had the habit of enjoying a weekly cup of tea together. The gentleman always came to his companion's home precisely at four o'clock; his friend always served the tea in a cherished tea set, which had been passed down from generation to generation. The night before he was due for his weekly tea appointment, the gentleman had a crystal-clear dream. As he watched his tea partner bring the tea set into the room at their appointed time, she suddenly dropped it, smashing everything. He awoke from the dream disturbed but forgot about it during the day. Later, when he kept his tea

> We must accept that time is not completely separate from and independent of space, but is combined with it to form an object called space-time.
> STEPHEN HAWKING

appointment, he still remembered nothing. But just as his companion was carrying in the tea, the dream flashed before him. He shouted, "Watch out!" His friend was so startled at his outburst that she promptly dropped the tea set, destroying everything. Unfortunately, the gentleman's dream had omitted one crucial fact—the role his shout was to play in the accident!

This story evokes many questions about non-linear time. Did the precognitive dream in fact cause the accident? Would the outcome have changed if the gentleman had not shouted? Was the ancient tea set destined to be destroyed regardless of how the accident happened? Could the accident have been avoided if the gentleman had been more proactive, e.g., called his tea partner after the dream and suggested they use a different tea set on that day? Stripped down, these questions revolve around the traditional debate between destiny and free will. In other words, once you've seen what will happen ahead of time, assuming it is an accurate precognition, is the event destined to occur or can those involved create an alternate reality?

The truth is that this debate is only relevant in the context of linear time. Non-linear time suggests that the past, present, and future are all going on at once rather than occurring sequentially. I've found it useful to view non-linear time, and intuitive life in general, as interactive, constantly moving probability fields. Clear cameo images about the future or past (whether they come visually in dreams as this gentleman's did, in quick daytime snap shots, by kinesthetic knowing, or through other means) are strong invitations from the Universe for you to interact consciously with the relevant evolving probability field. How you interact (recognizing the invitation or not) and when you interact (immediately following the dream or just before the tea set shatters) is crucial. Non-linear time does not stand still; it exercises a lot of freedom, and so can we, if we embrace the reality of its many different dimensions.

Before we go on to explore setting time free from strictly linear points of view, select your guiding illustration to work with in this chapter.

Your Guiding Image for "Set Time Free"

- Create a section of your Intuition Journal and label it "Chapter Seven: Set Time Free."

One of Einstein's brilliant contributions to modern physics was his intuition that linear time, along with everything happening in it, is superficial.

DEEPAK CHOPRA

- Reach into your Image Vocabulary envelope and, without looking, pull out a guiding illustration for this chapter.

- Paste this image on the first page of the new section you've created in your journal.

TIME DIFFERENCES

Where is your future? Is it still ahead of you, yet to be lived, or does it arise from behind, hidden from view? If you're part of modern Western culture, you'll probably answer, "Ahead of me," because you've been trained to orient your body in space so that you are in the present, the past lies behind you, and your future is in front. But if you had lived in ancient Greece, you'd have answered the question with, "My future is behind me, of course. I can't see it, while I can see my past which runs out in front of me." If you had lived in the Indigenous cultures of South America, your language and actions might reflect a belief that you are in closer contact with and more influenced by ancient people, ideas, and cycles than you are with those that are physically present today.

If you're Dutch, mechanical time is so valuable that the arrival of a scheduled train is accurate enough to set your clock by. On the other

> People like us, who
> believe in physics, know
> that the distinction
> between past, present,
> and future is only
> a stubbornly
> persistent illusion.
>
> ALBERT EINSTEIN

hand, if you're from a Native American culture, timing is not determined by an external clock, but by the confluence of events such as the placement of the sun, moon, and stars, ceremonial traditions, synchronistic moments, and the "feel of right timing."[2] If you lived in one of the most rural and isolated communities of Appalachia, as I have, you'd determine the advent of spring by the blossoming of blackberry bushes because no calendar was ever as accurate as those plants. If you were part of Australian Aboriginal culture, you might search for a lost object by going into a special state called "Dreamtime" in order to find it.

The point of all this is that beliefs about time influence behavior. In large part, your world—your interactions with others, how you categorize experiences, what you make important—is determined by your subjective understanding of time.

You are experiencing this every day whether you realize it or not. Psychologist Harriet Mann offered an interesting perspective on how the four different types of people on the Jungian-based Myers-Briggs Evaluation (the thinking, feeling, sensing, intuiting types I mentioned in Chapter One) experience time. She noted that each type processes time differently and values different things on the time continuum. These differences have important implications for how each type develops intuitive skills. Look through the types on page 155 and identify the one which matches your time experience most closely.

Jungian Type	How Type Processes Time	Intuition Style
Feeling	Values the past and evaluates the present or future based on the past. Can either experience rich lessons from the past, or can become "stuck" in the past.	Uses emotions to garner intuitive information. Specializes in knowing the past.
Thinking	Values linear—past, present, and future—time. Loves organizing, strategic planning, researching the past, and evaluating the present. Has difficulty accepting precognition.	Uses the mind for getting intuitive information. Enjoys exploring the past, the present, and the future intuitively.
Sensing	Lives in the present. Past and future do not impact decisions. Finds planning for the future difficult, but makes great contributions to staying focused in the present.	Uses body sensations to get intuitive information. Experiences intuition as instinct.
Intuiting	Visionary and creative, this type values the future and is impatient with the past. Has difficulty prioritizing daily goals.	Uses intuitive body skills to access information. Specializes in the future.

Now imagine the discussions, if not arguments, that might occur at a family dinner table when people are unaware of their subjective time differences. Imagine that the mother in the family is a feeling type who wants to save money for the family's traditional summer vacation (past).

> *Time isn't a thing . . .*
> *I regard time as a product*
> *of consciousness.*
> LARRY DOSSEY, M.D.

The father is a sensing type who wants to spend money now on a new TV (present). The teenage daughter is an intuiting type who wants everyone to remember graduation is coming next year and she wants a car (future). The early adolescent son is a thinking type who wants to create a methodical plan for the extra money (past, present, future). While it is true that on the surface this family is debating how to spend money, the issue is how they each value time.

When you imagine this type of dialogue in an important political or business debate, you can understand how each person involved might believe that he or she has *the* right perspective and how miscommunication could take place. In a more ideal scenario, however, everyone would know the others' time strengths and would recognize the important role each perspective plays in decision-making. If you add intuitive skills into the ideal business meeting mix, you'd want someone who is sensitive to the future (intuiting intuitive), someone who can scan the past for the most relevant information (feeling intuitive), someone who keeps the focus on what intuition makes relevant to the present (sensing intuitive), and someone whose intuition can integrate and synthesize all three time zones (thinking intuitive).

If we valued all four types, we would stop judging each other's positions as irrelevant. Such an understanding of people's subjective time differences could not only increase our tolerance for all positions but add enthusiasm for, if not insistence on, the presence of each type at important functions. Once you are aware of these differences, your daily interaction with people who represent all four types multiplies your options in life, rather than serving as a point of contention.

Take a moment and do the following exercise, recording the results in your journal.

Exercise: Time Differences

1. Look over the different types of processing time. Which do you think most closely describes the way you process time most often? Are you evaluating everything in terms of the future or the past (intuiting or feeling)? Are you only interested in what is going on in the present (sensate), or do you like to make step-by-step plans (thinking)?

> *The evidence . . . suggests that we are still children when it comes to understanding time. And like all children poised on the threshold of adulthood, we should put aside our fears and come to terms with the way the world really is.*
>
> MICHAEL TALBOT

2. Write in your journal why you believe you're this type.

3. Can you think of an incident in your life where miscommunication based on different time styles may have occurred? Write in your journal what happened and who the players involved were.

4. Look over the different intuitive styles. Which matches your way of processing time? Why do you identify most closely with that style? Identify incidents in your life in which this type of intuition style may have been useful, or create a fictional account of how that style of intuition might work in your life. Record in your journal.

Although intuitive time—which can reveal the future, slow time way down, or stop time altogether—can appear complex or frightening to the ego or personality, *it is natural to your soul.* Simply put, your soul is not bound by time or space. Therefore, it makes sense that as you embody more soul, you will have more non-linear time experiences. If you understand and accept that fact, you won't feel afraid of intuition or the odd time experiences that can accompany it. In fact, you'll seek to experiment with subjective time travel.

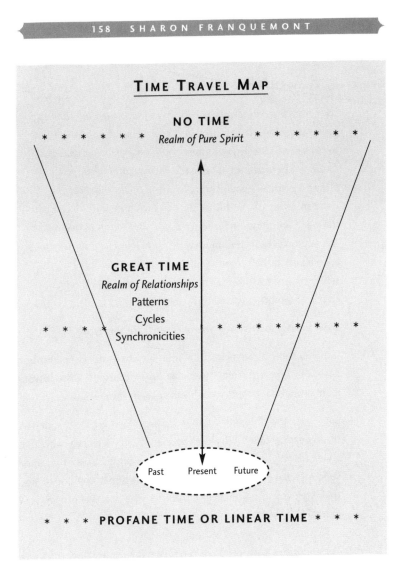

TIME TRAVEL MAP

NO TIME
Realm of Pure Spirit

GREAT TIME
Realm of Relationships
Patterns
Cycles
Synchronicities

Past　Present　Future

PROFANE TIME OR LINEAR TIME

TIME TRAVEL

Science fiction writers and Hollywood movie-makers have been playing with the idea of time travel for years. People have gone to the future and come back, visited the past and altered the present, and absorbed the challenge of time (past, future, present) going on all at once. The hero or heroine of these stories is usually completely in the dark about how to interact appropriately with the time alteration and simply longs to be back in the present. The interesting truth is that people really *do* travel through time with their consciousness.

In my opinion, you have the capacity to time travel in consciousness because your soul can travel at the speed of light or faster and, therefore, disappear into timelessness. This ability allows your soul to "go ahead of time," which is why you can get a glimpse of the future during a precognition. When you are identified even momentarily, with your soul—that part of you that can travel faster than the speed of light—it is a short trip from ordinary linear time to the realm of pure spirit or No Time.

This suggestion, that your soul travels at or beyond the speed of light, explains another commonly reported non-linear time experience—slow motion time. Some physicists believe that

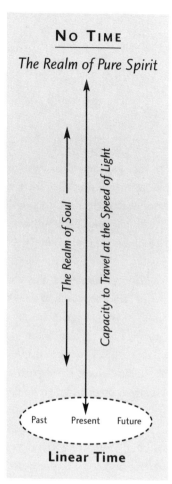

NO TIME

The Realm of Pure Spirit

The Realm of Soul

Capacity to Travel at the Speed of Light

Past   Present   Future

Linear Time

to a person standing on Earth someone going by who was traveling close to the speed of light would appear to be moving very slowly. In fact, the closer to the speed of light the traveler came, the slower he or she would appear to be moving, if he appeared to move at all. Perhaps if a person is identifying more with his or her soul, the observing personality self experiences time as moving in slow motion.[3] This is why people frequently report slow motion time during meditation, yoga, déjà vu, or moments of crisis. During these moments, a person is consciously or unconsciously enlarging his or her attention to include more of the soul.

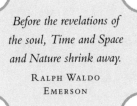

Before the revelations of the soul, Time and Space and Nature shrink away.

RALPH WALDO
EMERSON

The greater your soul identity, the more subjective time moves at speeds close to, the same as, or greater than the speed of light. You may encounter experiences with these soul-altering time changes as you go through this chapter. Time may even seem to disappear. One explanation is that you've entered a field of Oneness where demarcations such as time are non-existent. For example, runner Roger Bannister describes his winning moment as, "The world seemed to stand still, or did not exist." In the book *Tai Chi Ch'uan: The Technique of Power,* authors Horwitz and Kimmelman state, "There is a common experience in Tai Chi of seemingly falling through a hole in time."

The remainder of this chapter is dedicated to time travel experiments. Please approach *all* these exercises as Alice in Wonderland–type adventures—the experiments invite you to, as *Tai Chi* masters suggest, fall through a hole in time and into the arms of your soul. Some experiments will appeal to you more than others. You do not have to do them all: in fact, before you do any experimentation I suggest you read the chapter straight through and then do those exercises which attract you the most.

Each experiment invites you into a different reality; it contains a gift which I've listed to the right of the type of time with which you will be working. Your Time Travel experiments follow a preliminary warm-up exercise, and come in this order:

Type of Time You'll Be Working with	Gift
1. No Time or Timelessness	Experience profound peacefulness.
2. Probability Time	Co-create with the future.
3. Molasses Time	Slow down time to enhance productivity and enjoyment.

4. Elongated Time   Tap the power of the present.

5. Right on Time   Act in the moment.

All of the experiments are modeled after anecdotal reports of real people. This is not science fiction. Most of these reports occur in the context of spiritual development; creative moments or peak performances in sports, science, artistry of all kinds; or strong emotional connections or crisis. As you know, the purpose of our exploration is spiritual development. We want to make time experiences which are home base for your soul more part of your conscious experience. If you feel uncomfortable or overwhelmed by any experiment, stop it immediately, and, if necessary, skip to the next chapter. There is no reason to rush anything with intuition. Trust yourself.

Your warm-up experiment, "Expanded Time," serves to get you thinking in terms of the vast time vistas of your soul.[4] Its huge time images tend to wipe out your conscious mind's approach to time. This sets you free from preconceived notions and opens you to the variety of time experiences which follow. Do not skip this exercise.

Warm-up Exercise: Expanded Time

Before you begin, read the instructions completely. They are simple to remember.

1. Find a comfortable spot to sit where you will not be disturbed. Do the relaxation Basic Breath exercises (on p. 76) or whatever you need to do to clear your mind and heart. Settle into your body. Say today's date out loud.

2. Think about a thousand years. Ponder the concept. What does it mean? What is this period in human terms? How does pondering a thousand years feel in your body? Allow a thousand years to pass before your inner eye. How many generations is it? What is it to other creatures? What do you imagine it to mean in the life of a star?

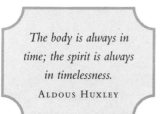

*The body is always in
time; the spirit is always
in timelessness.*

ALDOUS HUXLEY

3. When you've finished pondering a thousand years, double it. Ponder two thousand years. What does two thousand years mean?

4. Then, double that; ponder four thousand years. Follow that by doubling the number again so you are pondering eight thousand years. Then double that to sixteen thousand years.

5. Continue on until you *know* the feeling of timeless eons within your whole being. Is there a point where time itself becomes meaningless and disappears? At what point is that?

6. If time does disappear, look back at your daily life. What is and isn't important? Let things that you've made important which are actually not drift away from you as peaceful serenity fills you. Ask your intuition to help you remember these peaceful sensations.

7. If you are having difficulty, turn your attention to your soul. Remember that this vastness is its home territory. Relax and let your soul take over.

8. If time is vast but doesn't disappear completely, still note all the sensations you are having. How does it feel to be acquainted with such huge blocks of time? Can you experience the part of you that is comfortable with such a long view of life?

9. Complete your experiment by saying today's date out loud again, and bringing your attention back to your surrounding environment.

10. Thank your soul for any insights you receive, record your impressions in your journal, and tell them to someone else, if you want to.

Did you enjoy the warm-up? It is normal to have moments of discomfort during such an exercise. The ego is awestruck, if not frightened,

by the soul's immensity. Experimentation will help you get over this fear and
even make you yearn for adventures
with non-linear time, particularly the
peacefulness which can arise out of an
experience with timelessness.

No Time or Timelessness— Experience Profound Peacefulness

These individual life experiments have the makings of a true cultural revolution because of the new shared meaning they introduce . . . has an awesome power to change your lives.

WILLIS HARMAN

Buddhist philosophy names three types of time: Profane Time (there is no awareness of an active spiritual ingredient), Grand Time (time which is shaped by cycles, patterns, and myths), and No Time (an experience beyond time as the diagram on page 158 depicts). The closest experience we have in the West to No Time is timelessness.

Some people believe that only great mystics, spiritual adepts, or meditation experts can consciously experience No Time or timelessness. It isn't true. Human beings have been reporting disappearing time for eons. People making love, mystics, and peak performers all talk about it. So do people doing ordinary things. You can drop into these non-ordinary moments while gardening, working creatively on your computer, listening to music, playing sports, etc. Of course, what we are after is courting the timeless state through meditation or exercises. Students who have succeeded in this courtship describe it with phrases such as "time stopped; I felt so serene," "everything faded away and life itself went on forever," and "nothing was important in the light of eternity and I laughed out loud." Everyone can have these experiences. After all, they aren't very far away; they're already inside you. Of course, there is no guarantee that you'll feel the peace, serenity, and silence of No Time every time you reach for it, but that is true of everything in life!

The following No Time experiment is inspired by Albert Einstein's famous ride on a light beam, which some people believe provided the fundamental insights for relativity theory. It is also said of Einstein that he

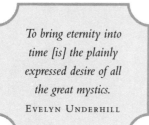

> *To bring eternity into time [is] the plainly expressed desire of all the great mystics.*
>
> EVELYN UNDERHILL

spent some portion of each day imaging or identifying with outer space, abstract concepts, and other things he wanted to understand. Einstein always honored his imagination.

You'll be using your imagination, too, as you move through these experiments. The purpose of your ride on a light beam, however, is not to discover new theories (although that could happen!) but to experience a basic component of existence—light—from a different perspective. You'll be riding again on the "light train" you meet in this experiment, so enjoy.

Time Travel Experiment #1: No Time or Timelessness

Read the instructions completely before you do the experiment.

1. Find a comfortable spot to sit where you will not be disturbed. Do relaxation breath exercises or whatever you need to do to clear your mind and settle into your body.

2. To begin, visualize yourself standing in a favorite spot. Imagine it to be a "station" for an imaginary small train like those you find in theme parks such as Disneyland. The sign at the station reads "Linear Time." The train you are waiting for is an endless light beam, and you've bought a ticket for a place called "No Time."

3. When the light beam train arrives in the station, hop aboard just as you would at a theme park. Travel for as long as you like. Let everything else in your imagination fall away; all that remains is you riding the beam of light. Ride until you have the sensation of time slowing way, way down. Notice everything you think and feel.

4. If you can, experience the train riding through the "light" barrier (an imaginary barrier like the sound barrier which is broken

when traveling faster than the
speed of sound), so you arrive
at a place which doesn't even
need a sign called "No Time."
Experience its expansiveness,
grace, and peace within you. If
the train doesn't go through a

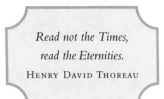

Read not the Times,
read the Eternities.

HENRY DAVID THOREAU

"light" barrier, don't worry about it. You never know when No
Time will find you.

5. Finish the experiment by getting back on the light beam train
   and traveling back to the station called "Linear Time."

6. Thank your soul for the experience and record everything of interest in your journal.

PROBABILITY TIME—CO-CREATE WITH THE FUTURE

While timelessness or No Time may be the most "far out" experience for
people, it is not the one I get the most questions about. The question
about time experiences I'm asked the most is, "Can I influence the
future?"

In the past, before modern physics, the question of whether people
can influence the future boiled down to wondering if mind could overcome matter.[5] Today, many physicists are united with mystics in the belief
that all life is related, an expression of one field. Therefore, perhaps the
question that should be asked is, "What relationships already exist in the
expression of mind as matter and matter as mind?"

The best advice I've been able to give people interested in approaching these questions is to think of future realities as part of one dancing
probability field. You, too, are part of that field and are interacting with
it. The more conscious you are of the field, the more opportunity you
have to co-create with it.

This is not a new idea. For example, some Native American tribes
honored the dreams of community members. When a dream arose that

> *Fullness of time . . . is the now of eternity, when the soul knows all things in God.*
>
> MEISTER ECKHARDT

depicted a future the tribe wanted to alter (e.g., a poor crop yield), they took action. They did not wait passively by to see if the dream became a reality. The tribe would come together and role-play the dream repeatedly. Each time they would make the critical event (the poor crop) slightly less serious. In order to appease the forces at work behind the dream, they did not try to eliminate the challenge completely but to reduce its impact through role-play (e.g., one field has a poor yield rather than an entire year's worth of crops).

We can find stories of such behavior in other sources. For example, in the Old Testament, Abraham queries God on His proposed destruction of Sodom and Gomorrah and step-by-step attempts to reduce the destructive impact. Or, consider the prophetic dream a truck driver reported having about a fatal accident involving his big rig. The following day, as he approached the crossroads he had seen in his dream, he immediately pulled his truck to the side of the road. Amazed, he watched at a safe distance as the exact make and model cars his dream had depicted came to the crossroads, stopped, and went on. Of course, he'll never know whether or not the accident would have happened if he *hadn't* acted on an alternate probability, but he was glad he did. We can legitimately wonder, then, about the English gentleman you met at the beginning of this chapter. If he had responded to his dream differently, would the cherished tea set still be with us?

Another interesting example of a person who literally rejected several probable realities until he settled on an acceptable one comes from Louisa Rhine's collection *Hidden Channels of the Mind*. A seasoned soldier in World War One had noticed that every time one of his buddies reported having a hunch that his "number was up," he unfortunately proved to be correct; he either died or was seriously injured shortly thereafter. When the seasoned soldier himself started having a foreboding that he was in for a "hit," he worked hard to ignore the feeling. But, no matter what he did, he couldn't shake the sensation. He states that, "I began to hope I would not be crippled in such a way that I would be useless and a burden. In my mind, I rejected wounds in this and that part of my body until, at last, I settled for a flesh-wound in the back of my left shoulder."

There was a young lady named Bright whose speed was much faster than light. She went out one day in a relative way, And returned the previous night.

ANONYMOUS

Two days later, when the soldier glimpsed a small knoll he was ordered to take, he recognized that this was the place where "it" would happen. The hit happened shortly after the battle began—a piece of shrapnel made a severe cut in the back of his left shoulder.

These stories suggest that the "fate" perspective of linear time may be a way we unconsciously co-create realities we would not choose otherwise. Many books, usually focusing on some aspect of positive thinking, have been written about the mind's ability to influence the future in a productive way. Experiment #2 is designed to help you practice being a co-creator with Probability Time.

Time Travel Experiment #2: Probability Time

1. Identify a future event you'd like to influence by either reducing its challenging aspects or building on its positive possibilities: for example, a stressful work situation, a dream which you do not want to come true, a promotion you would enjoy, etc.

2. If necessary, first do the warm-up exercise or the timelessness exercise to free your ideas about time.

3. Using your imagination, see yourself and everything around you as millions of dancing molecules floating around randomly in one field. Notice that when lots of molecules come together, an event occurs in the physical universe. For example, lots of molecules come together when you decide to get up and run your errands.

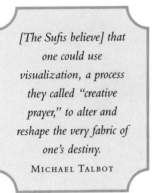

[The Sufis believe] that one could use visualization, a process they called "creative prayer," to alter and reshape the very fabric of one's destiny.

MICHAEL TALBOT

4. Put your imaginative inner eye to work. Place all your attention on the moment *just before* molecules come together to create the future moment with which you've chosen to work. Examples would be the moment before the shrapnel struck, the moment before the rain storm passed over the crops, the moment before you heard about a possible promotion, etc.

5. *Building on the positive future moment:* If you want to build on a positive future event, imagine yourself gently adding, in a co-creative way, more molecules to the mix. As you do so, bring the good sensations you will experience when your chosen future event occurs very *vividly* into your body. In addition to this, let some part of the future you envision be unknown. *Treat this activity with respect and perceive it as a type of praying.*

6. *Reducing a challenging future event:* If you are working to reduce a challenge you suspect may be coming in your future, go back to step #4, placing your attention on the moment *just before* the molecules come together. Have the molecules which represent the future you do not choose (e.g., the wounds the soldier did not choose) begin to float away. Reduce their numbers step-by-step as the soldier did until the remaining group is acceptable to you. *Treat this activity with respect and perceive it as a type of praying.*

7. Finish your exercise with Probability Time by getting on the light beam and riding it back to Linear Time.

8. Record everything of interest in your journal.

MOLASSES TIME—
ENHANCE PRODUCTIVITY
AND ENJOYMENT

My brother Ed used to live on an old New England farm. The wood stove in the kitchen heated up the house moderately well, but the molasses in the pantry didn't have that luxury. In the winter when I tried to pour the slow-moving, ice-cold molecules, which comprised that molasses on to my morning pancakes, I learned why people use the phrase "slow as molasses."

> *But we ought not to deny the reality of the future, either, for we can observe in the soul the intrusion of future events, although they have not yet happened.*
>
> RUDOLPH STEINER

Imagine time moving like a long, continuous, very slow-moving stream of molasses. The resulting experience would contain enough time between each moment for you to read the newspaper or take out your knitting. This type of time is what I call Molasses Time.

Molasses Time or slow motion time can even appear in the midst of chaos or rapid movement. Football player John Brodie describes this when he says that during intense plays, "Time seems to slow way down, in an uncanny way, as if everyone were moving in slow motion. It seems as if I had all the time in the world to watch the receivers run their patterns, and yet I know the defensive line is coming at me just as fast as ever . . ."[6]

Or, consider this story of one of my students at JFK University. "When I was younger, I had a Molasses Time experience. I was hanging out with a pretty rough crowd then, and one afternoon, while my friends and I were walking across a parking lot, a guy starting shooting a gun at us from the other end of the lot. I don't know what got into me; I started running *toward* the gunman.

"I wasn't worried a bit. I knew I wasn't going to be struck. Time was moving so slowly that I 'watched' the bullets flying toward me and had plenty of time to maneuver so they couldn't hit me. The minute I got up to the gunman and jumped on him, time snapped back into normal. I got really scared then even though everything was over."[7]

You do not have to turn to such intense moments to find Mo-

> The more a person is able to direct his life consciously, the more he can use time for constructive benefits.
>
> ROLLO MAY

lasses Time: many people report slow motion time experiences whenever they encounter intuition. Déjà vu experiences (the sensation of having already lived whatever is happening in the moment[8]) are by far the most common context in which people have reported slow motion time to me.

The important point is to notice the changes that happen to *you and your reality* during slow motion time. The advantages of cultivating Molasses Time are described by race car driver Jackie Stewart when he says, "Some days you go out in a race car and everything happens in a big rush. You don't seem to have time to change gears or brake. . . . You're not synchronized. And the most important thing [to do] is to synchronize yourself. . ."

From my perspective, Stewart is consciously inviting the capacities of his soul or best self to assist him in his peak performance goal. The more you identify with your soul, the more slowly internal time will move. Molasses Time can be very helpful in today's fast-paced, deadline world. When you're operating in the intuitive world, remember this rule of thumb: the greater the demand on your external time, the *slower* your internal time needs to go.[9]

You are now ready to begin your experiment with Molasses Time.

Time Travel Experiment #3: Molasses Time

1. Prepare for the experiment by identifying some area of your life where you are experiencing time pressure—getting that work project done, handling an unpleasant relationship, being needed in two places at once. You are going to use this as the context for your Molasses Time experiment.

2. Find a place to lie down where you will not be disturbed.

3. In your mind, go to the light beam train station in experiment #1, but this time buy a ticket to a place called "Molasses Time."

4. When the light beam train comes into the station, hop aboard. Your objective is not to arrive anywhere but to become thoroughly identified with the light beam itself.

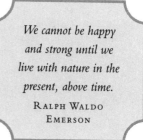

We cannot be happy and strong until we live with nature in the present, above time.

RALPH WALDO EMERSON

5. As you settle on board your train in whatever way feels natural to you, notice that you've been assigned a wonderful compartment for taking a nap! Beneath you is a bed made up of light beam molecules. Let yourself stretch out on this bed and imagine the light beams surrounding you like a warm, relaxing bath. Slow your breathing way down. Allow your experience of time to slow way, way down, too.

6. Relax every muscle of your body. Experience yourself as not only bathed in light but as *being* light itself. There is nowhere to go; there is nothing to be done. Slow time down even more.

7. Rest in this light nap as long as you want to.

8. Awake when you hear the light beam train pulling into a station. When you wake up, you find yourself, refreshed, at the Linear Time station. Amazingly, the slow motion time of your journey is still within you. It feels as if you've never left it.

9. Finish the imaginary journey by getting out your journal and recording your thoughts and experiences. *Do everything in slow motion* (reach slowly for your journal, pick up your pen, and write slowly). P.S. *If you fell asleep during the visualization, don't worry about it. You are probably tired and may be pushing yourself too much in daily life. Just keep practicing with it until you can do the whole experiment while you are awake.*

> *The natives dislike speed,*
> *as we dislike noise. . . .*
> *They are also on friendly*
> *terms with time and the*
> *plan of beguiling or*
> *killing it does not come*
> *into their heads.*
>
> DINESE (DESCRIBING
> AFRICAN NATIVES)

ELONGATED TIME—
TAP THE POWER
OF THE PRESENT

While the purpose of Molasses Time is to slow time down, another type of time experience subtly evokes slow motion time and permits you to tap the power of the present.

In the beginning of intuitive work, people sometimes get hooked on the exciting time experiences—timelessness, future time, slow motion, etc. The present appears boring and uninteresting. Of course, this isn't true. The present, where our bodies dwell, is the event horizon where your whole being shows up; you *are* only as real as the ability you have to live in the present. While you can describe the feelings and the meaning of time experiences from the past or future, you usually do not physically experience the events themselves.[10]

A Family Circus cartoon captures this well. Two children are sitting on the curb engrossed in conversation. The older child says to the younger, "The past belongs to yesterday, the future belongs to tomorrow, and the present is here today. That's why it is a present." Philosophers and many spiritual traditions agree: the present is where the great gift of life resides. Ram Dass popularized this notion over twenty years ago with the phrase "Be Here Now." Intuition follows these rules, too. While your soul is free to roam or read the time-space continuum, during your lifetime your body is its temple. This temple is the place where you "log in" what's happened and actualize your power.

The following story is about a speaker who actualized the power of the present. An active woman, she had a full schedule up until the moment she was due to give what she labeled "the opportunity speech of my life." Every time she worked on the speech she was dissatisfied with her ideas. As the time for her talk drew closer, she became more and more anxious. In this anxious state, ideas were forced, rigid, and dull. The talk she had planned put even her to sleep. She began to muse about the coming disaster and missed opportunity. Then, as she was showering a few hours before her talk, she recognized intuitively that "I don't need a thirty-minute speech—all I need is one good idea!" That flash set her free, and before she left the shower she had the foundation for her highly successful speech. She knew what to do.

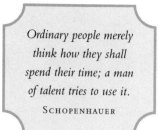

Ordinary people merely think how they shall spend their time; a man of talent tries to use it.
SCHOPENHAUER

What is important about this story is that the speaker did *not* "get" her speech because she was focused on the details of what to say. Nor did she "get" it when she had plenty of time to prepare. The truth is her flash came to her in the moment of her real need. The answer was found in *process* rather than content. The speaker's intuition told her that all she needed was one good idea; what that idea was and all the facts supporting it came later.

Intuition does this. It supports you from underneath; it provides the foundation you need for a fuller view. Pushing intuition to perform ahead of time doesn't work. It is most interested in the present and authentic needs. One way you can harvest the wealth of your intuition is to dwell in the present. In the present there is no separation between the moment of realization and the capacity to begin actualizing:—before that speaker got out of the shower she had the basics of her talk.

This is because the present is rich. It has all the answers. To find them, elongate the present; relax, and stretch it from horizon to horizon.

While the previous story is a spontaneous case, our goal is to develop techniques for conscious, intuitive access into what the present knows.

> *Samdhi is to know the synthesis of all cosmic time and space in an "Eternal Present."*
> WHITALL N. PERRY

Time Travel Experiment #4: Elongated Time

1. Identify an actual challenge which you would like either resolved or headed for resolution today (intuition doesn't work as well with trumped-up or trivial challenges). Write it in your Intuition Journal.

2. Relax. If necessary, use the Basic Breath relaxation technique on page 76. If it attracts you and you find it relaxing, take a shower.

3. Relax so deeply that your inner being is silent.

4. Affirm to yourself that the solution you seek is nearby in the present. Tell yourself with confidence that it wants to link up with you as much as you want to link up with it. If this attitude seems difficult to achieve, have patience with yourself. It takes time to trust the mutually attractive force of knowledge or truth.

5. Work with yourself as a whole unit—body, mind, spirit.

   • Using your imagination, create the primary feelings your body will have when you know the solution. Excitement? Relief? Satisfaction? Peace? Relax into the feelings so deeply that your body is saturated with them.

   • Recognize that your mind is going to have an Ah Hah! experience. It will find great meaning in something which is relevant to your solution. Using your imagination, re-experience your mind in the Ah Hah! state of crystal clarity and acute creativity.

   • Identify simultaneously with your chosen feelings and mental clarity, and then re-experience your spirit rushed with joy. Stay in this integrated and combined state for a few minutes.

6. Take out your journal and write about the challenge you identified in step #1 for three pages or more. If nothing comes, write about anything. Do not skimp on the writing. Even if you think you've had a breakthrough on page one, keep writing until you've finished three pages at least.

> The present . . . in which all times are included, is one: it is a unity itself.
> NICOLAS OF CUSA

7. Take a highlighter and go through your writing, marking insights, directives for action, and little clues. Act on what has been suggested.

8. As you see the results of your experiment, date and record them in your journal.

RIGHT ON TIME—ACT IN THE MOMENT

When my family lived in Suches, a secluded village in the mountains of Georgia, the local people taught me that nature was their most important clock. Alone with three children for six months during the winter, I wanted to know when feeding the wood stove for warmth might end. I called my neighbor and asked her how much longer we'd need wood heat. "Until the blackberries blossom," she answered without a moment's hesitation.

The blackberry blossoms, of course, arrive "right on time." It might be earlier one year, later the next, because their arrival time is based on a confluence of external and internal events—amount of sunlight, weather, conditions of the soil, age of the plants. Although people are not blackberries, our various cultural communities also organize time around a combination of external and internal factors, and every culture has a different definition of what "right on time" means. In all the cultures that I have investigated, however, intuition's sacred flashes do not vary; they are said to arrive "right on time" or "just in time" like the blackberries.

Your intuitive time clock tells you, when you listen, what to do and when to do it. For example, Erik had not spoken to one of his friends in many years but was plagued with the nagging feeling that he ought to call her. It was already after midnight when he gave into the urge. He didn't even know if the phone number still worked; all he knew was that the time for a call had arrived.

> Contact with eternity is in the present moment, but it is mediated by thought. It is a matter of attention.
>
> DAVID BOHM

"Hello, Jane. I know it's late, but this is Erik. I felt like I had to call you."

There was silence on the other end of the phone. When the woman did speak, she revealed that she was just about to take enough pills to commit suicide. Erik stayed on the phone for hours to help her out of her despair.

Right timing, in these situations, is directly tied to your willingness to live and respond in the present moment to what your intuition is suggesting. Erik might have waited hours, days, weeks, or months, but he didn't. He acted on what was *really* important. You can practice this, too.

Time Travel Experiment #5: Right On Time

This is the easiest experiment of the five I've listed, but it is often the one people avoid the most.

1. Date your journal page and then write these words on the page you've dated. "I, [your name], within reason, do promise to act on the next intuition I receive."

2. When an intuitive suggestion arrives, act on it immediately. Record the results in your journal.

When you commit to your intuitive clock, your inner time gears begin to operate differently. You find it important to feel the texture, immediacy, and laid-back nature of time. You look at the confluence of events and listen for good feelings in your body before you decided what "right on time" means for you. You're delighted to be a blackberry bush.

BEING TIME

> *But angels perceive in the light that is beyond time and eternal. They know in the eternal now.*
>
> MEISTER ECKHARDT

Remember, you are not undertaking these experiments—and they are just experiments—to escape clock time or fool yourself. Your purpose is to set free your ideas about time in order to acquaint yourself with the larger time frames of your soul.

Your activities may have profound implications for your health and well-being. Larry Dossey, the physician who wrote *Time, Space, and Medicine,* suggests that most mental and physical diseases "are a disorder of time perception . . . it is the goal of every therapy to reorder the patient's relationship with time." And Deepak Chopra, in *Ageless Body, Timeless Mind,* argues elegantly for a shift in our perception, saying, "In the final analysis, how you metabolize time is the most important aspect of this [aging] process, because time is the most fundamental experience."

Many of us have heard such words before, yet it is so difficult to imagine how they apply to daily life's profound testament to the passage of time. Again, a key to this application is greater identification with the soul. The soul knows how to metabolize time differently than does your body or personality. Time can become an expression of the state of your soul's being. For example, when your being is identified with its endlessness, you are comfortable with No Time or timelessness. When your being is focused on its ability to be aware of all times at once, you focus on the past, present, and future. You become a thinking type. When your being is focused on the future, you are interested in precognitions. They are natural for you. When your being is focused on images of the past, you are often valuing your emotions.

All these time frames are part of your health. You need the rest of timelessness, the thinking type's ability to plan, the capacity for vision of

The pure one (sâfi) is plunged in the Light of the Glorious; he is not the son of any one, free from "times" and "states."

RUMI

the future-oriented approach, and the wisdom to know your feelings. In this way, an intuitive, or soul, approach to time takes care of the needs of the body as it goes through your life journey. In the final analysis, intuitive time is good for your physical, mental, emotional, and spiritual health. This is because, at the core of your being, soul time is *being* time.

Final Exercise: Your Intuition To Do List

1. Complete the sentence, "Because I am accepting my soul's invitation to 'Set Time Free,' I already know to . . ." List 5 to 10 things you know to do. Remember, you can choose simple things such as "practice slowing time down by breathing very slowly," "look for articles on odd time experiences," "discuss intuitive time with a friend." When you've finished, read your list over, highlight the simplest activity which *will turn your ideas of time upside down,* and do it. Record everything in your journal.

2. Go back and look at your Guiding Image for this chapter. How does it capture what you had to learn about a different relationship with time? What specific part of it points to your expanded relationship with time? Record in your journal.

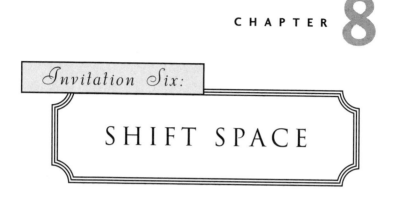

Invitation Six:

SHIFT SPACE

INTUITION AND THE RULES OF SPACE

Intuition doesn't obey the rules of solid space any more than it conforms to the rules of linear time. It is not constrained by boundaries, edges, limits, or the solidity of physical forms. Intuition flew through "walls" when it told Sarah that her friend Kathleen, who lived a mile away, was going to call in a few minutes. It observed no privacy when the figure of Andy's aunt appeared to pop in on his first date with his future wife. The shimmering, ghost-like image lasted for just a fleeting second, but Andy swore he'd seen his aunt. Later, when Andy asked his aunt, who was known in the family for doing such things, about the pop-in visit, she told him, "Yes, I 'saw' you, and I think you are going to fall in love with this new girl." Obviously, Andy's aunt had an unusual understanding of space and could shift her relationship with it, so that some part of her consciousness came in for a landing on Andy's date. In formal terms, Andy's aunt was adept at "remote viewing," the ability to see something at a distant location, and often at a distant time.[1] Besides sending her consciousness out to visit Andy, she seemed able to send an image, too. She was experiencing what is called non-local space, as similar experiences with time are called non-linear.

> *We enter an unbounded mental space, wide open to all potentials.*
>
> FRITZ KUNKEL

If you doubt such things really happen, I don't blame you. In 1978, my family and I drove to St. Louis, Missouri, to attend my first Parapsychology Associate meeting. Robert Jahn and Brenda Dunne of Princeton University presented a report with slides on their remote viewing experiments. Remote viewing is designed to test people's ability to observe something at a distance without actually going there. In a typical research example, person A drives to a target site which has been randomly chosen from a pool of fifty to one hundred places. Person B uses his or her mind to intuitively "see" what person A is looking at. As Jahn and Dunne presented slide set after slide set comparing the pictures of actual targets with their corresponding remote viewing drawings, I was amazed.

Consider these research results which come from the remote viewing work Marilyn Schlitz and JoMarie Haight did at The Rhine Research Center in Durham, North Carolina. Marilyn, who is now Director of Research for The Institute of Noetic Sciences, remained in North Carolina and attempted to remotely view the randomly selected sites that her partner, JoMarie, was visiting in Cocoa Beach, Florida. The picture on the left side of the illustration on page 181 was taken by JoMarie as she stood looking at some rocket ships to the right of a flat-topped, tree-rimmed building. Marilyn, who was sitting in a dimly lit room in Durham, drew the sketch on the right side of the illustration and wrote down the following impressions: "Mostly a feeling of sharp angles. First to the left, then upward to the right. This impression of something shooting up."

This research is unique in that it has held up under a lot of critical scrutiny, including commissioned reports by the U.S. Army and The National Research Council. The results indicate that under the right circumstances, a human being can travel to distant locations with his or her consciousness.

As strange as these intuitive, non-local space abilities appear to be, they are not as odd as experiences of bi-location or shape shifting. In these experiences, the physical body appears to undergo a transformation through

which it can alter its size, shape, and location. For example, Lama Govinda tells of Tibetan lamas who withdraw into seclusion and silence for nine years. At the end of this period, their bodies have become "so light and subtle that they exit their cells by going through a nine-by-ten-inch opening."[2] The first time I met a Native American Medicine man we had an intense discussion about his ability to bi-locate. He was adamant that I at least entertain the idea that his *body*—not just his consciousness, his imagination, or his mental projection—could be teleported hundreds of miles away to do the healing work to which he was called.[3] It was hard for me to understand and accept what he was saying, and he knew it. I thought it had to be a perceptual shift only, like the one described by golfer Jack Fleck in which "the hole looked as big as a wash tub. I suddenly became convinced I couldn't miss. All I had to do was keep the sensation by not questioning it." Author Michael Murphy once heard from a football player that "players sometimes changed their shape and size for a split second, and it wasn't just in the eye of the beholder. They *actually* changed, he had seen it, and he could get other players to say so too."[4]

Perceptual shift or not, these experiences or something like them

> *Knowledge is a function of being. When there is a change in the being of the knower, there is a corresponding change in the nature and amount of knowledge.*
>
> ALDOUS HUXLEY

may happen to you as you work with your intuition. You could find yourself traveling through space, hanging out on the ceiling, seeing things at a distance, or visiting the vast inner space of your soul. Although these experiences are not as common, or not as commonly reported, as the unique time adventures of the last chapter,[5] they, too, make sense in the context of soul embodiment. More soul equals more freedom from accepted encounters with time and space. And, as you may recall from Chapter Four, "Open Your Senses," your radiant, double, or resurrected body is capable of many things. As strange as it might sound, this body is your natural inheritance. All you need to do is be acquainted with some ways in which it holds space in the intuitive world.

To provide yourself a Guiding Image for this chapter, select your illustration now.

Your Guiding Image for "Shift Space"

- Create a section of your Intuition Journal and label it "Chapter Eight: Shift Space."

- Reach into your Image Vocabulary envelope and, without looking, pull out your guiding illustration for this chapter.

- Label which category the picture comes from at the bottom of your selected page.

- Paste your illustration on the page.

SHIFTING SPACE

This bi-location case, reported by Alan Vaughan in his book *Incredible Coincidence,* is my favorite example of how someone could experience a profoundly different sense of time and space through the simple act of gardening. The year was 1942, and San Jose State Professor Richard Szumski, a young man at the time, was raking leaves in the yard of his family's Chicago home. Space was about to shift for Szumski and his body was about to go with him.

> *There was a dizzy, sickening sensation of sight that was not like seeing: I saw line that was no line; space that was not space. I was myself and not myself . . .*
> EDWIN ABBOT

I enjoyed the sound of the rake . . . the sight of them [leaves] as they tumbled along the ground. I swung the rake in a steady rhythm and then, with no sensation of movement or passage of time, I was no longer there. . . . Instead, I was holding a brick and standing on a hard, light-colored surface that reflected the glare of the clear, bright sun.

"Hi, Daddy." The voice of a very young child came from behind me. I turned and saw a little girl riding a tricycle with a younger boy, his arms wrapped around her waist, riding on the platform behind her. Beyond them was an unusual-looking house . . . [it] seemed to be made mostly of glass, but I was having difficulty focusing my eyes on it, for it seemed to shimmer and waver. However, I could see the two children clearly as they rode their tricycle past me on what looked like a very wide sidewalk. . . . They were both facing back in my direction, smiling at me. I stood smiling at them in amazement, for I knew with an absolute certainty who they were. The scene burned itself into my brain. . . . That moment in time became a permanently etched picture in my mind.

Frightened and confused by this strange experience, Szumski related it in detail to Joan, his date that evening. When the two later married, they frequently wondered together if this was a picture of their future. In 1962, twenty years later, the dream was fulfilled at their San Jose ranch home with large bay windows. Every detail of Szumski's original 1942

> *For a moment of night we have a glimpse of ourselves—pilgrims of mortality, voyaging between horizons across the eternal seas of space and time.*
>
> HENRY BESTON

visit to the future was accurate except one: the whole 1962 scene was happening while he was standing in his neighbor's yard instead of his own. Until the 1942 reality came true in 1962, Vaughan states that Szumski wondered why such a trivial incident was "burned into his brain and etched into his consciousness." When he and Vaughan delved deeper into *how* the experience had served his life, Szumski stated that even when he was in dangerous Naval battles during World War Two, he believed he would survive because he had already visited his future self alive and at home with children. His wife also revealed that during many childless years she never gave up hope because he had already seen their children.

In this case, the meaning of an intuitive event influenced the feelings and beliefs not only for the participant but also for the closest witness, in this case Szumski's wife. Also notice that, unlike many spontaneous intuitive experiences, the setting of the event was peaceful. On the surface, a young man is simultaneously raking leaves in one yard and a father working in another yard twenty years later. In fact, it is the ordinary reality of the 1962 scene which serves to comfort the chief characters when they are in distress and danger during the intervening years. They focused on the ordinary within the context of the extraordinary.

I love this example, which raises some important questions. How do time and space intersect? Was Szumski merely visiting the future with his mind or was he *really* standing in it? If so, what kind of a body was he experiencing? How would most people respond if this happened to them? How could people be prepared for this and other potential intuitive experiences with non-local space?

This chapter explores answers to some of these questions. You will be experimenting with a body capable of non-local realities, just as you experimented with non-linear time in the previous chapter. These experiments can be powerful; don't do them if you find yourself feeling disoriented. Just read the chapter for its information and perspective. The truth is, some people may call the material in this chapter "far

> *The inherent baselessness of physical and mental objects is called reality.*
> AVATAMSAKA SUTRA

out," because you'll be viewing your body in very different ways. In experimenting with four experiences of space, you'll learn why they are important to intuition. You will:

1. experience the space inside your physical body.

2. hold personal and transpersonal identity as you encounter the immense space of your intuition and soul.

3. learn what to do when your enlarged, spacious identity intersects intuitively with others.

4. experiment with an out-of-body experience.

YOUR PHYSICAL BODY: NINETY-NINE POINT NINE HUNDRED AND NINETY-NINE PERCENT SPACE

Science has revealed that each atom of your body is 99.999 percent empty. What this means is that you are a bunch of empty space! To experience the full effect, consider the following rough analogy. Imagine that each atom of your body could be blown up to the size of the Houston Astrodome. Next, place the nucleus of the atom in the center of the playing field. Using your imagination, stand inside your nucleus. If you wanted to find the electrons circling around the rims of your edge as you stand in the nucleus, you'd have to look way, way out into the ends of the stands. There is nothing but space between your nucleus self (composed of protons and neutrons) and your electrons. Multiply this fact by the billions of atoms which comprise your body. Now you can more easily un-

> *We are perceivers. We are an awareness; we are not objects; we have no solidity. We are boundless.*
>
> CARLOS CASTANEDA

derstand how you are occupied by vast nothingness.

Most of us crowd our lives with millions of data points: people to call, plans to solidify, recreation to enjoy, money to make, projects to undertake, parenting to handle. But if we understood ourselves to be empty space, we might recognize that, rather than enjoying a natural state of nothingness, we make ourselves and our lives overstuffed closets. Plenty goes in; very little goes out. We deliberately abandon empty space in favor of solidity.

It is interesting to reverse things. Instead of focusing on your body's solidity, try focusing on its 99.999 percent space. I first learned about doing this during a 1981 parapsychology tour of China organized by Dr. Stanley Krippner. The trip was fantastic. China was just opening up to Westerners and our team had been invited to investigate reported psychic experiences and to meet with Chinese scientists and traditional doctors. The schedule was hectic, and after a few days I came down with a serious fever and cold. Not wanting to miss anything, I went out to dinner anyway.

I was lucky. Seated next to me was one of China's Qi Gong masters who, sensing my misery, leaned over and whispered, "Most people don't realize they can r-e-l-a-x themselves back to health." I was so surprised he spoke English that I hardly paid any attention to his words. He was quiet for a while and then once again said, "Let go. Let go into health. Open up. Let go." As he spoke, the room began to swim and I was aware of an immense sense of spaciousness entering my body. Everything slowed down and I grew bigger, as if I was looking at myself through a giant microscope. I was nothing but dancing molecules, and space washed through me, carrying the debris of my illness with it. I was letting go. But then, I couldn't hold the image any more. I struggled against the relaxation which was making me feel better and became acutely aware of the scientists and people surrounding me. Everything returned to normal, I smiled politely, thanked the master, and never forgot the moment.

Now I know, of course, that the Qi Gong master was teaching me about space, *my* space, and how I could shift my relationship to it.[6] This is a good skill to develop in the intuitive world because (1) it provides a visualization tool for letting go of things which can block your intuition, e.g., projec-

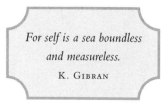

For self is a sea boundless and measureless.

K. GIBRAN

tions, negative emotions, or unpleasant sensations in your body, and (2) it helps you relate to the spaciousness which is your body. As you probably know, in addition to being mostly space, every seven years your body replaces every cell. Metaphorically, you are re-inventing yourself, a self which is literally a dancing collection of molecules, on a regular basis. And, so is everyone else. Change happens, evolution happens. Space tells us so.

One thing more: identifying your body as primarily space teaches you about meditation. As space, you recognize ideas and feelings as they touch, pass through, or occupy your empty space.[7] You know they are not you. You can view your inner space as a playground; things come in and go out. Some things you judge pleasant; some, not so pleasant. Eventually, you'll become accustomed to this constant movement, and you'll enjoy the freedom you experience when you're not attached to the different things moving through your space. And you can apply this whole teaching to the thoughts that come and go during meditation.

Exercise: Experiencing Your Body As 99.999% Space

1. Find a comfortable place to sit and do the Basic Breath exercise on page 76.

2. Using your imagination, see yourself as a dancing field of molecules (some students like to envision the shimmering way people look when they are being "beamed up" in Star Trek).

3. Now expand this concept. Pretend you are looking through a large microscope and your body is mostly space with molecules floating around. Pay attention to the space between molecules.

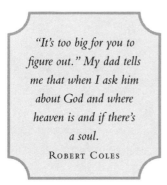

"It's too big for you to figure out." My dad tells me that when I ask him about God and where heaven is and if there's a soul.

ROBERT COLES

4. Loosen things further and let any debris (you don't have to know what it is) float away. There is nothing for it to hold on to. You're too spacious.

5. Next, let things get bigger until you are peering into your atoms. Enjoy the space you find there. Relax into your perceptual shift of space. Know that you are 99.999% space.

6. When you judge yourself ready, return your attention to your normal perception of things. Record your reactions in your journal.

IDENTITY AND YOUR SPACIOUS SOUL

A friend and student of mine, David Van Blake, told this story to a men's intuition group I was facilitating. The curriculum at Friends World College, where David was a student in his early twenties, was aimed at creating citizens of the world. David and his classmates were required to travel throughout the world for three years. The students, who were in charge of designing, executing, and completing the tour on their own, had landed in the heart of Africa. One ordinary night David went outside on the roof and lay down to enjoy the stars as he had done countless times before.

On this night, however, in the low light and crystal-clear air of the southern hemisphere, the sky seemed to start at the end of his nose. The cosmos was peeled open. The Milky Way traversed the Universe. Endless darkness, teeming with billions and billions of stars and galaxies, opened up to him. "I was shaken," David said. "I lost my Earth reference. I was on the fringe looking across my home galaxy edgewise. Suspended in space, out there with no tether, I was aware of how finite I was; how insignificant my life was. Simultaneously, I was overcome with vertigo and agoraphobia, forcing me to rush inside for the security of four walls. The moment has haunted me ever since."

As he told this story to the group, the room fell silent. None of us could speak; David's story had transported us from our day-to-day concerns to Africa and to similar encounters we had each had with either the external or internal cosmos. Either universe can be disorienting. You may get scared that you can't keep your personal identity intact

> By convention there is color, by convention sweetness, by convention bitterness, but in reality there are atoms and space.
>
> DEMOCRITUS

because it will be swamped by the endless space of your soul's inner universe. In fear, you may jump away from the cosmic encounter by ending meditation, answering the phone, going on to your next task, or anything else which switches your attention away from the vastness, just as David ran away from his nose-to-nose encounter with the heavens.

Your intuition can mediate this vast terrain for you. Shifting gears in spaciousness allows you to journey to the magnificent universes of your soul with your whole identity. You are no longer frightened for yourself and your significance. You remember something David either didn't know or never learned: soul space is as vast as the night sky which sent him reeling.

As you encounter more unusual experiences with time, space, relationships, or events, you may jump back, reassess, and wonder if you've lost your bearings in the midst of these changing perceptions. Your core identity isn't going anywhere; it is only being enlarged by the entrance of more soul. The most useful exercise I've discovered for maintaining your identity, your whole Self, while gaining the size of your soul's universe is the Circle and the Dot exercise. You are going to spend a lot of time on this exercise and its variations. In my twenty-eight years of facilitating intuition, I judge it to be one of the three most consistent, useful, longterm exercises I share.

The dot symbolizes identity, the Self. The circumference symbolizes the Universe. Around the world, this simple symbol is found in Indian mandalas, spectacular Norman stained-glass windows, New Guinea sun disks, Navaho sand paintings, Tibetan weavings, domes, games, art, mazes, etc. This image is so important because it suggests you can be inward and outward simultaneously; you are your Self (the dot) and the Universe of your soul (the full circle).

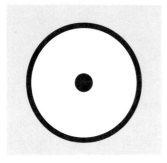

THE DOT: YOUR IN BREATH

When I was a child I played a game where one person lies down on the floor and a small group of people get on their knees, surround the person on the floor, stick two fingers each under his or her body, and slowly lift the person off the floor. The person lying on the floor, depending on whether he or she wants to be helpful to the group or make it difficult, imagines himself or herself to be light like a feather or heavy like a rock, respectively. With this game, which requires imagination and concentration, children test the power of the mind (whether a feather or a rock) as well as mind over matter (if they can use only two fingers each to pick a heavy weight up in the air).

The Circle and the Dot exercise also requires you to use your imagination and concentration. As the Circle you'll be open, vast, and spacious like your soul; as the Dot, you'll be dense and solid.

Exercise: The Dot

1. Take your journal with you and find a comfortable place to sit where you will not be disturbed.

2. Begin with a deep inhale. Listen to the sound of the air as it comes through your nostrils. Feel the air filling your lungs.

3. Take a deep breath in. *During the entire in breath,* identify your Self with the Dot in the center of the Circle.

4. As you are inhaling and identifying with the Dot, imagine that the air you are breathing in is the animating principle of life. God, spirit,

Allah, the Great Mystery, the Holy Spirit, power, qi, and The Force are some of the names people give to this principle.

> *The point is that the human needs the conviction of his [or her] own reality and without it he [or she] is deprived of life space.*
>
> JOSEPH CAMPBELL

5. Next, subjectively compress yourself. As you compress, imagine inauthentic things (you do not have to know what they are) being squeezed out of you or falling away from you.

6. Exaggerate your thick density until in your imagination every molecule of your soul-self is sandwiched together.

7. Be solid.[8] Be heavy like a rock. Say to yourself or out loud, "I am centered and present."

8. As a rock, you have earned your place. Know yourself as the Dot on your *in* breath.

9. Return to normal breathing for a few minutes and then repeat your deep inhale process. Repeat this exercise emphasizing the inhale as many times as you want.

10. When you've finished, record any reactions in your journal. Was it easy to identify with the Dot? Did you feel dense and solid? What did you experience when you were filling yourself with the animating principle?

Whenever you are experimenting with time or space exercises, it is important to keep your Dot, to stay centered in who you are. As Fritz Kunkel says, "The body is the soul's vehicle for navigating space and time." Without you solidly behind the wheel, your vehicle will not do as well traveling through intuitive domains.

> *The true quality of the soul is that of space, by which it is at rest everywhere. . . . But this space within the soul is far above the ordinary material space.*
>
> EDWARD CARPENTER

THE CIRCLE: YOUR OUT BREATH

The out breath is symbolic of the circumference and all its enclosed space, the domain of your soul. When people turn inward to do the Out Breath exercise, almost everyone goes to one of these two places: (1) The clear edge of our atmosphere or (2) Deep space.

Of course, some people only want to go to the edge of their skins, which is perfectly appropriate for them. But, since most of us choose to go to 1 or 2, and often encounter some resistance on the way, we'll focus on what I call the Blue Sky Space and the Black Sky Space. Remember that you're doing the Out Breath exercise to be spontaneously comfortable with your soul's vastness, whether you enter that awareness by choice or surprise.

To understand what I mean, ask yourself, "How would I respond if, when I went into my inner world, I was greeted by a vast, far-reaching clear nothingness where I couldn't get a sense of myself?" Or explore, "How would I feel about dropping into a gigantic, endless sea of absolute blackness?" Your soul may be comfortable in these domains, but often your personality is not. When you're comfortable with these soul spaces, you automatically open to the intuitive urgings you find there. The price of not becoming comfortable is simple: you'll miss opportunities.

Your Out Breath: The Blue Sky Space

In Tibetan Buddhism, transcendent consciousness is indicated by a clear blue sky. White clouds in the sky are said to be "life" with her ups and downs. Clouds can block our view of who we really are, the clear blue sky. Clouds come and go, but the blue sky endures, as does our true nature. The Blue Sky Space symbolizes that part of you which is boundless, free, and enduring.

Exercise: Your Blue Sky Space

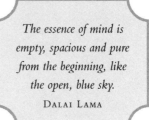

> The essence of mind is empty, spacious and pure from the beginning, like the open, blue sky.
>
> DALAI LAMA

1. Find a comfortable place to sit. Have your journal nearby.

2. Take a deep inhale and identify with the Dot.

3. When you are thoroughly identified with the Dot, allow your breath to slowly (very slowly, if you can) leave your body. Listen to it as it goes through your nostrils or your mouth.

4. Imagine your breath traveling outward to the edge of the Earth's atmosphere, to the Blue Sky Space.

5. Experience yourself as tremendously expanded and filled with space. Imagine yourself as the clear blue sky. You're light as a feather and almost all space.

6. When it is natural, take a deep breath in. As the air comes in, experience yourself becoming your dense, solid Self, the Dot, as you did in the Dot exercise.

7. Continue the exercise breathing into the Dot and out to the Blue Sky Space until you are enjoying both states of being and are completely relaxed.

8. End the exercise on an *in* breath and identify with the Dot.

9. The Blue Sky Space and the Dot both represent domains of your soul and its expression. Record any reactions you have in your journal.

This is a good exercise to do when you're seeking greater insight or a bigger perspective on your life. You can vary the exercise by identifying something that concerns you, using your imagination to visualize it somewhere in the circle between the Dot and the Circle, and then leaving it alone as you do the exercise. Your intuition will absorb information about

> *Narrow is the mansion of my soul; enlarge Thou it, that Thou mayest enter in.*
>
> ST. AUGUSTINE

the area of concern as you breathe in and breathe out. When you reach the Blue Sky Space, look back at your concern and ask the following: From the enlarged perspective of the Blue Sky Space, what do I observe? What do I know? What is still unknown? What is important about my concern? What is not important? After you have answered these questions and others you may think of, ask your intuition to give you a clarifying image, word, or sensation.

When one of my students, Mary Ann, did this exercise, she decided to investigate whether it would be wise for her to switch jobs. She was happy enough in her particular job, but she'd gone about as far as she could go and was feeling restless about her future. She placed her concern in the Circle, took a deep inhale, and then exhaled to the edge of her Blue Sky Space. After the exercise, Mary Ann examined the images associated with her concern and was confused because she'd seen herself on a beach. "This was about work," she wondered. Her journal record about the impression reads, "Perhaps I need to go on a vacation." She got on a plane to Hawaii. Two years later, however, something different unfolded: she quit her job and started her own travel business, specializing in the Pacific Islands.

Blue Sky Space is synonymous with clarity and the illumination of the soul. Evaluate your insights from that perspective as best you can.

Your Out Breath: Black Sky Space

The second most common journey is to the nighttime sky, the place David went, and I call this Black Sky Space. Interestingly, although many people's inner-world exploration takes them here, not all are comfortable with the choice. People often express fear not only of endless space but also of the blackness. But because I trust people's intuition, I always encourage them to experiment at least once with this destination, which is the one their intuition chose.

One reason people may fear Black Space is lack of familiarity. All human beings with sight have observed a clear blue sky illuminated by the sun. Millions of people have also flown through those blue skies in airplanes. In contrast, although all sighted human beings have observed very distant stars and the soft luminescence of the moon, only a handful have actually flown among them. Those who have report the immensity of black space. Astronaut William Pogue tells this story.

> *The eternal silence of these infinite spaces terrifies me.*
> BLAISE PASCAL

I raised my visor on my helmet cover and looked out to try to identify constellations. As I looked out into space, I was overwhelmed by the darkness. I felt the flesh crawl on my back and the hair rise on my neck. I was reminded of a passage in the Bible that speaks of the "horror of great darkness." Ed and I pondered the view in silence for a few moments, and then we both made comments totally inadequate to describe the profound effect the scene had made on both of us. "Boy! That's what I call dark."

This story captures not only the experience of absolute darkness, but the depth and breadth of it in space. Pogue's comments reveal a common association between darkness and horror. It is this association which we must address in order to welcome and be comfortable with the absolute blackness that going inward to your intuitive world can uncover.

In his book *The Man of Light in Iranian Sufism,* Henry Corbin describes two types of blackness. The first, he states, "is only Darkness; it can intercept light, conceal it, and hold it captive." This is the most familiar type of blackness. He describes the second as "another Darkness, called by our mystics the Night of light, luminous Blackness, black Light." Corbin goes on to describe a three-fold plane in consciousness: the day consciousness lies between the dark Night of the subconscious and the luminous Night of the supraconscious. Intuition is associated with the latter as it is the soul, the light of consciousness, which rises above the Darkness of the subconscious.

The sky was deep black,
yet at the same time
bright with sunlight.
ALEKSEI LEONOV

If you find yourself traveling to the blackness of space or want to visit there, focus on luminous blackness, a blackness which generates light. Give the blackness a texture such as velvet or satin. It may enhance your comfort to imagine warmth based on something besides the sun. For example, imagine taking your own internal sun with you as you exhale into the endless night sky. It may also help you to imagine a blackness which surrounds you with comfort, warmth, and safety. Sometimes the womb is a good metaphor for this.

I am spending more time on the luminous blackness than on the Dot or Blue Sky Space because I want those of you who arrive there spontaneously to understand that your intuition is taking you to a profoundly different understanding of "black" than the one with which you are probably most familiar. Most Westerners have never heard about the positive spiritual light dwelling in blackness, although Eastern traditions, such as Zen and Tibetan Buddhism, teach a great deal about a corollary experience: emptiness. Some spiritual writers have spoken of the phenomenon of the "Black Madonnas" found throughout the Catholic world and their relationship to Darkness and The Void.[9] In addition, Jungian analyst Marion Woodman and clinical psychologist Elinor Dickson, among others, have written about the positive power of the Dark Goddess.

Exercise: Your Black Sky Space

1. Find a comfortable place to sit. Have your journal nearby.

2. Take a deep inhale and identify with the Dot.

3. When you are thoroughly identified with the Dot, allow your breath to slowly (very slowly, if you can) leave your body. Listen to it as it goes through your nostrils.

4. Imagine your breath traveling past the edge of our atmosphere to the Black Sky Space.

5. Allow your awareness to be filled to the brim with stars and galaxies. Experience the luminosity of the blackness. Invite its velvety, mystical nature into your being.

> *The limits of soul you could not discover, though traversing every path.*
> HERACLITUS

6. When it is natural, take a deep breath in, choosing to again become your dense, solid Self, the Dot.

7. Continue the exercise, breathing into the Dot and breathing out to Black Sky Space, until you are enjoying both states of being and are completely relaxed.

8. The Black Sky Space and the Dot both represent domains of your soul and its expression. Record any reactions you have to them in your journal.

This is a good exercise to use when you want to find the light in an experience which you judge disappointing, bad, or sorrowful. The goal is not to eliminate or repress pain you might be feeling but to *add* positive luminescence to your understanding. Begin by experiencing the opaqueness of pain, which can literally eclipse your inner sun, shutting off light and joy.

When you are in this state, your goal is to transform the opaque blackness of the unconscious into the illuminating blackness of the supra-consciousness. Imagine that opaque darkness is a quality which does not know how to surrender to a deeper state and a healthier expression of itself, the luminescent state. Think of this state as a soft, black pearl. Don't try in advance to plan what insight you'll receive; trust that the luminous blackness will reveal a different perception of events.

The Dot and the Circle exercise, when done consistently, can add to your growing foundation of inner world experiences. You won't be surprised or left at a loss for how to maintain your identity should your soul's eternity decide to come calling. As you gain experience with the exercise, you may want to add a slight pause at the end of your *in* and *out* breaths.[10]

> *Soul is not in the universe; on the contrary, the universe is in Soul.*
>
> PLOTINUS

BEING, OTHERS, AND INTERSECTING SPACE

Activating your intuitive dimension implies a new sense of being. You've become multisensory. You know how to rest and feed your intuitive body with silence and joy. You are open to non-linear time experiences. You are more comfortable with the spacious domains of your soul. Your being is now much bigger both literally and figuratively.

Psychologist Robert Gerard drew the illustration on page 199 to depict how big some traditions believe your evolving Self will eventually be. Notice that when your transpersonal or soul self is developed, you have a physical, energetic, emotional, and mental presence. Information from all these levels is flowing to you; you are these levels. As you become aware of and operate from your soul nature and evolve toward your transcendental self, you have more access to your transpersonal mind, transpersonal love, and transpersonal will. Observe how big the transcendental field is and note where intuition is located—in the transpersonal love area. This explains why intuition thrives in the context of inclusive, unconditional love.

Imagine for a moment that your being is already in this state. Although you are not yet fully conscious of how to actualize your immense nature, you do know that some part of you can access the intuitive wisdom of the upper levels (other traditions have other descriptions for these high states, such as enlightenment, mystical oneness, transcendency). Obviously, as one of these beings, your identity extends far beyond the edge of your skin. In fact, when someone is standing close to you, he or she is literally standing *inside* your transpersonal field, and you inside his or hers. Your body spaces are intersecting. Depending on the level of awareness present in both parties, lots of information passes back and forth.[11] This is one reason why your increasing intuitive sensitivity allows you to know something about others by merely standing next to them.

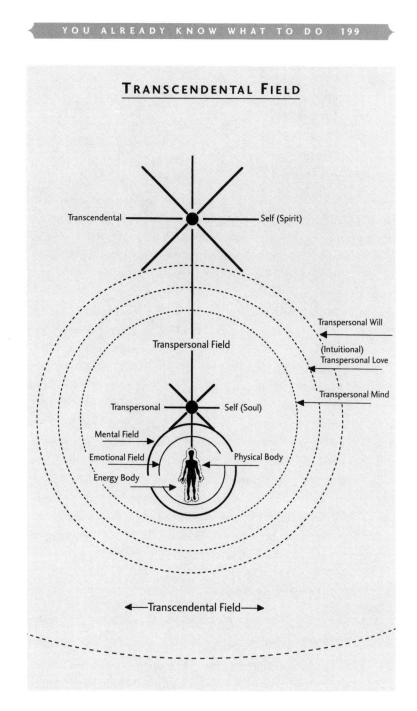

TRANSCENDENTAL FIELD

Transcendental ——— Self (Spirit)

Transpersonal Will

(Intuitional)
Transpersonal Love

Transpersonal Mind

Transpersonal Field

Transpersonal ——— Self (Soul)

Mental Field

Emotional Field

Physical Body

Energy Body

◄—Transcendental Field—►

> The galaxies exist in you . . . in your every cell, your every atom.
>
> GEORGE LEONARD

When you are awake and aware of this possibility, you're not surprised when you immediately receive information about your friend, partner, child, or colleague. Naturally, you need to verify this information in a direct and non-intrusive way. For example, you might say, "I'm sensing something *meaningful* has happened today. If so, would you like to talk about it?" (Substitute appropriate word for the italicized word in the example.) If you have a buddy with whom you are doing this work, you can give each other permission to say whatever you are feeling in each other's presence. This is a good way to start learning about separating your projections and wishful thoughts from your authentic intuitive impressions. The person will let you know if your impressions are accurate. If you are certain of an impression's veracity and the person denies it, *let it go.* It is none of your business.

When you are unconscious about the influence someone else's energy field might be having on you, you can find yourself feeling depressed, angry, or irritable for no reason. Uplifting qualities are conveyed, too, so the mere presence of a joyful person can enliven your spirit because you are literally bathing in his or her positive energy fields. Most of us do not complain when that happens, but it is important to learn how to conduct intuitive interactions with someone struggling with difficult feelings without absorbing his or her mood or attitude. In her book *Intuition Workout*, my colleague and friend Nancy Rosanoff presents the following exercise which helps people intuit the difference between their own energy fields and those of others when they intersect.

Exercise: Intersecting Space

1. Take your journal and go to a spot you've used before for meditation or visualizations.

2. Close your eyes and take a few deep breaths. Let each breath bring in sparkling, luminous energy. Let each exhalation release the ten-

sions of the day, the thoughts, the distractions. Keep breathing deeply, letting energy in and tension out.

> . . . that is we have two realities: one in which our bodies appear to be concrete in time and space; and one in which our very being appears to exist primarily as a shimmering cloud of energy.
>
> MICHAEL TALBOT

3. Imagine that you are completely surrounded by an egg-shaped bubble. Give yourself plenty of space. Make the bubble the perfect size for you, not too big and not too small. This bubble is made of a substance so strong that no outside energies can enter in. Make sure it is thick enough to guarantee this. It can still be clear, but is strong and thick.

4. Your energy is the only thing inside the bubble. Your energy emanates out from you, bounces against the inside of the bubble, and comes back to you. As your energy bounces back, you get stronger and stronger.

5. Bask in your energy for as long as you want.

6. Next, think of someone you know, someone you feel comfortable with. Imagine that person in his or her own bubble, and let that bubble float toward you. Reflect on the bubble as it approaches. How is it like your bubble? How is it different?

7. Now let your bubbles intersect. Notice how you respond. How does your energy change? How does the other person's energy change? Are you still comfortable? Do you know anything about him or her from the contact, and, if so, what do you know? What do you imagine he or she might be learning about you? Are you still comfortable?

8. Let the two bubbles become separate again. Thank your friend for doing this with you and let his or her bubble float away.

Love is the will to extend one's self for the purpose of nurturing one's own or an other's spiritual growth.

SCOTT PECK

9. Remain in your bubble for a few moments, feeling what it feels like to be just you again.

10. When you are ready, return your attention to the luminous in breath and relaxing out breath.

11. Record your experiences in your journal.

Optional: Do the whole exercise in the presence of a friend who is doing it with you.

You can also do this exercise with projects, events, or places, by giving these items bubbles and letting them float toward you. Always cognitively check out the information you receive before you assume it to be true or take action. Intuition doesn't suffer by being tested.

SHIFTING SPACE: AN OUT-OF-BODY EXPERIMENT

You are now ready for your final exercise with shifting space concepts. You know that traveling in these spatial domains is a normal human ability; it's just one with which you've had little practice. Experimenting with new ways of understanding the world is not new to you. As an infant and toddler you were experimenting all the time. The learning paths you chose back then were scattered with plenty of mistakes, but you probably don't remember any of them.

This is also true for learning how to shift space and set time free. You'll make mistakes, so the only thing you should ask of yourself is to have fun. And, in the spirit of fun, read the following true story and then do the experiment which is based on it.

In 1863 S. R. Wilmot set sail from Liverpool to New York. While he was at sea, a terrible storm struck and, although there was news back on land about the storm causing the loss of another ship, not a word about Wilmot's ship's fate was publicized. Still at sea, unable to sleep for eight nights, Wilmot finally slept soundly when the storm's fury abated on the ninth night. He reported dreaming of his wife, whom

Bring us back to our center and we will return there with gladness. Renew us now as you have in days gone by.
HEBREW PRAYER

he'd left in the U.S.A. She came to his cabin door, discovered that Wilmot's cabin-mate was in the room as well, hesitated a little, and then came in, leaned down, and kissed him.

In the morning Wilmot was surprised when his fellow-passenger remarked what an unusual man he was to have a lady come visit him in this way. They compared notes of their experiences, including how the lady had looked and what she did. Their accounts corresponded. Three days later Wilmot was further amazed when, reunited and alone with his wife, she asked him, "Did you receive a visit from me a week ago Tuesday?"

Back in the United States, Wilmot's wife had become very concerned about him when she heard that the steamer *Africa* had been lost at sea in the same storm. Unable to sleep, she lay awake until 4 A.M. when, it seemed to her, she went out to seek her husband. She crossed the sea, came to the ship, descended into the cabin, and was surprised to encounter a man in the upper berth of Wilmot's cabin. Nonetheless, as she recounted, she went in, leaned over, kissed Wilmot, and then went away. Her description of his odd-shaped stateroom was precise.[12]

Once again we encounter an experience where love, emotional connections, and crisis all converge to produce an unusual event. The interesting part of this tale is that for the three people involved, all of whom were probably preoccupied with the possibility of their own or someone else's death, the veil between what is possible and impossible, according to the accepted laws of physical space, was rent. Each of the three had an encounter they could describe as normally as if they were recalling sitting down for tea.

> All things in the world
> come from being. And
> being comes from
> non-being.
>
> LAO-TZU

You, too, are going to work with a partner on a remote viewing experiment. This will increase your chance of success (because intuition travels on love), and it will also raise the probability that you'll have fun no matter what happens. The focus of your work is on achievement rather than the resolution of a crisis.

There are big differences between knowing that unusual things can happen, knowing they can happen to *you,* and knowing they can happen under your conscious direction. Ordinary people do succeed at making remote viewing skills conscious, but they are often in a highly charged environment or in the laboratory or a workshop. Be patient and curious.

Exercise: Shifting Space and an Out-of-Body Experiment

1. Choose a partner to work with whom you love very much. It doesn't matter what role he or she plays in your life. What is important is that you love that person deeply and trust absolutely that he or she loves you. You do not have to live together or nearby. Distance is no object.

2. Discuss out-of-body experiences with each other (stories you've heard, experiences you've had, what you each think of the subject).

3. Working separately so your partner can't see what you are doing, select the greatest wish you have for the other and write about it on an index card. Only use one side of the index card to describe the wish.

4. Each of you pastes or tapes the index card to the very center of a plain white 8½ x 11 or larger sheet of paper.

5. Get out magazines, Magic Markers, crayons, or pens. Using words or pictures or a combination of both, surround the index card with

a collage that expresses the joy and love you have toward your wish for your partner. Have fun.

6. Pin the picture up someplace where your partner is not going to see it for at least one week.

7. When both of you are done with your collages, begin your out-of-body experiments.

8. Every night and every morning, when you are in that special state of almost falling asleep or just waking up, gently request that some part of your consciousness visit the collage your partner made for you at least *once a day for one week.* Tell your traveling "sidekick" (this is what I call that part of you) that it doesn't have to schedule the visits through you; in fact, you don't even have to know when the visit is happening.

9. Although you haven't seen it yet, once a day, any time during the day, sit down with your journal and write three full pages of intuitive impressions about the collage your partner made for you and his or her depth of support. If any images come to your mind, draw them. If you find it difficult to work with the assignment, write what it is you *hope* your partner wished for you.

10. At the end of every writing session, practice shifting your space by telling your "sidekick" to go visit your partner's wish for you. Using your imagination, pretend you are standing in front of the collage your partner made for you. Look at it with your intuitive eyes, feel it with your intuitive heart, and touch it with your intuitive hands. What do you see? What do you feel? Write precisely what you think it is.

11. If you have any dreams during the week, write them in your journal.

12. At the end of the week, compare notes with your partner and show each other the collages you have created. Share some moments of love.

13. Record everything of interest.

SPACE SHIFTERS

Space shifters who have at least some access to all the levels on page 199 can be simultaneously in the specific state of the "I," the transpersonal state of the "I AM," and, ultimately, in the transcendental Self, the "I AM THAT I AM." Intuition operates on all these levels, although each ascending level of awareness requires less and less effort to develop and use intuition. In fact, intuition is antiquated when your love opens to universal space because universal love is omniscient, all knowing. When you are with it, there is no need for out-of-body visits because you are so soul embodied that you are one with all bodies through the auspices of your own. Rumi, the great thirteenth-century Sufi mystic, summed up the relationships between love, space, and intuition when he wrote:

The clear bead at the center changes everything.
There are no edges to my loving now.
I've heard it said that there's a window that
opens from one mind to another.
But if there's no wall, there's no need for fitting
the window or the latch.

Final Exercise: Your Intuition To Do List

1. Complete the sentence, "Because I am accepting my soul's invitation to 'Shift Space,' I already know to . . ." List 5 to 10 things you know to do. Remember you can choose simple things such as "go out and really enjoy the stars," "read up on atoms," "practice the Dot and the Circle exercise every day." When you've finished, read your list over, highlight the simplest activity which *will bring more space into your body,* and do it. Record everything in your journal.

2. Go back and look at your Guiding Image for this chapter. How does it capture the principles of spaciousness? What is the most striking thing your image now teaches you about shifting your identity to include the spaciousness of the soul? Record in your journal.

CHAPTER 9

Invitation Seven:

DISCOVER
YOUR PURPOSE

A NEW BEING

Your experiments with greater soul embodiment, intuitive skills, and expanded time and space dimensions have altered your perceptual world, and changes in perception always lead to changes in being and vice versa. These changes are probably leading you to automatically examine your life with new eyes, asking yourself questions like: Am I the best person I can be? What habits or addictions am I strong enough to eliminate? How can I keep my body healthy? Is there anyone I need to forgive or ask for forgiveness? But perhaps the most universal question asked by people during times of increasing soul identity is: *What is the purpose of my life?*

This questioning process may begin as a gentle yearning inside you for something different, or as a nagging irritation with your present job, locale, or relationships, or as a global dissatisfaction with your entire life style. The question: *What is the purpose of my life?* is a signal that your soul is calling you to something that is more appropriate for the new you; it is beginning to evoke your unique purpose. Your purpose may have to do with the acquisition of character—enhanced courage, joy, passion, integrity—or it may be related to the things you do in the world, or some combination of character development and personal accomplishment.

> One's deep intuition is
> an infallible guide to
> purpose and
> accomplishment.
>
> WILLIS HARMAN

One thing is certain: your soul is interested in helping you discover your overall purpose and the next best step toward actualizing your destiny.

In his best-selling book, *The Soul's Code,* author and psychologist James Hillman talks about each of us having an inner "acorn" encoded with our destiny, life path, and purpose much as an actual acorn holds all the information necessary for the mighty oak tree to fulfill its destiny. Intuition is designed to reveal to you this kind of authentic destiny; it calls you back to a part of yourself which never left. Because intuition knows the language of your acorn, it helps you discover and design your life purpose.

In this chapter, you'll learn ten principles which guide intuition's role in unfolding your purpose. To demonstrate these principles in action, I'll tell you one person's unfolding purpose story and then show you how it illustrates all these principles. I guarantee you that these principles are already at work in your life. Understanding them alerts you to the common ways intuition works with life purpose and gives you confidence in your soul's ability to assist your unfolding in an elegant and methodical way.

In these pages you'll also see how to identify the best next step you can take to support your destiny, and you may get at least a glimpse, if not the total picture, of your grand dream or overall life purpose. To begin peeling away the distractions between you and your destiny, you will do exercises for one week (Monday through Sunday) from the previous six chapters, but this time you'll apply each exercise to discovering, developing, and growing your purpose. This concentrated effort will certainly pay off, because these exercises fertilize, water, and activate the wisdom of your inner acorn.

To prepare for your work, select your guiding illustration for this chapter.

Your Guiding Image for "Discover Your Purpose"

1. Label the next page of your Intuition Journal "Chapter Nine: Discover Your Purpose."

2. Without looking, reach into your Image Vocabulary envelope and pull out your guiding illustration for this chapter.

3. Note which category it comes from on the bottom of the page you've labeled.

4. Paste the image on the page.

> *To know how to choose a path with heart is to learn how to follow intuitive feeling. Logic can tell you superficially where a path might lead to, but it cannot judge whether your heart will be in it.*
>
> JEAN SHINODA BOLEN

Never forget that your destiny is fashioned out of a consistent intuitive dialogue between your inner acorn and your evolution as a person. The story you are about to read reveals how this conversation between one person's inner acorn and personal evolution developed across time. An oak tree doesn't appear overnight; it follows a step-by-step process. Purpose, too, has its own sense of destiny and timing.

ONE STORY OF PURPOSE

There are ten principles which guide intuition's role in unfolding your purpose. The basic facts of Nancy Rivard's story illustrate one or more of these principles and demonstrate intuition in action.

The story begins when Nancy Rivard was working as a flight attendant supervisor with higher management positions in the airline she worked open to her. Better pay, more regular hours, and increased status came with any of these positions, but Nancy intuited that taking advan-

> *Wander where there is
> no path. You lay a
> path in walking.*
> A. MACHADO

tage of these job openings would be the wrong move for her. In fact, her intuition kept inviting her to go back to her old, less prestigious job as a flight attendant.

Since her father's death, Nancy was in a deep evaluation of her life and what purpose it might have. She found herself asking her soul these related questions over and over: "How can I be useful?" and "How can I put love in action?" Although she didn't know the answer to her questions, Nancy decided to listen to her intuition and returned to flight attendant status. Professionally, it was a step down from where she was, but attendants had flexibility, time off, and access to the entire globe. Nancy knew she needed those things, but even as she took the plunge and let her advancement possibilities pass by, Nancy was mystified.

Years passed. Nancy enjoyed her life as a flight attendant, began to travel all over the world, and continued to develop her spiritual life. Then, in 1991, while she was in deep meditation, Nancy received guidance that she was to participate in the 1992 Earth Summit in Rio de Janeiro. The Earth Summit had a profound impact on her. She felt a tremendous camaraderie with the human beings she met, and she wanted to contribute to the global community that she saw emerging. She realized that traveling for a profession had embedded her with a deep love for humanity and a conviction that there was a larger plan at work in the world—one designed to promote sustainable life and the evolution of consciousness. She saw that the travel industry could play a more fundamental role in building a better world, but felt crazy whenever she intuited herself influencing the industry. "You're just a little flight attendant," her logical mind kept expressing. "How can you make a difference?" "By example," her intuition would reply.

In the fall of 1993, an integrating vision began to appear in Nancy's consciousness. Why not start a volunteer organization of airline personnel that would give them a chance to serve others? Nancy became convinced that this was precisely what she needed to do. She'd call her or-

ganization Airline Ambassadors. Nancy
also remembered that years earlier,
while consulting intuitive Kevin Ryer-
son, she had received guidance that she
was to be an ambassador. At the time
the insight had little meaning, but now
it fit.

Nancy quickly realized that she'd
have to get her vision off the ground on
her own, so she cranked up an old computer, carved a work space out in her

> There is no need to run
> outside for better seeing.
> Nor to peer from a
> window. Rather reside in
> the center of your being.
> The more you leave it,
> the less you learn.
>
> LAO-TZE

small studio, and began creating brochures, mission statements, and a ros-
ter of interested airline personnel. Participants could use their ability to fly
all over the world for free, or for reduced fees, in order to become ambassadors of love and goodwill for those in need.

For the first few years Nancy's fledgling organization moved along
slowly, but today the organization has over a thousand members representing eight airlines. The all-volunteer Airline Ambassadors participate
in four main activities: (1) delivering humanitarian aid such as medical
supplies to clinics all over the world; (2) escorting orphans to new homes
or bringing children to medical care in other countries; (3) participating
in special events and conferences; and (4) providing at-risk youth with educational opportunities. One youth, nineteen-year-old Gerard from
Guyana, recently helped deliver three tons of medical supplies to Brazil.
Later he told Nancy, "This is the most pivotal experience of my life." Affiliated with the U.N. and recognized by the U.S. Congress as a NGO
(non-governmental organization), Airline Ambassadors was part of a U.S.
Presidential Conference on volunteerism.

INTUITION AND PURPOSE: TEN PRINCIPLES

The acorn trusts that it is encoded with the directions necessary to become an oak tree, rather than, say, a blue spruce. Like a real acorn, you,

> *This is the true joy in life, the being used for a purpose recognized by yourself as a mighty one.*
> GEORGE BERNARD SHAW

too, must trust the wise messages encoded in your inner acorn. When you trust, your destiny is assured. When you withhold trust or remain ambivalent, your progress with purpose is slow. Even if you hesitate to trust, but sincerely experiment with trusting, you'll achieve results. Trust of any kind is fundamental to each of the ten principles.

As you read through these ten principles and see how they have operated in Nancy's story, think about your life. Explore how intuition might be helping you at this moment actualize aspects of your purpose.

TEN PRINCIPLES OF HOW INTUITION WORKS WITH YOUR PURPOSE

Your Intuition:

1. Guides you one step at a time.

2. Responds to guiding questions.

3. Builds on skills you've already developed.

4. Stays in contact with you through spiritual practices and exercises.

5. Unfolds a larger purpose slowly.

6. Reveals how everything fits.

7. Asks you to begin where you are.

8. Is in it for the long haul.

9. Has mini-purposes nestled inside your larger purpose.

10. Welcomes your input.

Principle #1: Intuition guides you one step at a time.

Nancy Rivard's journey to purpose began with one simple step: she needed to listen to her intuition and let her present advancement possibilities go. Mother Teresa described a similar moment when she said that in spite of years of intuitive guidance that she'd be involved in street work, nothing happened to direct her toward her purpose until she dared to take the first step and help someone on the streets of Calcutta.

> *All individuals . . . have, therefore, the whole universe as their common ground, and this universality becomes conscious in the experience of enlightenment, in which the individual awakens into his own true all-embracing nature.*
>
> LAMA ANAGARIKA
> GOVINDA

Sometimes your intuition may ask you—as in Nancy's case—to take a step without knowing why. Other times you may, like Mother Teresa, have a glimpse of why that one step is important. In either case, intuition only asks you to take one step at a time.

Principle #2: Intuition responds to guiding questions.

As Nancy evaluated different aspects of her life, she found herself asking over and over, "How can I be useful? How can I bring love into action?" Repetitive seed questions like these imply that you are staying open and flexible: you are willing to live in the unknown. Sincere self-inquiry provides a path along which intuition can flow. In short, Nancy's soul was going to answer her question. She could rely on that.

Principle #3: Intuition builds on skills you've already developed.

Notice that Nancy's repetitive question was about usefulness. As a flight attendant, she served a useful purpose in her work, providing food and

> *If we could only see reality more as it is, it would become obvious what we need to do.*
>
> JOSEPH JAWORSKI

drink, comfort, information, and care in emergencies. It's not surprising that Nancy's core question reflected the skill base she had already developed. Intuition will build on your present skills, often redirecting their application to a different or a broader context.

Principle #4: Intuition stays in contact with you through spiritual practices and exercises.

During the "silent" years, when it appeared the answer to Nancy's question was not forthcoming, Nancy continued to grow her spiritual life through prayer, meditation, and celebration. It was during one of these practices that Nancy received key guidance to go the 1992 Earth Summit.

Spiritual practices build inner pathways for your acorn's intuitive messages. Until these pathways are solidly in place, you may miss, ignore, or distort intuitive messages. During a quiet period in terms of your purpose, focus on strengthening your spiritual practices.

Principle #5: Intuition unfolds a larger purpose slowly.

It was many years after her initial inquiry before Nancy began to fully weave together her acquired skills and aspirations for global work. The integrating vision for Airline Ambassadors emerged out of years of work as a flight attendant, years of spiritual practice, and the glimpse into her potential future which the Earth Summit provided.

Spiritual traditions frequently warn that the light of your soul and your soul's full embodiment is so extraordinary that it might temporarily blind you, strike you dumb, hurt you, or even kill you. For this reason, the path of your purest light is revealed slowly to yourself and to others. Be patient with the workings of your soul; it has its own time line.

Principle #6: Intuition reveals how everything fits.

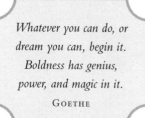

Whatever you can do, or dream you can, begin it. Boldness has genius, power, and magic in it.

GOETHE

As Nancy's grand dream for Airline Ambassadors unfolded, she perceived how working as a flight attendant had prepared her for founding an organization dedicated to global service. Everything fit.

Your intuition will pull together the pieces of your life puzzle so that everything fits. When an integrating vision begins to emerge, make sure you write down in a list all the parts of your life which are being tied together. This will help you weave things together and empower you to claim all your talents and abilities.

Principle #7: Intuition asks you to begin where you are.

When the Airline Ambassador vision began to coalesce, Nancy had no computer equipment or skills, no secretary, little spare time, and only a few extra dollars. She began anyway. She rearranged her home, accepted a friend's offer of out-of-date computer equipment, and contracted interested colleagues.

Intuition urges you to begin where you are and with what you have. If your quest is authentic, the basic necessities for a simple next step will always be provided.

Principle #8: Intuition is in it for the long haul.

The years that passed between each of Nancy's steps demonstrate that intuition is in it for the long haul; it won't abandon you or your dreams. You can rely on the actions of your soul.

> Be alert, be self-aware,
> so that when opportunity
> presents itself, you can
> actually rise to it.
>
> DAVID BOHM

Principle #9: Intuition has mini-purposes nestled inside your larger purpose.

When Nancy first created Airline Ambassadors to spread love and goodwill throughout the world, she didn't know how those lofty ideals would translate into practical applications. The four main activities of the organization today grew organically out of her founding members' interests and the requests for help that the world presented.

Remember this: although "purpose" is a big-meaning word, many mini-purposes are nestled inside it. Nancy's story exemplifies that as you finish one purpose, your intuition will reveal the next one.

Principle #10: Intuition welcomes your input.

As the language of the soul, intuition is a communication highway between your soul and your personality. Never forget that intuitive communication is conversational; it is not dictatorial. Nancy's soul conversed with her about founding the Airline Ambassadors; it didn't order her compliance. Nancy's input and that of her colleagues gave final definition and direction to the organization.

Like the oak tree's acorn, the blueprint for your purpose is inside you. But it is your welcome input which gives full shape to your destiny.

Remember that trust is a prerequisite for these ten principles to operate successfully. Sometimes it takes courage to trust because your soul, which sees your purpose in the uncut marble of your life, asks you to cut out areas of your life which are not contributing to personal and collective evolution. You may be attached to the areas the soul identifies. However, I urge you, within reason, to take your soul's advice and cut out out-dated parts of your life because your soul's purpose is to allow the real you—the passionate, present, purposeful, and powerful you—to emerge. When you exercise such deep trust, you are acting in accordance with your *artha,* a Sanskrit term meaning purpose, or that which you are born to do. According to this teaching, once you sense your *artha,* life becomes very simple. All you need do is strive to remove everything that is not *artha,* and then your *artha* will come into radiant focus.

> *I have a sense of destiny as though my life was assigned to me by fate and had to be fulfilled. This gave me an inner security. . . . Often I had the feeling that in all decisive matters, I was no longer among men, but was alone with God.*
>
> C. G. JUNG

Exercises: One Week Dedicated to Your Purpose

Background and Preparation

To explore your purpose and intuition's role in depth, you will practice purpose exercises each day for a week. This work will help you get a glimpse of your larger purpose, catalyze an integrating vision, and identify your next best steps.

Purpose has to have something to hang its hat on, some guiding structure which is part of your inner architecture. To establish this structure for your week, design a guiding inner question or an affirmation about purpose.

A guiding question about purpose should be simple and get at the core of your inquiry. For example, Nancy, who wanted to be of service, asked about usefulness. Dennis wanted to succeed at art. His question was, "How can I create an art which speaks intimately to others?" Joan, who wanted to be a leader, asked, "Who do I need to be to evoke the best in people?" Charles sought a role in transforming business and asked, "How can I assist positive change in organizational communities?"

Affirmations declare a truth whether that truth is a present reality or a desired one for your future. As a software program for the hardware of

> The "resurrection" is not of the so-called dead, but of the living who are "dead" in the sense of never having entered upon true life.
>
> HONORÉ DE BALZAC

your consciousness, your affirmation's words should also be simple and direct. For example, the affirmation that scientist, businessman, and author Willis Harman (*Higher Creativity* and *Global Mind Change*) shared with thousands of people is: "I have no other desire than to know the deepest part of myself, and to follow that."

Harman promised people that if they "vividly imagined this to be true and repeated it many times daily over some months, the results would produce changes that were startling." Willis Harman could promise you that because his own life had been augmented and transformed by this affirmation.

Either of these techniques establishes the inner architecture necessary for the investigation of your life's purpose.

Exercise: Preparation

1. Take out your journal and decide whether you will repeat a question or an affirmation during your week of work.

2. Write your question or affirmation in your journal.

3. Repeat your question or affirmation aloud or to yourself many times a day throughout your week.

You are now ready to begin your week dedicated to purpose.

MONDAY: A LOGO FOR YOUR PURPOSE

Your intuitive eye is powerful; it is visionary. Sometimes the visions which it reveals can surprise even you because they arise from so deep within. Other times you choose a vision and send it inward to your intuitive eye.

The logo for your purpose is an example of the latter—it programs your intuitive eye and ignites your vision. Every time you look at your logo, your intuition gets tuned into your purpose. This is true whether you know what your purpose is yet or not. Purpose, like the sun, is within you even if the clouds, rain, snow, or fog of your development make it difficult to see. Slow and methodical work with your logo will always evoke opportunities for you to fulfill the meaning behind your logo's image.

> *When the activities of life are infused with reverence, they come alive with meaning and purpose.*
> GARY ZUKAV

Working with a logo can empower new directions in your life. In January 1996 Sherry None took a class that focused on Julia Cameron's book, *The Artist's Way.* During one of the exercises, she surprised herself by declaring that within five years she would move to the mountains and would be doing something to dispense wisdom. At the time, Sherry, a business woman, was earning a very comfortable income and had no plans of leaving her company. A chance encounter with Nancy Rosanoff's book *Intuition Workout,* which she read from cover to cover, led her to pursue intuition training with me in May of 1996 and the logo exercise. She drew a small self on the left side of her paper, a much larger and brighter self on the right, and her transition symbol was a trash basket. Above the basket, she wrote, "In one year my old life will be in the basket." After a few more encounters with her wisdom, she spent ten minutes in a parking lot drawing up where she was going and what she needed to do to get there. She wrote (1) retire; (2) enroll in school; (3) rent or sell my home; and (4) pursue teaching intuition.

Sherry accomplished all these things in less than the year she gave herself. She was in school, living elsewhere, and retired. Her business, which she registered as "Intuitive Concepts," focused on the role intuition plays in career choices, and started immediately. Within a few weeks she had five teaching engagements on the East and West Coasts.

Other people, such as Janis Marshall, have converted their future logo exercise into something more than just an exercise; their future logo liter-

> *Spiritual practice always involves going beyond simply finding out who one is to a level of finding out what one needs to do in the world.*
>
> GERALD MAY

ally becomes their business logo. But you don't have to change jobs or open a new business to gain from relating your logo to your purpose. Your logo can provide insight, direction, and empowerment wherever you are now and whatever you are doing now.

Monday's Exercise, Part A: Identify Your Visionary Logo

1. Go back to the logo exercise you did on page 50. Find the corresponding logos you drew in your journal. Look at the future logo you drew at that time (on the right-hand page of your journal).

2. Unless you strongly object or think you've already actualized the meaning behind that logo, this logo represents your work with purpose. If this just can't work, draw a new logo.

3. Draw another picture of your logo (or use your new one) and pin it near your front door.

4. Look at your logo every time you enter or exit your home or any other time that you think about it.

5. As you look at your logo, imagine that it is helping you identify the next best steps for actualizing your purpose and the overall vision for your purpose. Remember, the latter may emphasize character development over doing things.

Maximo Kalaw, director of the Earth Council, inspired another way for you to work with your logo or purpose when he told me, "The Indigenous Philippine word for work meant seeking a vision. When someone went to work, it was understood that he or she left to seek or fulfill a vision."

Borrow from this tradition. As you leave for work, look at your logo and tell yourself, "I am seeking my vision today." If you live with others, consider doing this work together. Share logos with each other and, as you leave for work, wish each other well, saying things like "Have a nice day fulfilling your vision," or, "Good luck with your visionary purpose today." When you come home at night, share what discoveries about purpose you've made that day. If this happens in your household or among your friends, before long you will all have a wealth of wise strategies for discovering purpose, creating path, and actualizing vision.

People should not consider so much what they are to do, as what they are.

MEISTER ECKHART

Monday's Exercise, Part B: Sharing Your Visionary Logo

1. Share your logo with others with whom you live or are in close communion.

2. Wish each other well with unfolding your purpose as you leave and return from daily activities.

3. Record in your journal anything of interest.

TUESDAY: SAY "YES" AND OFFER A PRAYER

The word "Yes!" has a strong presence. Technically, saying "yes" implies agreement or confirmation. Or, the word can be seen as a type of benediction, meaning "so be it." When you say "yes," you are saying, "let it be so," "let it happen," or "I confirm that . . ." Saying "yes" to the meaning behind your logo blesses your purpose and signals your intuition that you want its help.

Tuesday's Exercise, Part A: Say "Yes"

1. Say "Yes" to your purpose by standing in front of your logo and chanting "Yes" as often and for as long as you desire.

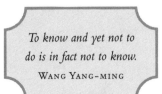

To know and yet not to do is in fact not to know.

WANG YANG-MING

Another thing that you can do to affirm the meaning of your "yes" is to get up early, go to a high hill before sunrise, and pray for or converse with the larger forces of life about the purpose within you. If you can't bring yourself to get up early and do this, you may not have the dedication necessary to achieve your goal. There is no failure in this; you simply haven't found the purpose which would make you *want* to get up and participate in a helpful, symbolic conversation with the rising sun.

You can always use the "as if" technique recommended by Ralph Waldo Emerson. Emerson believed that if you acted "as if" you had what you really wanted, you stood a better chance of *getting* what you really wanted. So simply ask yourself, "What would I be doing about this sunrise activity, if I thought it would make a big difference in my life?"

Tuesday's Exercises, Part B: Offer a Prayer

1. Find a high spot where you can observe the morning sun rise. As it rises, converse with or offer a prayer to the rising sun about your purpose. Talk over anything else you want.

2. Record notes about your experience in your journal.

WEDNESDAY: MANIFEST POWER

Purposeful intentions are born every day. Most of them don't make it to bed with you at night because by evening they've already been discarded. Power has not manifested behind them. Focusing on purpose for a week will change that.

An important tool for enlisting your intuition's help with purpose is embodiment. Your purpose must live in your body, not just in your mind. Thus far, you have called on your intuitive eyes and hands in drawing, visualizing, and imagining your logo. It is time to call your intuitive power centers into action. You've explored your upper intuitive power center as a ball of light or fire (page 82). To energize your purpose with the power found in this power center, visualize your logo, your sense of purpose, inside

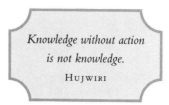

Knowledge without action is not knowledge.

HUJWIRI

the center of this fiery ball. When it's at the center of your intuitive upper power center, your purpose acts like the sun and brings a galaxy of possibilities to you.

Wednesday's Exercise:
Manifest Power

1. Stand up, spread your feet apart so they are directly below your shoulders, bend your knees slightly, and then, bending your knees more as you go, "sink" into your lower body cavity until you reach a comfortable stance.

2. Imagine a fiery ball inside your abdomen two or three fingers down from your belly button. Feel its heat and warmth inside you.

3. Visualize your logo, your purpose, in the center of this intuitive power center.

4. Take a deep breath in and imagine the air going all the way down to this power center and stoking your fiery center of purpose with its presence.

5. As you exhale, imagine everything that is irrelevant to your purpose being carried out on the air.

6. Repeat steps 4 and 5 until you've maintained a natural, relaxed rhythm for 5 or more minutes.

7. Complete the exercise by removing your attention from your upper power center, breathing normally, and taking out your journal.

8. Write and complete both these sentences in your journal: "Now that my purpose is energized, I know that the next step I need to

> God changes not what is
> in a people, until they
> change what is in
> themselves.
>
> THE KORAN

take to unfold my purpose is . . ." and "This activity contributes to my overall purpose which I believe is . . ."

9. Record anything else of interest in your journal.

THURSDAY: JUST LET IT BE

Purpose sometimes benefits when you silence yourself and just let it be. There comes a time to leave your purpose and your interactions with it alone. This "time out" is undertaken in a conscious, clear way. It is not stumbled upon because you are too busy or neglectful. Either of these reasons saps energy and momentum from your week-long program. But if purpose is set aside properly, silence has the opportunity to gift you with direction.

In his book *Kahuna Healing,* Serge Kahili King tells that once, when he was sleeping in the wilderness with a few friends, his inner voice awakened him in the middle of the night and urged him to walk into the silence of the wilderness. Doing so, he became aware of "a deep humming sound that seemed to vibrate through everything." Eventually, his inner voice advised him to sit down. Suddenly the entire night—the stars, the air, the plants, the Earth, his own body's cells—transformed themselves into millions of murmuring voices which began to speak to him about life. The voices told him that "love is the key to all. Love is the Path, Love is the Secret. Teach Love. . . ."

Silenced by the majesty of it all, Serge was unable to speak but sent his love back into the Universe. Years later, Serge still strives to live the message of that night's vision. The purpose that was revealed to him that night had nothing to do with activities, but rather out of the silence arose words about character, ethics, and high aspirations.

Whenever you find yourself agitated or worried about your purpose, remember to say this to yourself: "When I let everything go, my intuition invites in the most important part of my purpose."

Thursday's Exercise: Just Let It Be

Be silent about great things; let them grow inside you.

BARON FREIDRICH
VON HUGEL

1. Find a silent place to sit or walk in the night. If you chose inside your home, turn off all the lights.

2. Silence your thoughts, your emotions, your body, and your questing.

3. Using your imagination, wrap the loving arms of your silence around your purpose. Cradle it for 10 to 15 minutes.

4. Record in your journal how it felt to be silent and anything else of interest.

FRIDAY: CELEBRATE

When you realize an inner dream because you dared to listen to your intuition, you get a dose of joy which lasts forever. You understand that any purpose which truly belongs to you can't be taken away; your acorn is yours and yours alone. No one else can do what is uniquely yours to accomplish.

In 1987, Colleen Mauro debated how to participate in a large, world-wide prayer for the evolution of humanity, and she eventually decided to spend it alone at the beach. Although it was a beautiful day the beach was empty, so she spread out her blanket in order to commune with the sand, sky, and crashing waves. She found herself saying, "Please, God, let me be part of the transformation. I want to be part of the transformation, God. Please, may I be part of the transformation." She chanted, sang, and repeated this question over and over for hours. As night began

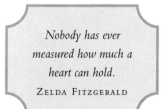

Nobody has ever measured how much a heart can hold.

ZELDA FITZGERALD

to fall, she realized that she'd spent her day exactly as she had hoped.

In 1988, after years in the magazine industry, Colleen was unemployed and worried that she might have to relocate to continue her career. "What am I going to do?" she asked herself. "Am I going to have to leave San Francisco, the city I love, to find an appropriate job?" Colleen's request on the beach a year earlier was far from her mind, when her inner voice said very clearly, "Call the Center for Applied Intuition." Colleen was startled; she had enjoyed meeting the Center's director, Bill Kautz, several months earlier, but couldn't imagine why her intuition would be sending her back. Curious, Colleen called and made an appointment to speak with Bill.

"Our conversation about the Center's activities was interesting, but the minute I saw their little in-house magazine I knew what I was going to do with my life," Colleen said. Certain that a magazine about intuition would succeed, Colleen revamped and distributed the first edition of *Intuition* magazine herself. She loaded up the back of her little car with magazines and hand-delivered them to small, local stores. When the magazines sold out, she knew her intuition had been correct and that her opportunity to contribute to the transformation had arrived. There was reason to celebrate.

Friday's Exercise: Celebrate

1. After you wake up and before you get out of bed, turn to Leila's Laughter Workout on page 141 of this book.

2. Do the exercise with this variation: pretend that you're laughing because you've found, like Colleen did, the perfect, absolutely perfect, way to explore, learn about, and actualize your next step in the purpose process.

3. When you're done, record how it felt to laugh over this in your journal.

4. Jot down something that might happen to help you actualize your purpose and that would make you laugh. For example, I finally meet a colleague I believe crucial to my career and then discover her/his name was already in my Rolodex. We'd met

> *To me, wholeness is the key to aliveness. It is more than just physical vitality. It is radiance.*
>
> RICHARD MOSS

years earlier, but I didn't realize who I was meeting. Or, a television comedy presents a professional situation similar to mine. I realize how humorous everything is and arrive at work open and relaxed.

SATURDAY:
MAKE TIME YOUR FRIEND

Timing and purpose are deeply intertwined. Think of the acorn. It must unfold its destiny with the right sense of timing, sending roots into the soil and reaching for the sun and rain at the right time of year, or it will never succeed. Fortunately, the knowledge of how to do this is innate to the acorn; it doesn't need to work at it.

This is true of your purpose, too; it may bloom early, or late, or somewhere in between, but your purpose knows the timing which is innate to your being. When you trust your soul, you do not try to push purpose ahead or hold it back. If you do not trust your soul's timing, and if you doubt you'll ever know your purpose, you may become forlorn, frustrated, disillusioned, or angry. If purpose comes quickly and you are not prepared, you can be overwhelmed by the power of your own destiny.

Bill spent hours during his youth studying the insects in his backyard. He particularly loved watching the bees make their hive in an abandoned shed, followed them harvesting the flowers, and relished the sound of their hum. Spiders caught his eye, too. He created a home for one of them and fed it insects until his parents made him let the creature go. As he grew and his attention shifted to sports, his love of insects and nature faded into the background of his life.

In our play we reveal what kind of people we are.

OVID

At college Bill was elected captain of his basketball team. He was a natural leader: Bill could convince anybody of anything. When school ended and his skills did not earn him a place on a professional team, it seemed natural to follow his leadership and sales skills. He was eventually named head of sales for a large industrial supply firm. On the surface everything seemed perfect. His job was going great and his family was thriving, but he was bored.

One night he had a dream in which he was running through a dark and dangerous woods trying to get away from something he couldn't see. Spying a clearing up ahead and fearing he'd be exposed, Bill dove into what looked like a secret hole in the ground. To his horror, once inside he found himself in the middle of a bee hive. Magically, however, the bees didn't sting him; on the contrary, their fuzzy bodies walking all over him tickled and felt friendly. The dream ended as he was observing the workings of the hive with fascination.

Tears ran down Bill's eyes when he woke up. "I both saw myself as a little boy and a grown man looking for his roots, his home, a place where he belonged. I was embarrassed by how womb-like it was, but I knew inside the dream's beehive that my childhood love was still inside me and that now was the time to pick it up. It had been waiting for me all this time. I talked it over with my family and, with their support, decided to look into what I could study that would provide me with opportunities to work in nature."

Time was Bill's friend. It held his love for nature until the moment when he could pursue his deeper dreams. When time is a friend, you relish how it works. You know that your purpose is within you and that eventually time will unfold a dream, an integrating vision for your life purpose.

Saturday's Exercise:
Make Time Your Friend

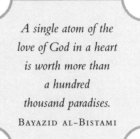

*A single atom of the
love of God in a heart
is worth more than
a hundred
thousand paradises.*
BAYAZID AL-BISTAMI

1. Take your journal with you and find a comfortable spot to sit where you will not be disturbed. Do relaxation breath exercises or whatever you need to do to clear your mind and settle into your body.

2. To begin, visualize yourself standing in a favorite spot. Imagine it to be a "station" for an imaginary small train like those you find in theme parks such as Disneyland. The sign at the station reads "Linear Time." The train you are waiting for is an express light beam, and you've bought a ticket for a place called "Integrating Purpose Vision."

3. When the light beam train arrives in the station, hop aboard just like you would at a theme park. Let everything else in your mind fall away; all that remains is trusting the beam of light.

4. Ride until you have the sensation of time slowing way, way down. When the train comes to a stop in the station, imagine stepping off the train and instantly closing even your visionary eyes.

5. Be blind to all visual processes. Experience that your integrating vision is waiting at the train station for you, but that you must understand it in a different order to average sensory input.

6. Without searching visually, ask yourself questions such as: How does my integrating vision make my body feel? What character traits are embedded in my vision? Do I get a sensation of complexity or are things simple? Are there any surprises? What aspects of my life are tied together? Sense the answers in your body.

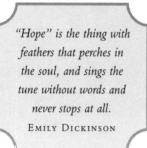

> *"Hope" is the thing with feathers that perches in the soul, and sings the tune without words and never stops at all.*
>
> EMILY DICKINSON

7. Slowly open your visionary intuitive eyes. Can you see an integrating vision or some part of it? If so, note it carefully and, when you feel ready, record your impressions in your journal. If you see nothing, do not be disturbed. Record whatever feelings you've experienced in your journal. If you see something which doesn't appeal to you, reject it. Do the exercise again another day.

8. After you've finished writing in your journal, return to the visualization, get on the light beam, and travel back to the Linear Time train station.

9. Thank your soul for your experience.

SUNDAY:
OPEN YOUR SPACIOUS HEART

Your heart is spacious. It has room to manifest your purpose in a loving way. In fact, love provides the loyalty and stamina necessary to fuel your destiny. Purpose needs love in order to succeed because, if events follow a normal course, you may face a lot of obstacles on your path to purpose.

Tami Simon was depressed; she believed that she wasn't making use of her life and that all the gifts she'd received in life—a prestigious education and a wealthy family—were not being utilized. After traveling through India and Sri Lanka, she started working as a waitress. Inspired by a prolific reading of Hermann Hesse's books from the age of twelve on, her dreams of contributing to the world through philosophy or mysticism lay shattered on the shoals of not knowing what to do next. It seemed that the way of life she loved and adored had no practical application in the world. Everything felt blocked, and Tami was distressed that she was such a disappointment to her mother, to her highly successful business father, and to herself.

Discouraged, Tami quit her job as a waitress and began to pray. Every day, many times a day for three months, she said, "God, I am willing to do your work; show me what it is." Meanwhile, the only thing she was doing that she really liked was hosting a local, all-volunteer, public radio interview program, but after months she knew that work wasn't going to provide income. With her savings running out and her direction unclear, Tami's last journal entry for that period reads, "I guess I'm going to have to get a regular job."

Although her father had a history of serious heart disease, Tami was unprepared for his death. When the dust cleared, Tami found herself with a small inheritance. She wondered what to do with the money. When she consulted a professional for help, he advised her, "Invest your money in yourself." When she protested that she didn't know what to do, he responded, "Yes, you do. You know what you want to do."

Tami did know what to do. "I want to disseminate spiritual wisdom," she heard her soul self say as she left the consultant's office. "I can start a business which combines my love for spiritual teachings with my love for sound." Tami, who had always rebelled against business, was surprised at herself. She recognized that she inherited more than money when her father died; she felt that part of his business acumen had intuitively entered her.

Most important, Tami's love for inner work and wisdom had carried her through doubts, painful events, and depression. Today, as the founder of the successful audio tape company Sounds True, Tami says that discovering her purpose has changed her life. "I may hit obstacles or wonder how to proceed, but I am never filled with despair like I used to be. My purpose sustains me; I know where I belong and am filled with joy."

Tami is tapped into the love for her work, which dwells in her soul. When your love flows, you know what to do. You are resilient. If one plan or idea about your purpose doesn't actualize, you already know that another one will. You are not attached to any one outcome. Dwelling in your spacious heart, your intuition can manifest your destiny.

Sunday's Exercise: Open Your Spacious Heart

1. Stand in front of your logo which you have taped to the wall.

2. Review all the uplifting and inspiring meanings it has for you.

3. Open your intuitive heart like the aperture of a camera. Let love flow out to your purpose, to your logo which symbolizes it, for 5 or more minutes.

4. Reverse the flow of love. Keeping your heart open to receive, imagine that love is flowing back to you from your purpose for 5 or more minutes.

5. Record anything of interest in your journal.

The Gift of Purpose

Most people believe that the greatest gifts of being connected with your purpose are personal—a sense of fulfillment, clear direction, and focused energy. But the gift which I believe is the most important in today's world is the gift of partnership, of community, of tribe. As a species, we gather around purpose like bees to their queen. The hive is alive with activity, and, eventually, everyone who is fully aligned with the core purpose knows precisely what to do. Years ago this couldn't happen because people's loyalties were to a piece of land, to family members, to a set of beliefs, or to their employers. While these loyalties are still central in contemporary society, another kind of loyalty is growing. Today many people's loyalties are to their skills or their callings.

A loyalty to skills is usually built on planning or circumstances. As thousands of people face unemployment due to the downsizing or reorganization of businesses, many articles have appeared discussing how people are now identifying with their skill base rather than with the corporation with whom they are affiliated. Loyalty to callings arises from a passion for your purpose. Organizations whose membership or events is based on this most ancient of self-selection processes—apprenticeship with your soul—have an electric quality. Like the Earth Summit which Nancy Rivard attended, these organizations or events quietly anoint and consecrate new members, and invigorate the old. If you ever attended a conference, concert, or seminar because your purpose, your soul, was guiding you there, you probably met others and became part of a collective energy which reinforced your purpose.

Author Carol Adrienne, co-author of *The Celestine Prophecy: An Experiential Guide* and author of *The Purpose of Your Life,* talks about people participating in a soul group. Soul groups generate synchronicities, intuitive pathways, and right timing. For example, Jane, a colleague, felt she came alive when she found her "people," a local women's business group which was as perfect a match for her talents as their talents were for her. Even before she first walked in the meeting room door, synchronicities began to happen. She ran into a fellow member named Ginny and had a conversation about printing rates for brochures that the two had been meaning to have for weeks. As she entered the meeting room, she felt a surge of warmth and welcome unlike with any other group she had ever belonged to. She was drawn to a cluster of women talking in the corner, and, as she approached, she realized they were discussing the possibility of forming a support network which would supply information, insights, and aid for new female CEOs in the area. Everyone laughed when Jane asked if the organizing members could also be the recipients of advice. Jane had just been made the CEO of a small bank.

The gift of your soul group's identity is also encoded in your being; you will "recognize" the people with whom you are destined to have profound interactions. And you don't have to work at forming or finding your soul group. Soul groups are a natural by-product of following your purpose because your intuition will lead you to places and people which are pivotal to your purpose, as you are to theirs. The network which you create together provides information, strength for going forward, and illumination of your best next steps.

Once you enter these purpose-oriented partnerships, a whole new domain of intuition opens to you—collective or collaborative intuition.

You become ready to explore the subject of the next three chapters: how intuition works in intimate relationships, in organizational life, and in your relationship with the Earth.

Final Exercise: Your Intuition To Do List

1. Complete the sentence, "Because I am accepting my soul's invitation to 'Discover Your Purpose,' I already know to . . ." List 5 to 10 things you know to do such as "call my new business contact," "start a scrapbook about purpose," "remember what I wanted to be when I was a child." When you've finished, read your list over, highlight the simplest activity which *provides the most meaning*, and do it. Record everything in your journal.

2. Go back and look at your Guiding Image for this chapter. Does it capture any of the ten principles of purpose? If so, which one or ones? Why are these particular principles important to you? Record in your journal.

CHAPTER 10

Invitation Eight:

MATE WITH SOUL

MATING WITH SOUL

Joseph Campbell and others credit the twelfth-century story of the Holy Grail with fertilizing the seed which would eventually revolutionize traditional European ideas of love. In the story, the hero Parcival's search eventually leads him to fall in love and select his own partner. This concept—using love as the criteria for selecting marital partners—was a radical departure from the prevailing norm of the time, which favored arranged marriages. It wasn't until six centuries later, with the success of the Industrial Revolution in the late 1800s, that these concepts began to flower.

Therefore, while your parents, grandparents, and maybe great-grandparents selected each other as partners, your great-great grandparents most likely did not. As a culture, Westerners have had at most three full generations to master selecting partners on the basis of love and mating from the soul. This is not very long, compared to prior centuries spent basing our selections of a spouse on wealth, family relationships, land ownership, or perceived fertility. It is no wonder that we are still in the learning process.

Intuition, as the language of the soul, is the unspoken dialogue of in-

> *And now abideth faith, hope, and love, these three; but the greatest of these is love.*
>
> THE BIBLE

timacy, and it is central to the new soul mating process. Partners of all kinds—marital, friendship, family, and professional—can develop soul-to-soul, intuitive communication, so that it is a conscious part of the relationship. When intuition is an accepted, sought after, and conscious part of relationships, it helps you and your partner (1) deepen intimacy; (2) work well as a team; (3) assist in each other's healing and growth process; and (4) establish a strong foundation for mutual success in the world. When intuition remains unconscious in a relationship, partners usually miss opportunities to understand each other's minds, identify what each partner needs for support, know in advance what the other is going to do, or tap shared intuitive dreams.

This chapter is designed to help you to make intuition conscious in your soul mate partnerships whenever and wherever they occur. To identify the Guiding Image for your capacity to accomplish this, do the following exercise.

Your Guiding Image for "Mate with Soul"

- Create a section of your Intuition Journal and label it "Chapter Ten: Mate with Soul."

- Reach into your Image Vocabulary envelope and, without looking, pull out your guiding illustration for this chapter.

- Label which category the picture comes from at the bottom of your selected page.

- Paste your illustration on the page.

This idea of connecting and mating at the level of the soul goes along with the resurgence of intuition as an important component in our life choices. Before you go on to fully explore intuition's role in partnerships,

it is important for you to (1) understand
the impact that a conscious or unconscious awareness of intuition has in a
relationship; (2) how intuition can operate in a relationship; and (3) the most
common misunderstanding people have
about intuition's role in soul mating.

> *It is with the soul that
> we grasp the essence of
> another human being, not
> with the mind, not even
> with the heart.*
> HENRY MILLER

INTUITION IN PARTNERSHIPS

The following two true stories illustrate the difference between one couple's experience when intuition was an unconscious, relatively unim-
portant part of the relationship, and another couple's experience, when
intuition was a conscious, valued part of the relationship.

The first story, where intuition is relatively unconscious, concerns a
bank's executive officer and his wife. The executive, who had granted a
large outstanding loan to a prominent department store, came home from
work one day and was greeted by his agitated wife. When the banker
asked his wife what was wrong, she shared that she'd just come back from
a shopping trip to that same department store and was upset by her experience. The employees had followed her around and appeared bored;
something seemed wrong, but she didn't know what. Smart enough to be
alarmed by his wife's impression, the banker requested an immediate
analysis of the department store's financial state. When the spread sheets
indicated no trouble, he dismissed his wife's strange impression. Yet, unexpectedly, this large national department store folded within the year.

If these partners had agreed to honor intuition, however and whenever it might show up, the spread-sheet results would not have been
enough to deflect concern. Perhaps the officer would have gone to the
store himself, contacted other resources familiar with the department
store's financial condition nationally, or monitored the store's financial
state for several consecutive weeks.

Now consider this story where intuition is a conscious, valued pres-

> *When you really want love, you will find it waiting for you.*
> OSCAR WILDE

ence within the relationship. After two years spent planning, building, and designing their Houston home, Joseph and Mavis Jaworski finally moved in. The architect had even included a place for Mavis to set up her medical practice in a few years, when she finished her residency at Baylor College of Medicine. The couple vowed to never move again and were relishing their nine stable months in the house, when the unexpected happened: Renata Karlin of the Shell Oil Group showed up in Jaworski's office to ask if he wanted to apply for a job as the head of Shell Oil's worldwide scenario planning. The position lasted four years and was based in London. It was confusing. Joseph had been dreaming of taking his work to the global level, but he was committed to helping Mavis complete medical school and they had just moved into their house. Telling Karlin he'd get back to her in a week, Joseph went home to discuss the proposal with Mavis. In the midst of telling her, she broke into a big grin saying, "I told you so—remember, in front of St. Paul's Cathedral."

Five years earlier, Mavis had had an intuitive flash as she walked up the church steps with Joseph. She had said, "Joseph, I want you to know something I am certain of. In the next few years you will move back to London with the family and me. You'll be doing important work for a very large multinational company." For Mavis, the Shell Oil proposal validated this flash, this inner voice, and meant things were moving along exactly as they were intended. Confident that everything would work out for all of them, Mavis already knew what they needed to do: get their affairs in order so that they could move when Joseph was offered the job. Later, as Joseph thought about all the possible reactions Mavis might have had if she had not intuited the future, or, if she didn't trust her intuitive flash, he was amazed. But, the intuition *had* occurred, and their ability to consciously trust it led the couple to align themselves around Mavis's flash and chart their course for destiny.[1]

Both these stories demonstrate one important point about how intuition can operate in partnership and, to some degree, how it operates in general. Intuition does not always follow a straight and direct course; if the fastest way to get information to someone is through his or her partner, friend, child, or co-worker, so be it. In this way, intuition behaves like a river cutting its way

In Love no longer "Thou" and "I" exist. For self has passed away in the Beloved.

ATTÂR

through land—if it hits hard territory to go through (someone is too busy, distracted, or preoccupied), it searches around for the easiest path to follow (finding a partner who is open). When you understand this, you pay conscious attention to the intuitive information that shows up in your partnerships, regardless of who receives the messages, and you test their relevance to your life.

Many people use the amount or kind of intuitive experiences in a developing relationship as an indication of whether or not they have found *the* right partner or soul mate. In these cases, intuition is used to validate or officially stamp a relationship as soul mate material. This is the most common misunderstanding of intuition's role in the soul mate process.

I have strong feelings and opinions about this. I don't believe that selecting a person with whom you will share your deepest intimacies should be left to intuition alone. Intimacy, especially spiritual intimacy, cannot be trivialized or used as a "sign" that you've met your beloved. In love, like everywhere else, intuition is part of the assessment package, not the whole thing.

The creation of a positive and productive relationship is hard work; the acquisition of your full intuitive powers is also hard work. So, connecting from soul-to-soul or mating with another on an intuitive life path can also be very, very hard work. It requires mutual love and appreciation, dedication to yourself and your partner, curiosity, a good sense of humor, and a willingness to learn. Of course, apart from all the hard work, traveling in these domains consciously with another person offers one of life's richest rewards as well as being sheer fun.

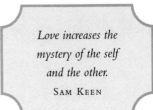

*Love increases the
mystery of the self
and the other.*
SAM KEEN

It is normal for soul-to-soul communication to contain intuitive experiences which are very numinous (spiritual, sacred, shining). Be aware that these shining, radiant experiences sometimes lead people to become unconscious in their relationships. For example, when Justine saw Bill's full radiance, his charm and accomplishments, she was so mesmerized that she subconsciously chose to cut short her own development and merge with Bill's idealized self. She stopped meditation, lost interest in therapy, and wanted to serve her partner in any way she could. In short, she wanted Bill's shining to illuminate her insides instead of doing the work herself. This behavior can also work the other way around. Joann was mesmerized by Roger's brash and daring ways. Her devotion filled Roger's low self-esteem needs, so he didn't pursue developing other aspects of himself or working with his challenges.

Both Justine and Roger responded to their yearning for personal numinousness in unconscious ways.[2] Should you ever suspect you are doing this, remember the radiance tools I talked about with the intuitive heart (Chapter Four) and get your heart back in your body. It has its own radiance and can illuminate and help you heal even your deepest wounds.

A key point to remember is that *every* experience with another holds the capacity to be numinous. In fact, numinosity is central to soul-to-soul relationships of all kinds, just as the presence of intuition is natural when people open their hearts to each other.

INTUITION: THE SOUL MATE PROMISE

With this background, we are ready to proceed. At the end of this section you are going to choose someone with whom you can make a Soul Mate Promise (found on page 245). I am defining "soul mate" as a person with whom you want to develop soul-to-soul contact and communication. This person could be a friend, your buddy in this work, a new love interest, a relative, a co-worker, your life partner, etc. In addition to enhanced intimacy skills, the Soul Mate Promise can increase your productivity, catalyze your creativity, or just make you feel more alive. The important point is to share with another all the reasons why

Ya Azim. *Behold, the God we reflect to each other.*

HEBREW GREETING

you'd each like to make this contact. Choose someone you want to work with for at least a month. Useful criteria for your selection are: mutual trust, a history of open and honest communication, basic curiosity about intuition, responsibility (you need someone who will really do the exercises with you), and loving appreciation. The promise you are going to make to each other is based on the following three broad principles necessary for a successful soul mate process.

Principle #1: You are a soul-to-soul learning team. Never forget you are both learning. Learning is not always even; one of you may do better in one thing while the other does better in something else. This is natural. On the other hand, the sensation by either partner that he or she is more advanced, more natural, or better than the other for any reason is to be avoided. In my experience, an inflated sense of expertise is often used to avoid true intimacy. Should you feel this happening in your relationship, talk it over immediately. It is irrelevant who is doing it. If you can't mutually stop this behavior, find another partner. This work requires a sense of equality.

A soul-to-soul learning team recognizes that building a sacred relationship with another human being is a rare and wonderful opportunity. You commit to "beholding" each other—to seeing each other with the sacred eyes of love and to remembering that you are in relationship with a living soul.

Principle #2: Honor and respect each other's need for privacy. Intuition is intimate, and, by definition, it implies that you might stumble upon something your partner considers very private. So it's a good idea to understand how intuition interacts with intimacy, secrecy, and privacy. Never forget

> *We find rest in those we love, and we provide a resting place in ourselves for those who love us.*
>
> ST. BERNARD
> OF CLAIRVAUX

that the first intuitive intimacy you experience is with your soul. This entire book is designed to build on that relationship. Until you are intimate with your soul, soul-to-soul communications can only occur during random moments when you access soul briefly. In fact, it is not possible to carry on a conscious conversation, verbal or non-verbal, from soul-to-soul without being intimate on some level with your own soul. Once you are committed to a conscious, intuitive relationship with a partner, your intuitive eyes, ears, and hearts usually uncover any secrets lurking about. Dishonesty or secrecy do not last long in a mutually intuitive relationship—they don't feel comfortable to the soul.

While intuition does not enable secrecy, it does respect privacy. Many traditions teach about a place in your heart where no one, including a soul mate, is allowed in unless he or she is expressly invited in by you. Sometimes called the cave of the heart, this place functions as a retreat, a getaway, a sacred space, and an inner temple. Your Soul Mate Promise contains a pledge to respect each other's cave of the heart and the quality of privacy it symbolizes. While intuition promotes transparency among people, it is not an invader. If you should ever feel invaded or be accused of invading, sit down and talk over the situation. Make the boundaries for the cave of the heart very clear; everyone is entitled to his or her private inner space.

Principle #3: Accept that walking the intuitive path together means that you have agreed to help each other evolve and heal. Although the purpose of the spiritual path is not healing, healing opportunities are a by-product of going forward. In my experience, one of the key components of soul mate healing is the ability of a couple to see each other's essential nature or soul nature without becoming mesmerized, attempting to reduce each other's radiance, or looking the other way. Soul natures are magnificent. In fact, the interior vistas of the soul are every bit as breathtaking and majestic as any wilderness, undersea cavern, or outer space quadrant. You'll learn that the architecture and structures of each person's inner world are as intricate and varied as anything your physical eyes could observe.

Just as you might in the wilderness, you can also intuit dangers lurking about in a partner's inner nature: wounds which have not healed and places where you may be unpleasantly surprised. Your intuition is correct. When you open yourself and experience more soul, you take the lid off buried wounds. This is why it is natural to feel both excitement and vulnerability as you venture into your inner world in the presence of a soul mate. The process is revealing. To succeed, both members of the soul mate team must commit *equally* to their mutual healing. To not do so leaves one person very vulnerable. On the other hand, a commitment to participate in each other's healing process really enhances both partners' ability to profoundly trust truth, intuition, and the web of life.

> *But marriage and family may provide the best hospital for our ancient wounds.*
>
> SAM KEEN

When I work with life partners whose relationships are going through challenging times, I ask them to each ponder this question for a moment: "Imagine a time in the future when your relationship has passed through this rough passage. What would your souls want to say to each other?" They always intuit very healing answers. For example, one might say to the other, "I knew that you were ignoring me in order to pursue your own development and I know my personality gave you a hard time. But I hope you remembered how much I loved you and missed you," or, "I realized that you are working with an old wound from childhood but was scared my personality didn't know how to support you through it and was worried that I'd desert you. I didn't want to do that because I love you."

Interestingly, even during a brief consulting session, people are quick to move away from these soul-speak, healing answers. Feeling vulnerable and unloved, they very quickly shift from integrating their soul-speak answers, which imply they truly do know what is going on, to the more

> *We are not primarily put on the Earth to see through one another, but to see one another through.*
>
> PETER DEVRIES

ignorant, "We don't know what's happening." As odd as it seems, individually and collectively people tend to downplay their most soulful features or deny the power of their souls.[3]

Your goal in the healing process is to help your partner *get out of the habit* of dismissing the soul-speak dimension where intuition really flourishes and *into the conscious act* of integrating and honoring what intuition has to contribute. Therefore, your job is straightforward: (1) you provide protection, support, and truth when your partner leaves the soul-speak dimension and some part of him or her is feeling vulnerable, and (2) you encourage renewed access to soul-speak behavior by reinforcing the courage, love, beauty, and health which already exists in your partner. If the latter were not so, he or she would not have signed up for this work with you.

With this background, select a partner and do the following exercise.

Exercise: The Soul Mate Promise

1. Read over the Soul Mate Promise (p. 245) with your partner. Xerox a copy for each of you and paste one copy in each of your journals.

2. Decide if there are any points you want to eliminate or anything more you want to add. Custom design your Promise so it works for you.

3. *You must check in weekly with each other.* Even if you live together, do not leave this to chance meetings. Be specific. Set up how your check-in times will happen, e.g., when, where, how (on the phone, e-mail, in person, etc.).

4. Date and sign your Soul Mate Promise.

When you have both signed and dated the Soul Mate Promise, you are ready to work on exercises which build shared intuitive skills.

INTUITION: THE SOUL MATE PROMISE

Beginning on today's date, _____, we the undersigned promise to fulfill the following statements to the best of our ability as we develop our soul mate relationship.

- We seek to be a soul-to-soul learning team.

- We promise to share our experiences on the path to a more intuitive life openly and honestly with each other.

- We will listen to each other's stories and responses with openhearted love and respect.

- We acknowledge that the visions we share with each other are sacred.

- We promise to keep all the information we share with each other private unless we are given permission or invited to tell others.

- We regard each other's need for privacy as sacred space especially because we seek to live a more transparent life with each other.

- We recognize and honor the vulnerability inherent to opening to each other's interior worlds.

- We state our intention to serve each other's physical, emotional, mental, and spiritual evolution and welcome each other's dazzling soul natures.

- We understand and accept that participating in each other's healing is part of mating with soul. We pledge to help each other heal to the best of our abilities.

- We promise to keep our lines of communication clear and tell each other any problems we encounter in our soul-to-soul relationship.

_____   _____
Soul Mate signature   *Soul Mate signature*

> *Love one another as*
> *I have loved you.*
> THE BIBLE

SHARED INTUITIVE EXPERIENCES

When star race track driver Daphne Greene contracted Epstein-Barr disease and had to learn to walk again after spending two years bedridden, she refused to accept her physicians' pronouncement that she couldn't expect to return to her peak performance years.[4] She checked with her inner physician and began to visualize and *feel* her body healthy, vital, and balanced. As she says, "I 'rehearsed' wellness at the core of my being." The results were mixed because as Daphne began exercising, her disease returned.

In spite of these setbacks, she wouldn't take no for an answer and she continued to work on her inner wellness images. The disease, she says, forced her to hone a deep inner knowing where intuition was not some "exotic category of experience separate from everyday life." In the end, she triumphed and was the first American woman to be selected from two thousand applicants to compete in the Camel Trophy Adventure, a physical endurance team event pitting nineteen countries against each other in thirty continuous hours of activities.

Intuition was not just part of Daphne's individual skill base; she and her partner, Jim Swett, demonstrated extraordinary intuitive communication skills in a special part of the Camel Trophy where Green had to drive blindfolded with only the words of her partner to guide her. Describing her experience, she said, "You learn quickly, in that situation, what it means to embody intuition. My race partner and I learned to communicate on a moment-by-moment basis. Your partner's subtle, unexpressed thoughts become yours. You anticipate each other's assumptions in uncanny ways. . . . We reached a level of unity and selflessness that made success possible."

Daphne Greene was ripe for this experience; she had already learned to trust intuition during a challenge to her physical wellness. Fortunately, you do not have to be in such circumstances or be blindfolded to bring forward the best of your intuitive soul mate potentials. You can start building intuitive networks with your partner immediately.

After you've signed the Promise, discuss *every* intuitive experience you have with your partner, even if it doesn't involve him or her directly. Bring both your journals to your weekly discussions so that you can record all the details of your experiences. This activity creates an experiential data bridge between you both and reveals what type of experiences might be your strong suit as a soul mate partnership. Read over the following list of examples of intuitive experiences you might share.

> *I add my breath to your breath . . . that we may be committed to our own and each other's growing and that we may finish our roads together.*
>
> LAGUNA PUEBLO PRAYER

Types of Intuitive Experiences Available to Soul Mate Teams

__Heart-to-heart communication

__Mind-to-mind communication

__Spaciousness and freedom

__Spontaneous healing actions

__Right timing in the world

__Right timing between you

__Shared visions

__Precognitions

__Shared synchronicities

__Spiritual insights

__Shared symbols

__Intuitive sensitivity to each other's bodies

__Soul-speak talk

__Shared non-linear time

__Shared inner guidance

__Specific needs for healing

__Spontaneous worship

Exercise: Types of Experiences

1. Discuss with your partner what might happen in each of these types of experiences.

2. Identify the types you'd most like to share.

> *O soul repressless, I with*
> *thee and thou with*
> *me. . . . We too take*
> *ship, O soul. . . . With*
> *laugh and many a*
> *kiss. . . . O soul, thou*
> *pleasest me, I thee.*
>
> WALT WHITMAN

ESTABLISHING A SHARED INTUITIVE DISCIPLINE

Many partners like to do things together—dance, play tennis, go to movies, enjoy concerts, eat out. Soul mate teams benefit tremendously by finding some type of shared spiritual practice they like to do. Some teams I've worked with have designed their own exercises or used one of the following activities: doing the same meditation, praying together, reading sacred texts, reciting the same chant, taking up tai chi or yoga, saying chosen affirmations, or consulting the same learning tools (e.g., the *Tarot, I Ching*).

It is not important that you are always together when you do your chosen activity. Just communicate your experiences with it during your weekly check-ins. Your chosen discipline builds a base for intuitive dialogue into the partnership and will be augmented by more exercises throughout this chapter.

Exercise: A Shared Intuitive Discipline

1. Decide with your soul mate partner what your shared intuitive discipline will be.

2. Design a schedule for the discipline and write it in your date books.

3. At your weekly check-in time, report to each other your progress with your shared discipline. Are you doing it? Is it easy? Do you still like your choice? If either of you is having trouble sticking to the schedule, try contacting each other for encouragement and support just before your discipline is scheduled.

4. Keep a record in your journal of all your experiences with the discipline (not just the successful ones). Record some of your partner's experiences, too.

LOVE IS THE KEY

The English language contains one word, love, to mean a wide variety of experiences. But the love of a partner for a child feels different from the love between siblings, good friends, or life mates. Love for your work represents another category of experience. In contrast to English, the Greek language classifies three different kinds of love: *eros,* which emphasizes a sensual love of life; *agape,* which describes an unconditional love that cares for another irrespective of sex, age, or other differences; and *philia,* that quality of love between friends and comrades which, according to Stanford University professor, Nel Noddings, implies the "drawing together of seemingly incompatible substances to create a new entity."[5]

> *Love is the bond between heaven and earth.*
> PICO

The love behind the success of the Soul Mate Promise combines the ideas of *agape,* unconditional love for another, and *philia,* love which creates a new entity. The new entity that unconditional love creates can empower your mutual exploration into the unknown, support each other's healing, and stand fast on the path of partnered evolution. It doesn't get distracted because its nature is essentially unemotional. Remember when I asked you to fill your heart with love for someone, someplace, or something and then *remove all emotion from the sensation?* As people practice with this unemotional love, they commonly report feeling their chests being flooded with light, a sense of caring with no agenda, openness, being big, or a heightened sense of presence.

At first, removing emotions from love may seem like a confusing request. People ask, "Doesn't love mean that my heart beats faster or leaps at the sight of my beloved?" Yes, of course, this is one experience of love (which is found in love for work, family, creativity, as well as in romance). But this is not the depth of love we are after. What we are after endures the loss of fast-beating or leaping hearts, and truly makes a commitment to help another and one's self in the acquisition of a more effective soul life.

With this in mind, you are ready for a soul mate exercise designed

> *The more souls who resonate together, the greater the intensity of their love, and, mirror-like, each soul reflects the other.*
>
> UNKNOWN

to increase your intuitive intimacy. The secret to success with this exercise rests on your ability to focus on *your own love nature*. You do not have to probe into your partner's nature in order for information to be revealed.

Exercise: Love Is the Key

1. Working separately in your journals, both you and your soul mate first prioritize five outcomes, in addition to improved intuitive communication, that you would like to gain from soul mate work. Write down anything of interest. Examples include: making time for myself to meditate, discovering things which will provide genuine support for my partner, finding more recreational outlets, discovering new friends, loyalty, a sense of being loved and taken care of, tolerance.

2. Exchange sheets with your partner and read his or her list without judgment. Talk over any questions you may have about the items listed. Make sure you understand not only what your partner wants as outcomes but also why these things are important to him or her, if it isn't obvious.

3. Decide who will be the "receiver" and who will be the "sender." Only one thing is required of the "receiver," Person 1. To the best of his or her ability, Person 1 needs to maintain silence of body, mind, and heart throughout the entire exercise. Person 1 *does not* consciously focus on his or her list of outcomes.

4. Person 2, the "sender," reviews Person 1's list of desired outcomes. Then Person 2 puts down the list and forgets about it. Person 2's main task is to focus on his or her *own* love nature. This is done by filling the chest area with love. When the chest is full, Person 2 simply keeps his or her attention on the love. Love is all that exists. Do *not* focus the love on Person 1 or on the desired outcomes.

5. When 3 to 5 minutes have passed, Person 2 picks up Person 1's desired list of outcomes again and writes down any immediate impressions to the items.

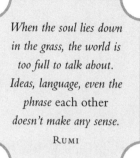

When the soul lies down in the grass, the world is too full to talk about. Ideas, language, even the phrase each other doesn't make any sense.

RUMI

6. Person 1 and Person 2 discuss the first impressions, any other insights, creative flashes, or ideas of interest. Record in your journals everything that happens, even if it appears to have no relationship to the list of outcomes. If you find your minds wandering, don't be discouraged. Record even the dissatisfactions you feel. You can write impressions in each other's journals, too.

7. Reverse roles and start at step #4 again.

One of the interesting things about human beings is that sometimes we do not know what we need in order to receive love and healing. Because this is true, when people identify outcomes they would like to reach through soul mate work, I encourage them not to hold on to the specifics too tightly. Instead, I ask them to think of their work with their soul mate as an offering or healing gift rather than as a way of achieving targeted specific outcomes. This perspective gives intuition room to maneuver.

Sometimes your intuition will reveal a deeper level of insight or healing, one that you didn't even prioritize. For example, one of my students, Ellen, wanted to establish a better relationship with her mother, but during the month of our work, the relationship which underwent the greatest transformation was that with her daughter Alice. Ellen's delight about the improved relationship with Alice and the things she learned changed her attitude toward her mother. Ellen felt greater compassion and understanding, which paved the way for a far different approach to her mother (one with a lot less anger). Ellen's intuition knew that the order of events which would best serve her desired outcome—an improved relationship with her

> One makes mistakes:
> that is life. But it is never
> quite a mistake to
> have loved.
>
> ROMAIN ROLLAND

mother—included *first* enhancing her relationship with her daughter.

Soul mate partners sometimes encounter other ways in which intuition doesn't work in a straight line. It can circle around and come in for a landing on a person who is least expecting it. My favorite example of this was told at a spiritual retreat by Rev. Edgar Jackson, a well-known distant healer. Distant healers send intuitive healing to clients even though they may be thousands of miles away. A woman facing surgery had called Rev. Jackson for a distant healing appointment. As was his custom, on the evening before her surgery, they established a time when he would enter his study and focus on her healing. After the session, he went to bed satisfied with the session but awoke in the middle of the night with a terrible pain in his toe. Years earlier he'd mangled his toe in an accident. When he checked to see why his injured toe was hurting so much, he was shocked to see that his toe no longer appeared mangled. It had spontaneously returned to normal and was better than it had been in years! He raised the question with us, "Why on that particular night, after years of absentee healing, did my own toe receive healing?"

No one at the retreat had an answer for him, but the story is a perfect example of how intuition can change its target. This is why it is most productive to make a love offering for healing rather than presume that our conscious minds have all the facts at hand. This allows your soul to direct intuitive care toward the highest priority.

The Love Is the Key exercise is good to do with your partner as often as you both enjoy it. In your record keeping, notice if you encounter (in newspapers, on the radio, on TV, or through the internet, or in conversations) things relevant to each other's prioritized items. You are now operating as an intuitive unit, and information can come to either one of you like it did to Mavis and the bank officer's wife at the beginning of this chapter.

It is also important for you to start creating the shared "entity" found

in the definition of *philia*. The next section is devoted to doing just that.

BUILDING A BRIDGE

> *To love deeply in one
> direction makes us more
> loving in all others.*
> MADAME SWETCHINE

Bob and Ginny, a couple I work with,
were dissatisfied with the level of inti-
macy they had reached in their relationship. Following a brief discussion,
I sent them home to design together a symbol which would represent
their intuitive understanding of how to achieve the intimacy they sought.
They took a big piece of paper and both drew a cross-section view of a
deep but narrow chasm. A river ran at the bottom.

Next, they created a bridge over the chasm, and in the middle of the
bridge was a house with many different floors, decks, and stairs. An elevator descended down to the river. Some rooms in the bridge house were
designed for deeper intimacy, some for privacy, and others for family
gatherings. The house symbolized the "entity" Bob and Ginny were
wanting so much to create; it had room for everything including intimacy.
When they brought the image in, we discussed everything, and then I encouraged them to take it home, hang it up if they could, or at least think
about it from time to time.

Less than a year later, the silent image they intuited had done its
work. Bob and Ginny had established a strong foothold in a new path of
intimacy and had begun wiping away years of reactive habits. In fact, their
work went further than that, and they began to manifest what Barbara
Marx Hubbard calls a "suprasexual" relationship, one where the souls
share a destined life path of service. Bob, an environmental activist, and
Ginny, an artist, started finding ways to integrate their lives, so Ginny
sculpted bird perch pieces which were placed in the creek waters and designed to serve the creek's threatened habitat. Bob incorporated her in-
stallation into a long-term eco-political campaign to preserve the wildlife
habitat of the creek. Notice that their first strong collaborative community project involved water, although it was a creek rather than the river

> Some say we are
> responsible for those we
> love; others know we are
> responsible for those
> who love us.
>
> NIKKI GIOVANNI

of their intuitive drawing, and perches surrounded by water where birds could land rather than the bridge house where the couple could build their intimacy. This is a typical way that intuition symbolically pictures a suggested direction and shows how physical reality can eventually assume a similar, but not precisely the same, shape. It is my conviction that the couple's drawing, which represents one map to deeper intimacy, depicts non-verbal clues about their blocks to closeness and suggests paths for unlocking the creative, intimate power of their union.

You, too, can build an entity bridge with your partner. In fact, you will be doing this whether you are aware of it or not, because every union creates a third "force," the combined personality and soul of the union. If you are aware of that, together you can shape the character of the entity, nurture its evolution, and evoke collaborative intuition—intuition which flows freely in a partnership or group setting.

To enhance the creation of collaborative intuition and get a peek at the entity you and your partner are creating, do the following exercise. It is based on something you have already begun to experience: the non-verbal vocabulary of images.

Exercise: Building a Bridge to Collaborative Intuition

1. Go to your local copy center and get a few sheets of 14 x 17 white paper. If they don't have sheets this large, you can work with an 11 x 14 piece.

2. Divide the piece of paper vertically into three parts. The center third, which you and your partner will share, can be slightly larger than either of the two ends.

3. Get out some rubber cement, scissors, magazines, Magic Markers, and your Image Vocabulary envelopes.

4. Without looking in your envelopes, each of you pulls out
one image and pastes it on the
end thirds of the opposite end
sides of the paper. These images represent your intuitive relationship with each other.

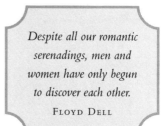

*Despite all our romantic
serenadings, men and
women have only begun
to discover each other.*

FLOYD DELL

5. Discuss your images, exploring
what they might symbolize about your presence in a soul mate
partnership.

6. Now turn your attention to the blank center section. This is where
you'll create a symbol (they range from the simple to the complex)
which represents your third entity and your ability with collaborative intuition. Draw this image with Magic Markers or select
magazine images together and paste them in the center section in
a meaningful way. This image can be anything; for example, an animal or animals, flowers, trees, abstract shapes, or a building floor
plan.

7. When you've finished, look at your center section as if it were a
separate entity. What character traits do you see in that entity?
What are its interests? How might it support the growth of your
collaborative intuition? Is there anything which suggests healing?
What dreams and visions are depicted here? What aspects
evoke power, passion, or purpose? Discuss as many angles of
the entity as you can and then relate to each other how you see
your separate images (the ones on the ends) interacting intuitively with this entity. Jot anything you don't want to forget in your
journals.

8. Hang up the collaborative image somewhere in your daily environment. It should be a place where you'll at least glance at it regularly,
even if you don't focus on it. Xerox a copy if necessary so that both
of you can do this if you don't live together.

> *The pathway of love is the ordeal of fire. The shrinkers turn away from it.*
>
> GUJARATI HYMN

Optional: You can augment your work by holding the entire image in your mind for a few minutes. Follow that by focusing on your individual love nature for 5 minutes.

Your partnership entity—the power behind this image—is a deep well you can return to for strength, comfort, and insights. This well is important to establish because intuition doesn't stay in a neat box called "I'll only reveal easy things to deal with." When space is created (and love creates space), wounds which need healing arise. This happens for two reasons: (1) feeling love from within and without, people have the self-confidence to work on dysfunctional issues. In fact, the desire to do so is an indication of the depths of love present in a relationship. And (2) intuition is sensitive and, when made conscious, it reveals areas where we all feel incomplete and in need of healing. This is why the Soul Mate Promise contains a commitment to your own and to your partner's healing.

ILLUMINATING BOGEY MEN AND BOGEY WOMEN

Depending on how you look at it, one of the greatest gifts intuition offers in a relationship is its ability to reveal your own and your partner's outdated, inner scripts. These scripts are usually filled with rejections and wishful thinking based on the wounds and joys of previous relationships.

For example, Sally projects "superman" all over her partner, Bob, ignoring or obliterating the challenges of his personality. Bob likes her idealism, so he resents it when she begins to point out the inconsistencies in his behavior. If she is not aware of intuition's ability to reveal buried wounds in a loving partnership, she might be projecting how ineffectual he is all over him, which is particularly scary for Bob because deep down it activates an inner fear that he can't make positive changes or succeed.

Or in another case, Jeff thinks his wife is an amazing woman. Patty can do it all: succeed professionally, provide spiritual direction, keep the household together, take care of the children, entertain, etc. Jeff doesn't recognize Patty when she collapses and wants his

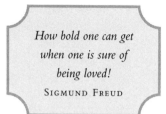

How bold one can get when one is sure of being loved!

SIGMUND FREUD

support, so he subtly withdraws support from Patty the moment she reaches out. Patty, feeling like she has to "do it all," becomes angry and acts out by ignoring some of the household chores. Meanwhile, Jeff starts projecting memories of a messy house and a needy woman from his childhood all over his partner. What's going on here?

Psychologically, Jeff and Sally are responding in present time to inner wounds based on past events. I call these "bogey man" or "bogey woman" scripts. These scripts are more drama-laden than a bad soap opera and always contain a story about how your soul mate partner is a bogey person and might, or could, or will (depending on how much one believes in it and how conscious both people are in the relationship) deal you a terrible blow. This belief is often reinforced because partners can unconsciously intuit each other's bogey person script and act it out unerringly without the slightest clue of what they are doing!

This is why it is so important to be awake and responsible in a soul-centered partnership. Fortunately, if your souls are committed to each other, you are not left alone with each other's scripts. A silent partner arises out of the shared entity you've created because *intuition also knows this script.* Casting the light of the soul onto the story, intuition can illuminate the bogey man or bogey woman script, stripping it of its power over you and the relationship. This is true even if you are working with another person for only a short period of time. The following exercise is designed to help you illuminate these scripts and work cooperatively toward mutual healing.

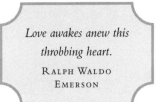

Love awakes anew this throbbing heart.

RALPH WALDO
EMERSON

Exercise: Illumination and Healing

1. Working alone, each partner writes at the top of a journal page the phrase, *"The behaviors which make me feel most unloved in partnership are . . ."* List three or more bogey man or woman behaviors. For example, "not communicated with," "taken for granted," "treated as a distraction."

2. Circle the one or two which represents each of your greatest fears and deepest needs. At the bottom of your page, write the phrase, *"I am asking my own and my partner's intuition to help me begin healing so that I can give and receive more love."*

3. Read each other's list and discuss the one behavior you identified in step #2.

4. Taking turns, formally ask your partner to assist in the healing process. Say aloud, *"I invite you and give you permission to fulfill your healing role as I am working with my inner scripts. I accept that I am ultimately responsible for my healing and appreciate any assistance you can give me toward that goal."*

5. Taking turns, say a prayer for your partner's healing aloud.

6. Agree that for the duration of your work together you will alert your partner immediately if you find yourself or your partner in any way encouraging the dreaded inner script.

7. Tell each other any insights you have about your partner's or your own inner script. Record relevant facts concerning the exercise in your journals.

This work can be very intense. Sometimes we travel with our partner into the depths of our personal hells in order to rediscover or reconstruct our inner temples. Growth depends on two things: (1) curiosity and (2) commitment. It's important during this work to maintain an attitude of inquiry, asking questions such as, "I wonder why I am acting or thinking this way?

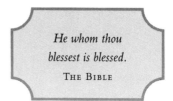

He whom thou blessest is blessed.
THE BIBLE

What connections do I intuit between this behavior and my background, family, or personal experience? Where have I seen behavior or encountered beliefs like these before? Do I remind myself of a movie or TV character, or an animal? When I meditate on my healing symbol, what images come up? What successful models for soul-to-soul partnering do I have?"

Soul mate partners fall in love with and are committed to the truth. They employ their intuition to sniff it out together like blood hounds. Furthermore, the truth they seek about themselves and each other is not wielded like a sledgehammer but is always infused with kindness and respect. If you are in a long-term, committed relationship and your work with intuition reveals places where you feel "stuck," it is advantageous to seek therapeutic help. You have everything to gain by clearing out old debris and holding out for real soul-to-soul communion.

THE BLESSING SIGHT

The soul is dazzling. Spiritual literature tells us that the mere sight of it can blind people temporarily, set them spinning, or knock them to the ground. Some texts warn us to be careful in handling the soul because its light is so intense. Soul mates know this. They are aware that each other's beauty can be so resplendent that feelings of fright or envy may rush to the foreground. Inadvertently, just as our partner is needing more space to expand into, we can run away, numb out, become mesmerized, or be completely unsupportive.

If you are mutually serious about your soul mate goals, you will commit to resisting these responses and pledge to welcome each other's dazzling soul nature. You have one great advantage doing this work: you'll

> Dazzling and
> tremendous how quick the
> sunrise would kill me, if I
> could not now and always
> send sunrise out of me.
> We also ascend dazzling
> and tremendous as
> the sun.
>
> WALT WHITMAN

understand what is happening even if your partner starts to run away or criticize as your dazzling nature begins to shine. All you have to do is remind your partner of the Soul Mate Promise and say, "I need you to help me be comfortable with my soul nature by not resisting it now. Can you do that for me?" This discussion alone brings the purpose of your work together into focus again.

The purpose of the Blessing Sight exercise is to provide you with an opportunity to practice seeing your partner's dazzling nature.[6]

Exercise: The Blessing Sight

1. Sit across from your partner. Close your eyes, and use your imagination to behold him or her as a radiant soul. (If you don't "see" things, let yourself feel what it would be like to sense your partner as dazzling light.) Transform your partner's body into nothing but radiant light with light molecules dancing in all this for 2 to 3 minutes.

2. When that time is up, talk to each other about your experiences.

3. For a week at least (a month is better) *every night*, just as you fall asleep, and *every morning* as you wake up, visualize your partner as you did in step #1, seeing him or her as a dazzling soul. Experience this sight as a blessing for you and a blessing for your partner.

4. After that week or month, check in with your partner, speaking from your hearts. How has it been to see your partner as dazzling light? How has it been to know someone was seeing you as dazzling light? Share the strengths and joys you see in your partner. Acknowledge any inner work that you and your partner have been working on or

is feeling completed. What insights do you have for each other?

5. Do the exercise for the prescribed time and then exchange with your partner one character trait you worship or adore in the other.

6. Record everything in your journals.

> *Life has taught us that love does not consist in gazing at each other but in looking outward together in the same direction.*
>
> ANTOINE DE SAINT-EXUPÉRY

Two cautionary notes: First, just because you can see your partner's soul nature doesn't mean he or she will choose to actualize it. No one can make that decision for another no matter how much inner world support is supplied. Second, be careful not to label as "intuitive insight" any agenda you may have for how you think your partner ought to change. Doing so amounts to manipulation of the deepest kind. Your partner's soul nature has its own sense of timing and priorities; you can discuss and contribute to the healing process but not control it. Conversations from the heart with your partner will help keep you from these two problem areas.

A friend of mine, Djann Hoffman, calls this type of work with a partner "seeing into being." I have been with him when he's listened to someone's story of difficulties or doubts and then heard him gently say, "I see that things are difficult now, but I *see* into your being. I know who you truly are and know ultimately you'll know what to do." He also believes in another interpretation of the phrase "seeing into being"—seeing another as a radiant soul can bring forward an actual quality of being. Therefore, seeing your partner in such a light can help actualize his or her soul nature.

> I think we had the chief
> of all love's joys only in
> knowing we loved
> each other.
>
> GEORGE ELIOT

LIBERATION

A famous picture of Krishna shows him unwinding the rope which is binding the body of his beloved. The purpose of our work in this book and your work with your soul mate is to liberate or unwind your intuitive skills. Although none of us pretends to be fully enlightened beings, the soul mate team can role-play this "unwinding" in order to reduce or eliminate any limitations imposed on intuition—your own and your partner's. This activity, which I adapted for intuitive development many years ago from Jean Houston's and Robert Master's work, is particularly fruitful after you have completed a week or more of the Blessing Sight exercise. I've used it with hundreds of people, all of whom have really enjoyed it.

Exercise: Liberating Intuition

1. Decide who is Person #1, the person reading, and who is Person #2, the person being read to or repeating the phrases (see page 250). First do this exercise for Person #1, then reverse roles and do the exercise for Person #2.

2. Person #1 reads aloud to Person #2 the following statements and does the prescribed actions as he or she goes. Or tape record the following (use both your voices) ahead of time and then play it as you do the prescribed activity.

Liberating Intuition

- You are about to participate in an ancient ceremony designed to free you from any restrictions that may be placed on your intuition by your family, your friends, your colleagues, your culture, and yourself.

- I, your soul mate partner, representing all that has restrained you and tied you up, now act to unwind the ropes of your capture and liberate your soul's passion, power, purpose and presence.

- I place my hands on your feet and free you to follow your inner path.

- I hold your hands and consecrate your full capacity for intuitive healing and touch.

- I touch your ears and release them to know the sound of your soul's voice.

- I close your physical eyes and activate your intuitive vision.

- I place my hands on your chest and release the love that lives in your soul.

- I touch your forehead to acknowledge and awaken your deepest wisdom.

- I behold you as the sacred soul you already are and clear you to embody what you already know to do.

- I, a liberator, welcome you as the beloved of your soul and free your intuition to harvest the wealth found in every aspect of your life both now and forever more.

- It is finished.

4. End each ceremony with a big hug and record your reactions in your journals.

It is important to remember that you are doing the Blessing Sight and Liberation Intuition exercises not to sweep problems under the rug but to bring forward the reasons why you are soul mates into the foreground. Souls know what they are doing. There is a reason you've come together for this work.

SHARED DESTINY

Soul mate learning teams take place in the context of a world bigger than themselves. Because both your souls have long, inclusive views, your team may have the makings of what I mentioned earlier, the suprasexual relationship, and, therefore, share a life work destiny. To explore the potential reasons why you've selected each other as soul mates beyond the reasons you might now list, go back to the "Love is the Key" exercise. Look over the original five priorities you each selected and pool them together. Then evaluate all ten priorities from this perspective: is there one which you now realize is a seed of future work or specific growth you'll do together or separately? If so, discuss what it means to you and how you might go about supporting its actualization as a team. If not, identify the most important thing you've gained from working together, record it in your journals, and give thanks to each other for this golden opportunity.

Final Exercise: Your Intuition to Do List

1. Complete the sentence, "Because I am accepting my soul's invitation to 'Mate with Soul,' I already know to . . ." List 5 to 10 things you know to do. You can choose simple things such as "tell one person I love him or her today," "practice the Blessing Sight exercise every day for a month," "find someone else with whom I'd like to make a Soul Mate Promise." When you've finished, read your list over, highlight the simplest activity which *gives you the feeling of being mated soul-to-soul,* and do it. Record everything in your journal.

2. Go back and look at your Guiding Image for this chapter. What part of the image best symbolizes your soul mate experience? If this picture was a slogan for soul mating, what would the caption read? What is the most striking thing your image now teaches you about your intuition's ability to mate with other souls? Record in your journal.

CHAPTER 11

Invitation Nine:

PARTNER
EXPONENTIALLY

One morning when I was commuting to a speaking engagement, I tuned into a radio interview with peak performance expert, Charles Garfield. Commenting on the efforts of NASA and its subcontractors to achieve one of the great dreams of humanity—to walk on the moon—Garfield spoke eloquently about the power, passion, and purpose which inspired the NASA team to new heights of innovation and creativity. As I thought about the power driving the men and women united behind that dream, I couldn't help but wonder what their intuitive stories had been. In spite of the tremendous ideological and social changes which were sweeping the country at that time (the late '60s), I had a hard time believing anyone was thinking about or making use of intuition as such. Yet I was confident that intuition had flourished in that dedicated environment because I believe intuition is the glue that unites us when we partner exponentially to form family units, groups, organizations, and nation-states. As a soul-to-soul communicator, intuition electrifies inner pathways among people and can fuse all into one diverse, yet focused spirit.

> *This moment I shall start*
> *a divine life; this moment*
> *and not later. This*
> *moment is in my hands.*
> *My soul will show*
> *me the way.*
>
> LORENZO

MAGIC CLICKS

Stories about the accomplishments of such unified groups abound in science and technology, business, and sports.[1] For example, in 1979 when the Ford Motor Company was facing dark days, chairman Donald Peterson had the insight to put his industrial design department on equal footing with the engineering, marketing, and financial departments and get rid of the "committee car" approach. The designers were inspired to produce Ford's Taurus, the best-selling American car for a decade or more. Basketball player Bill Bradley talks about the electric moment when his team, nineteen points behind with only five minutes left in a particular game, experienced a rush of collective energy, which was so effective that they ended up winning the game by three points. Figure skater Toller Cranston describes a similar moment except he had shared it with his audience: "I felt an electric shock run through the crowd. They understood. In that brief instant we fused. Reality no longer existed and time became suspended. . . . It was something beyond love, beyond reality." In his book, *Joy in Sports,* Michael Novak implies that these moments of collective unity are the meaning of existence and reflect life as it ought to be.

> When a collection of individuals first jells as a team, and truly begins to react as a five-headed or eleven-headed unit rather than as an aggregate of five or eleven individuals, you can almost hear the *click:* a new kind of reality comes into existence at a new level of human development. A basketball team, for example, can click into and out of this reality many times during the same game; and each player, as well as the coach and the fans, can detect the difference. . . . For those who have participated on a team that has known the click of com-

munality, the experience is un-
forgettable, like that of having attained, for a while at least, a
higher level of existence: existence as it ought to be.[2]

While the last chapter focused on
intuition in your one-to-one soul mate
partnerships, this chapter zeroes in on
intuition in your soul-to-*souls* relation-

> *Never one thing and
> seldom one person can
> make for a success.
> It takes a number of
> them merging into one
> perfect whole.*
>
> MARIE DRESSLER

ships. In these soul-to-souls relationships, you, too, can know the electric
joy of magic clicks and life as it ought to be. Magic clicks are not new;
they are also in part what people refer to when they speak of being "in
the zone" or "with the Force." These phrases are in our language and
myths because they are in our reality. When you've done your home-
work—collected yourself, committed to a path, and undertaken the intuitive life—your soul automatically unites you with multiple others with
whom you know the zone, feel the Force, and can live in magic clicks.

Imagine for a moment that your intuitive sexual-body power center
is emitting powerful energy for your purpose; your intuitive heart is
radiating messages about who you are and what your purpose is; your
intuitive eye is scanning for others who are relevant to your life; and
your intuitive voice, feet, and hands are ready to introduce you to
whomever your intuition identifies. Take this image and multiply it by ten
people, then a hundred people, then a thousand, and so on. In the world
of like-attracts-like, others are seeking partnership with you as you are
seeking it with them. Your partnerships will multiply exponentially in an
intuitive atmosphere because recognition and linking is going on at a deep
level.

To identify the Guiding Image for your capacity to partner exponentially and know magic clicks, do the following exercise:

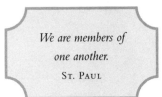

We are members of
one another.

St. Paul

Your Guiding Image for "Partner Exponentially"

- Create a section of your Intuition Journal and label it "Chapter Eleven: Partner Exponentially."

- Reach into your Image Vocabulary envelope and, without looking, pull out your guiding illustration for this chapter.

- Write what category it is from on the bottom of your chosen page.

- Paste your image on this page.

COLLABORATIVE INTUITION

It is important to make intuition a conscious part of your teams, organizations, or groups because, as an inner communication pathway, intuition helps members of a group know where the others are, what the others are doing, what's coming next, and what to do right now. This is collaborative intuition—intuition which arises *only* because two or more people have come together around meaning—in action.

Collaborative intuition is the capacity for a group or team of people to work together intuitively and to use their collective intuition to manifest new levels of insight, creativity, and productivity. Although historically, intuition has been identified primarily with an individual's ability, the truth is that *intuition thrives in a group context.* Intuition loves meaning, and people tend to gather around meaning—family and friendship occasions, recreational pursuits, professional life, community events, or national activities. This is one reason why intuition flourishes when the members of an organization are all committed to a common purpose, such as getting humanity to the moon. Another reason why intuition thrives in a group context is that love, love between and among group members or love for the task they are performing, is always present in a highly functioning team. When you bring meaning and love together (intuition thrives in meaning; intuition travels on love) in a team situation, the culture is ripe

for collaborative intuition. Creative insights, enlightened solutions, and new
visions are natural by-products.

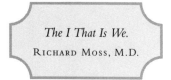

The I That Is We.
RICHARD MOSS, M.D.

An analogy for the collaborative
intuition process comes from the growth
pattern of vines which cover the ground in South American jungles. The
thick canopy in such jungles is very high, and the vines must fight to get
enough light to survive. As a traditional story goes, one maverick vine
tries to "go for it" and plunges upward toward the top of the canopy.
Other vines around the maverick are attracted to the possibility and join
in by wrapping themselves around the maverick. This process continues
until so many vines have joined the effort that their combined diameter is
as thick as a tree trunk. Growing together, the slender vines have enough
strength to break through the canopy and receive the light.

This light is like the illumination of the collaborative intuition process. What this story suggests is that working with others can help you
achieve a level of enlightenment. This chapter offers you experience with
collaborative intuition skills and shows their use in three different settings:
(1) small-scale groups of people such as occur in your business teams, your
family gatherings, your parties, or your study groups; (2) medium-scale
groups of people like those you work with in business or professional organizations; and (3) large groups such as those you might encounter in
community or national activities. As the following list indicates, you'll
work with some specific benefits of collaborative intuition in each setting.

Settings for Collaborative Intuition	Benefits of Collaborative Intuition
1. Small-scale groups (business teams, family, etc.)	1. Purpose/Creativity for Transformation
2. Medium-scale groups (business or professional organizations)	2. Intuitive Leadership
3. Large-scale groups (community/nation)	3. Intuitive Vision

> *Heaven is all around us . . . the unitive life is more possible than was ever dreamed of.*
>
> ABRAHAM MASLOW

The three benefits I've listed are only part of the picture. In my experience, the first setting (teams or small groups) catalyzes healing because intuition's ability to make life transparent means that you cannot hide from others the areas where you feel incomplete. Members of a group have the potential to assist each other in transformational healing. The second setting (business or professional organizations) allows you to exercise your intuitive eyes and heart in order to stay in contact with your group's soul, or what is often called the oversoul in mystical literature. The term "oversoul" refers to a cohesive energetic field that operates in conjunction with the goals, aspirations, and character of each member of a team and that embodies the wisdom of the whole. In the third section (large-scale groups), you'll learn about intuitive vision. Since you are likely to have some type of intuitive vision as your skills grow, it is important for you to understand the principles behind a successful intuitive vision process, how it differs from the traditional vision process used in most businesses, and how to work with others whose visions have relevance to yours.

In addition to learning about these three aspects of collaborative intuition, you'll (1) explore how understanding intuition's role in group process helps you and your colleagues maintain a productive relationship, and (2) practice a meditation which has the capacity to link you intuitively with groups of people who are part of your destiny.

As you read through this chapter, recognize that collaborative intuition is not a linear process. Cause-and-effect thinking has to go out the window. No one knows when or how to predict when the Force, the zone, or a magic click will occur in your group's life. Teams which consistently utilize intuitive exercises, however, seem to create an invisible intuitive field or way of being to which the group as a whole and every individual in it have access. Members can come into or out of this intuitive field at any given moment, and sometimes one exercise in this chap-

ter may cause your group to click into
the intuitive field while other times
that same exercise may produce nothing. What is definite, however, is that
using collaborative intuition in a team
or group setting produces insights; insights lead to new actions; and new actions create a transformed life. This you
can count on.

> *The soul knows only the
> soul; the web of events
> is the flowing robe in
> which she is clothed.*
>
> RALPH WALDO
> EMERSON

TAKING THE PLUNGE INTO COLLABORATIVE INTUITION

The Brown Bag exercise which follows is my favorite exercise to give
groups. This particular version focuses on creativity and is designed to be
done with your small business team (five to seven people), although you
could also use it (1) to identify creative solutions for family projects; (2) as
a game at your next party; or (3) in an intuition study group. If you are
interested in one of the latter three settings, before you begin the exercise
read all the directions and the *Options* section at the end of the exercise.

In the spirit of exploration, it is important to make certain that every
member of your chosen small group wants to experiment with intuition.
If there is unspoken resistance to or resentment of the exercise, the team
may get lost in philosophical debates, personality conflicts, or heady discussions about intuition. The Brown Bag exercise requires a hearty plunge
into collaborative intuition, and through it your group will begin immediately to build intuitive pathways among members.

To begin the exercise, have your team or group choose *one* problem
the members are facing for which they want to find a creative solution.
Then each member of the team prepares a brown sack "lunch" by placing inside the bag an object which symbolizes a new solution to the problem (one they believe in) or an index card with one or two written
sentences about the new solution on it. Next, each person takes a turn
putting his or her brown bag in the center of a team circle. He or she says

> *Don't go outside yourself,*
> *return into yourself, the*
> *dwelling place of truth*
> *is in the inner man.*
>
> St. Augustine

absolutely nothing as the fellow members (1) go around the circle they are sitting in and one-by-one answer questions designed to help them intuit what is in the bag, and then (2) continue to make comments about what is in the bag in "popcorn" fashion (whoever has something to say) and carry on a conversation about what they, as a team, intuit is in the bag.[3] By the conclusion of this exercise, the group understands the collaborative intuition process much better, and, most important, all kinds of creative ideas have been flushed up *regardless of* whether anyone intuits precisely what is in the bag (although most groups are amazed at how correct they are). As you will learn, even this small experiment with intuitive collaboration sets the stage for creative collaboration at a much higher level.

Exercise: Collaborative Intuition and the Brown Bag Exercise

1. You and all the members of your group bring with you a brown bag which contains a symbolic object or an index card with 1 to 2 sentences which *represents a creative solution to an agreed-upon problem.*

2. If your group has worked with each other for long enough to "guess" what each other's solutions might be, begin by first holding an open, random discussion in which you list *all* the possible solutions your logic suspects members will propose.

3. Following the discussion, your group forms a circle and does the Basic Breath exercise found on page 76 together for 10 to 15 minutes or until everyone is quiet and relaxed.

4. Taking turns, one member *at a time* puts his or her brown bag in the center of the circle. The person whose bag is in the center *can't speak at all* and tries not to make any gestures which would give clues to the group.

5. A volunteer agrees to record everything the group says on a piece of paper or flip chart large enough for everyone to read. These notes will eventually go to the person whose bag is in the center.

> *The wise ones, who see that the consciousness within themselves is the same consciousness within all conscious beings, attain eternal peace.*
>
> KATHA UPANISHAD

6. Working with one question at a time, group members go around the circle one at a time (each person answers one question or cluster of questions) and intuit things about the brown bag in the center. If you have more members than questions, when you reach the end of the questions, start with the first question again. If anyone can't work with a particular question, give him or her the next one.

7. Remember: don't try to be *right*; just talk. The purpose in answering these questions is *not* to identify right or wrong answers but to open yourself to other modes of knowing as a community.

   • What attracts you about what is in the bag? (Answers can start, "I am fascinated by . . .)

   • What do you intuit the owner believes or feels about the solution in the bag and why? (e.g., "I intuit that the owner believes that this creative solution will work well with our previous project and wants to build on a proven product . . ." or "I intuit that the owner feels this is the most elegant solution possible and that it will enhance our effectiveness").

   • How is this solution innovative or creative?

   • Why is the proposed solution *perfect* for the owner? How does it fit into his or her life with the team or company as a whole?

   • What do you admire about this solution?

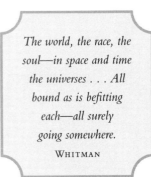

The world, the race, the soul—in space and time the universes . . . All bound as is befitting each—all surely going somewhere.

WHITMAN

- How does this solution stimulate your creativity?

- What other creative solution does this solution remind you of? Why?

- What does the owner already know to do to implement this solution that the team could really support?

- How might you contribute to implementing some part of this solution?

- If you need more individual questions, start at the beginning again.

8. The team once more intuits things about what is in the bag, talking in popcorn fashion (whoever has something to say), and then holds a team-wide conversation addressing these questions:

   - Evaluating everything everyone has said (look at the notes the scribe has taken), what does the team think is most important about the object or index card in the bag?

   - What does the group think the object is or sentences are?

   - If different, what is the creative solution?

9. When all the answers have been given, the owner of the bag takes out his or her representation, shares it with the group, and gives the group feedback on what has been said.

10. After choosing a new volunteer scribe, the group continues to do steps 2 through 8 until everyone has had a chance to put his or her bag in the center. (If you have a large group, split into groups of 5 to 7 members.)

11. When everyone has finished, the team lists all the possible creative solutions which have come out of the exercise, selects one or two

to pursue, identifies steps which need to be done, and assigns particular tasks to those who volunteer.

12. Each person keeps the notes which were generated from their bag and records anything which stands out in their journals.

> *Let a beauty full of healing and a strength of final clenching be the pulsing in our spirits and our blood.*
>
> MARGARET ABIGAIL WALKER

Option: You can use this exercise with your family to seek a creative solution to problems or decisions you are facing (this exercise will not resolve psychological dilemmas). If you do this exercise at a party, with friends, or in a study group, each person chooses to work with his or her own creative solution to a problem. Everyone doesn't work on the same problem. For step #11, each person lists creative solutions which have come out of the exercise for his or her own problem.

After you are familiar with the exercise, you can vary what is in the bag—a favorite moment, something deeper you'd like your group members to know about you, or a purpose you want to have the group support—and create relevant questions modeled after the ones I gave you.

The Brown Bag exercise can be repeated by your team once a quarter. Do not do it more often because intuition and logic need time to implement the creative solutions the team identified as well as any ancillary insights obtained. In the interim, the team can adapt any of the previous exercises in this book to collaborative intuition in one of three ways.

In the first option, each of you does your favorite exercise at home, and next time your team or group meets again you openly share all your experiences and results with each other. After all the members have shared their experiences and results, one-by-one each member says and completes this sentence aloud, "My experience is valuable to my intuitive development because. . . ."

In the second option, you can convert individual exercises to the collaborative intuition process by having your group select one exercise you

> In and through
> community lies the
> salvation of the world.
> M. SCOTT PECK

want to do together during a meeting. When your chosen exercise has been completed, you list all the results on a big sheet of paper that everyone can see *without interpreting the results for each other.* Then each of you selects from the list the result(s) which has the most mean-ing for you. It does *not* have to be your own result. Once you all have se-lected the most meaningful result, one-by-one you fill in the blanks of the following sentence and say the entire thing aloud: "The intuitive message I find most meaningful is . . . because . . ." Sometimes a majority of your members will choose the same result. If this happens, discuss what infor-mation the oversoul of your group might be emphasizing and what im-portance it could have to the evolution of the group.

In the third option, your group adapts individual exercises to collab-orative intuition by doing the exercises as a unit. A favorite adaptation for this purpose is the Guided Image exercise you've been doing at the be-ginning of every chapter. To do it as a group, each of you reaches into your Image Vocabulary envelope and, without looking, pulls out an image. You then pool all your images together and collaboratively create a collage, the final product of which represents the character and aspira-tions of your group's oversoul. Conversing together, your team interprets the collage from this perspective and can even give your group's oversoul a name.

Each of these three ways continues to pool intuitive information and abilities so that your team's knowledge and wisdom also begins to multi-ply exponentially.

MAGIC CLICKS AND HEALING

This expanding wise and intuitive field always reveals needs for healing. Al-though personality conflicts, cultural misunderstanding, ethnic stereotyp-ing, and strong differences of opinions can remain constant undercurrents in ordinary group situations, a group dedicated to collaborative intuition will find them flushed to the surface. This is because your group's oversoul is interested in building a cohesive, effective, and healed unit. In order to do so, the oversoul provides opportunities for your membership to eliminate subterranean problems which might generate internal criticism, gossip, suspicion, self-pity, and power plays. These behaviors can destroy a group faster than physical problems such as a poor locale for meetings, shortage of funds, or large distances between members.

> *We are at the center of a seamless web of mutual responsibility and collaboration . . . a seamless partnership, with interrelationships and mutual commitments.*
>
> ROBERT HASS

There is a big difference between the groups you belong to which recognize the healing actions of the oversoul and those which do not. In the latter groups, where the actions of the oversoul are not recognized, healing opportunities tend to be treated as distractions from the primary goals of productivity or usefulness. When you are in a group whose membership recognizes the actions of the oversoul, people welcome healing opportunities and realize that the group is together for individual and collective evolution; members want to become an effective healing and learning team. It is important for you to know that the healing opportunities I am referring to are not in the same category as an individual's need for therapy. In fact, personal, repetitive issues in a group setting may signal a need for private therapy and are part of a healthy learning process for those involved. The healing I *am* talking about is a by-product of your group going forward and can be effectively dealt with by yourself and the group over a short period of time. After this latter type of healing, your whole group functions at a higher level, and individuals find their longings fulfilled and new directions launched.

The following example, which centers around a woman's longing for a baby rather than just a business setting, gives you a chance to see how diverse individuals can come together and contribute to a healing process. Lynne had reason to be frightened of pregnancy because, after successful

> *There is a rainbow in you stronger than steel.*
>
> MEGAN DOHERTY

artificial insemination, she had lost her first child at five months. She faced fifty-fifty odds that her next pregnancy would end the same way. A member of one of my intuition focus groups for women, Lynne's story catalyzed the joys, frustrations, yearnings, and rewards of motherhood—or lack thereof—within group members. After the facts of everyone's separate lives were shared, the group began to "dream" together and sought to bring intuitive support to Lynne. The group recommended that she communicate intuitively with the soul of her future baby by playing the flute, naming and talking to her child, praying for guidance, and visualizing a positive outcome for herself, her partner, and her potential child. In addition, the members agreed to visualize along with her and to hold Lynne's goal in their thoughts and prayers. Lynne decided to try again. You can imagine how excited the group was when Lynne conceived some months later, the joy felt by everyone when in utero tests revealed that the baby was developing normally, and the group's delight when McKenna, who looks a lot like Lynne, was born. The members believed that their work had played a role in the events and they had become, at least partially, a collective mother.

Every member of another small group that I facilitated made important personal strides and achieved goals they had set out to accomplish in spite of the fact that the group only met one Saturday a month for eight months. Various members achieved these types of things: launching a business; getting started on finishing a long-delayed Ph.D.; selling a house and moving to a new area; going into private business; and finding a job where their talents were recognized. By the second meeting, everyone had shared what their goals were, and the remaining five meetings were spent developing contact with the soul, the oversoul, and doing collaborative intuition exercises.

Lynn's healing results and the achievements of the former small-group members are another kind of magic click you can experience in your work team or any place else where you focus on collaborative intuition. This is because collaborative intuition allows you and every person in the group to tap into the group's oversoul, which is an endless source of energy for all. It is this endless energy which fosters the skills necessary for intuitive leadership to emerge in business organizations.

> When we speak of informal leadership, we describe . . . the capacity of the organization to create the leadership that best suits its needs at the time.
>
> MEG WHEATLY

INTUITION IN BUSINESS ORGANIZATIONS: A SURVEY

Until the beginning of the 1990s, the number of Western people openly committed to intuition in business—teaching it, studying it, or applying it—was very small.[4] Most business professionals didn't consider it safe to refer to their intuition unless they described it as "my gut told me to . . ."; therefore, it was generally assumed that intuition was not particularly relevant to business operations. In the early 1990s, Jagdish Parikh and his colleagues at Switzerland's International Institute for Management Development conducted the largest, worldwide survey of business professionals (1,312 non-governmental managers from nine countries). The survey aimed to uncover how "those on the front lines of coping with world business" understood and used intuition in their professional and personal lives.

Survey results, recorded completely in Parikh's book, *Intuition: The New Frontier of Management,*[5] revealed some surprises. For example, 78 percent of the U.S.A. managers rated themselves very high/high on the use of intuition, and 76 percent could back that up by citing a specific example from their lives. Also, in an objective test of their intuition, U.S.A. managers were second only to Japan. Managers from every country identified that intuition was most *relevant* in business environments to (1) corporate strategy and planning; (2) marketing; and (3) human resource development, in that order. There was also high agreement in all countries about intuition's role in decision-making, in increasing probability of success, and in almost all facets of life.

These facts shed some light on intuition's actual and potential contribution to business environments. Two further points are relevant to

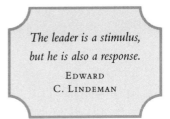

The leader is a stimulus, but he is also a response.

EDWARD
C. LINDEMAN

our work together: managers from the U.K. and the U.S.A. believed that intuition can be cultivated or enhanced, and 49.8 percent of U.S.A. and 40.6 percent of U.K. managers believed there is a possibility that *intuition is a group process* (my italics). Your work on collaborative intuition in this section is based on the idea that you can enhance your intuitive leadership skills by understanding how intuition operates in and as a group process.

UNDERSTANDING INTUITIVE LEADERSHIP

The best metaphor I know for understanding the impact of collaborative intuition on intuitive leadership comes from nature. Theodore Schwenk, in his book *Sensitive Chaos,* reports on R. Schieferstein's research into the flying patterns of birds. When birds fly in an arrow or wedge formation, they create one totality that includes the air which connects them. Like baby swans that glide on the waves of the wedge made by their mother, birds glide on the edge of the waves created in the air by their leader. The surprising thing is that the formation creates a field of energy which is even available to the lead bird. According to Schieferstein, "The current error, that the bird flying at the apex of the triangle has to work considerably harder than those following it, must be corrected. The field of air streams, created reciprocally by all the separate birds, spreads out in space with the speed of sound and therefore, as the speed at which the birds fly is much slower, it precedes them considerably, so that the lead bird can if necessary take energy from the field just as all the others can."

An intuitive human leader, like the lead bird who draws energy from the air streams which are created reciprocally by all the separate birds, draws on the energy of the group's oversoul. And, like the birds again, successful intuitive leadership is based on one's acute awareness of and sensitivity to (1) the group's soul or oversoul, and (2) how to tap the over-

soul for the good of the whole rather
than on the traditional sources of leadership—one's personal intuition or logical expertise, power, or charisma. In
addition, intuitive leadership is understood to be a shared phenomena; the

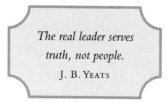

*The real leader serves
truth, not people.*
J. B. YEATS

active, intuitive participation of each member is necessary to go forward.
For example, World Soccer Champion Pele's ability to intuitively participate in collaborative intuition and tap the oversoul lead others to say of
him, "He seemed to always know where all the players are on the field"
and, as a result, could choose the best play. This was true even when the
players were behind him or otherwise out of his field of vision. In short,
Pele's collaborative intuition skills allowed him to tap into the oversoul,
read the oversoul, and energize himself in the oversoul. He was an excellent "lead bird."

This has practical implications for those working in business settings.
When Alain Gauthier, the Executive Director of Core Leadership Development, is hired to assist organizational change nationally or internationally, he often uses his intuition to identify patterns which suggest new
perspectives for the group to explore. "My intuition usually comes
through a spatial understanding of a group. It's hard to explain, but when
I stand up, observe what is going on, and reflect on the implications, I
often know a penetrating question to ask that will re-orient the meeting
and uncover new perspectives."

In these situations, Gauthier is taping the wisdom of the group's collaborative intuition field (noticing the spatial patterns) and the energy of
the oversoul to stimulate collective insight (the group identifies new directions). Gauthier explains that he has taught himself to identify and trust
the authenticity of his intuition when his voice is lower, more resonant
and relaxed, and coming from a deep place inside him. I believe the authenticity of Gauthier's voice is due to his ability to link his own soul with
that of the group's oversoul *and* the group's ability to intuitively communicate with him. Although it is not for him to know in advance the answer the group seeks, Gauthier's question unites their individual souls

> *In the simplest terms, a leader is one who knows where he wants to go, and gets up, and goes.*
>
> JOHN ERSKINE

around a collective direction, stimulates their collaborative intuition, and invites the magic click of insights to occur. When he asks such a question, his intuitive leadership is spreading the waves and allowing his clients to, like the birds, ride upon them until they come to their own answers.

Susan Greene, CEO of Greene Alliances, Inc., has a different story to tell about collaborative intuition. Susan was hired by a Fortune 100 company to help an executive team get moving. Although it was a hand-picked, highly skilled group, team members had been unproductive for months and appeared stuck. Susan took them to a relaxing retreat center, but an entire day and a half was spent on team members defending, blaming, and passing the responsibility for poor performance from one situation to the next. Frustrated, Susan opened herself to direction and insight from intuitive realms. She needed a larger perspective, one which could be provided by the group's oversoul.

The next day, as the team began to explore the issue of trust, a train roared by. The noise was deafening; all discussion stopped because people couldn't hear the person next to them. The thundering, long train went on and on, silencing the room for a full seven minutes.

"The issue which is causing the problems is trust," Susan announced confidently when the noise receded.

Team members asked her immediately, "Why do you say that?" They had a lot of trust with clients and customers. Trust was an unlikely candidate for the cause of their productive slump.

Mustering her courage to be honest with the team, Susan said, "The train told me it was trust with a very loud voice. You were discussing trust when the train came roaring by. I listen to what the intuitive connections in the world around me are saying; I listen to nature. That train told me in seven minutes what two days of exploration didn't reveal."

Team members realized what she was saying very quickly and began to explore trust at a more profound level. They soon conceded that although they trusted their customers, they didn't trust each other. This lack of mutual trust was "de-railing" and "side-tracking" their productivity, so they decided to spend the final two days building trust with each other. One team member was so impressed by the impact of Susan's intuitive interpretation of the train that he went to the window and announced to all, "We had better pay attention to what we are talking about when the next train comes." During the last hour of the retreat, when insight and enthusiasm had returned to the team, he got his chance as the train made its once-every-two-days return trip. The team member could now say with assurance, "That is *our* train. We are ready."

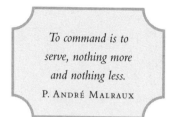

To command is to serve, nothing more and nothing less.

P. ANDRÉ MALRAUX

This story shows Susie's intuitive leadership skills in action; they enlarged the group enough to include the synchronistic relevance of a passing train's roar. Her individual soul read the collaborative intuition field and insightfully realized that one blockage (personality/trust issues) was related to another blockage (noise, which prevented people from hearing each other). Without help from her intuitive world, Susie might have classified the train's presence as an annoyance or an interference rather than a wave team members could ride together to the truth.

Exercise: Intuitive Leadership

1. Date your journal.

2. Review the actions of teams or organizations you have participated in for examples of collaborative intuition or being "in the zone or with the Force," and write them in your journal. For example, a time when your work team went "into the zone" and produced a report in record time; or a moment during a meeting when an insight by one team member electrified the atmosphere, and, subsequently, the whole team became creative. If you have never personally experienced collaborative intuition, describe at least one way that

*We pay tribute to those
to whom we open
our hearts.*

BALTASAR GRACIAN

you would like to experience it and write about it in your journal.

3. The next time you are in a group setting in which you are free to *experiment* (other than your intuition group), go inside yourself and ask your intuition to guide you to a new perspective on what is happening, one that is free from judgment about people's behavior. Frame the information that your intuition provides into a useful question. For example, if your intuition tells you that the group is missing important facts, you could ask, "What would we focus on if we assumed we were still missing important facts?" Or, if your intuitive guidance led you to believe your organization is holding too small a vision for its future, you could ask, "If we expanded our idea of who we were and what we were about, what do we think the company would look like?"

4. Record the results in your journal. Important note: *results include more than the literal answers to your question.* Among other things, results include the energy which greets the question (enthusiasm, caution, etc.), ideas which spin off from the discussion, and new alliances in the team.

5. After one month, evaluate the results of your question. Did your intuition have longevity, birth new directions, link souls, etc.? If you said you'd never had a collaborative intuition experience in step #2, have you had one now?

Alain's and Susie's stories are examples of how intuitive leadership can guide an individual to ask questions of a group which (1) focus collective energy; (2) access collaborative intuition; and (3) tap the power of the group's oversoul. In each of these cases intuition operates in a field which is shared by all; the leaders simply opened a door to what the groups already knew to be true.

THE OVERSOUL: THREE WAYS TO STAY IN TOUCH

> Vision is the art of seeing things invisible.
>
> JONATHAN SWIFT

To fully develop your intuitive leadership skills, you need to learn how to connect with the group's oversoul just like Schieferstein's lead bird does. As a living independent, yet dependent entity, the oversoul emerges out of a collective pool of souls who have gathered together. As with individuals, a healthy oversoul always seeks to embody more soul and grow; therefore, successful leadership requires that you learn how to stay in contact with this evolving oversoul. Three models, coming from Indigenous, religious, and nature teachings, suggest ways to establish and keep this contact.

Some Indigenous tribes have believed in a concept similar to the oversoul or collective soul. They envision the tribe as one, energetic "long body." This long body stretches to allow its members to travel great distances, while remaining part of the tribal body. A tribal representative might be sent out like a hand to retrieve something for the tribe. A scout might be sent as an eye to observe something. This way of organizing experience suggests how tribal members explained the workings of natural intuitive connections such as mental telepathy and ESP. From this perspective, you can stay connected to your organization's or team's oversoul by imagining yourself as part of the organization's or team's long body. Ask yourself, "What part of the body am I playing, and how does this define or contribute to my role as a leader?" and, "Why am I this particular part of my team's long body?" and "What is the best way for me to communicate to the long body and vice versa?"

In Christianity, believers are said to comprise the church, the body of Christ. Some Christians also believe that once Jesus was resurrected, His heavenly presence began to act like a gigantic field of energy wherein believers reside. They are connected and joined in the "body of Christ." As living cells within His body, believers comprise Christ's church on Earth. This is another conceptual framework you can use to connect with your

> *When God is our teacher,*
> *we come to think alike.*
> XENOPHON

oversoul. Imagine that you reside inside the energetic body of your organization's oversoul. What does its heart have to say? Where does it want to "walk"? What does it want to voice? What are its ethics, values, and aspirations?

Besides birds flying in an arrow or wedge formation, nature provides another analogy for understanding the concept of the oversoul. One of the largest living organisms on Earth is a grove of aspen trees covering thousands of acres in Utah. Author of *Leadership and the New Science,* and speaker Meg Wheatley tells us, "When we look at them, we think, 'Oh, look at all the trees.' But, when botanists look underground they said, 'Oh, look at this system, it's all one. These trees are all one.'" Intuition reveals the "underground" system, the system through which you are connected to the oversoul and are One with all life. When you want to establish a communication link with your organization's oversoul, pretend that one of your roots goes directly into it. Once you've tapped into the root system, examine the soil or concepts which tie you all together. Ask yourself the following questions: How deep are my roots in this organization? What part of its soil nourishes me and where do I need to go, or what do I need to develop, to nourish me more? If I made a statement which expressed my Oneness with the oversoul, what would it be?

INTUITIVE LEADERSHIP AND JUST PLAIN TALK

Another way in which intuitive leaders stimulate and utilize collaborative intuition is in talking circles, which is an Indigenous method for sharing your spiritual self, learning from others, practicing observation, and making decisions. In a circle format, every voice is valued equally—from the child to the adult, from the stock room employee to the company president—and everyone is listened to respectfully. Traditionally, a talking stick or other object is held by the person who is speaking and then passed to the next speaker. Talking either proceeds in a linear way around the circle or individuals speak up when they have something to say. Everyone is invited to contribute.

As odd as it sounds, this simple procedure for talking to each other as equals is very transformative. In fact, the after-glow of a talking circle often releases your intuition and provides the impetus for you to do what you already

> *You never know how something you may think, say, or do today, will influence the lives of millions tomorrow.*
>
> B. J. PALMER

knew to do without knowing what has directly influenced you to do so. These actions are a perfect example of a non-linear result of collaborative intuition. In a book entitled *On Dialogue,* British physicist David Bohm advocated we all participate in a similar process, which he called dialogue. Bohm pointed out that Indigenous tribes gathered on a regular basis and formed a leaderless circle to "just talk and talk with no apparent purpose." Such meetings would go on for hours and appeared to end for no obvious reason. But afterward, the people would know what to do about very important issues.

Hired by the Institute of Noetic Sciences[6] to help with their strategic planning process, including designs for embodying the concepts they had been researching for twenty-three years (e.g., meditation, guided imagery, and the role of intentionality in healing), consultant Sharon Lehrer initiated a weekly Bohm-type dialogue in a middle management cross-departmental team. During this activity, which the team called "check in," the group remained open and leaderless in order to invite what was important and meaningful to emerge organically. Although Sharon knew that the Institute's CEO had some ambivalence from time to time and wondered about the fruitfulness of the activity, he remained supportive of the process. In this safe container, the team developed greater collaboration, trust, and honest communication with each other. They also practiced guided imagery and focused on the practical application of intuition in planning and decision-making.

Very soon into the process, Lehrer reported that the team began to develop shared leadership and became a living community rather than a group of individuals who came to work without their spirits. The man-

> *The world would have you agree with its dismal dream of limitation. But the light would have you soar like the eagle of your sacred visions.*
>
> ALAN COHEN

agers began to offer substantial ideas to the organization and initiated more use of intuitive processes for accessing innovation, creativity, and deeper wisdom. They also joined the whole organization around the question: "What is my deepest purpose and how it is aligned with the deepest calling of the Institute?" As their beliefs and actions shifted, money began to flow, projects were completed more easily, and creative and shared leadership emerged. This pivotal team, which incorporated intuition into their meetings, became a cohesive force whose history suggested a noetic model for transformation within the Institute as well as in other business organizations and communities.

Exercise: Just Talk

1. Working in the context of an organizational team or small group, members create a talking stick together. It can be made from anything, e.g., wood, metal, crystal, etc. You may enjoy tying objects such as feathers, rocks, paper clips, or pictures to the stick. The finished talking stick will become a sacred object to the extent that the membership imbues it with meaning.

2. Spend some time in every gathering using the talking stick and "just talking."

3. Record your experiences in your journal.

While you are talking, be sensitive to an appropriate amount of time for your contribution. Don't monopolize the conversation. Also, avoid any tendency that the group may have to reproduce encounter groups or undertake therapy. Don't tell each other what to do or try to "fix" it if healing needs arise repeatedly. Remember the group's oversoul is bringing up healing in order to achieve it quickly and move forward.

INTUITIVE VISIONS:
PERSONAL CALLING CARDS

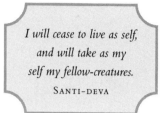

*I will cease to live as self,
and will take as my
self my fellow-creatures.*

SANTI-DEVA

You've explored how to use collaborative intuition in a team setting and how collaborative intuition contributes to intuitive leadership. Your final exploration of collaborative intuition focuses on intuitive vision.

Intuitive visions arrive from the inner world of your soul. As part of the soul's calling card they act as reservoirs of energy. You can always dial them up and tap their presence for guidance, understanding, strength, and courage. The subject matter of intuitive visions ranges from what would be good for you to do in the next ten minutes to large-scale callings such as working on community, national, or global issues. Visions help you know what to do; visions help us know what to do.

We all have intuitive visions, although we may not recognize them as such at the time. One reason you may not recognize your visions is because you expect them to come only through the more traditional methods of nighttime dreams, prayer, or meditation. The truth is that visions can arrive as simple, knowing wishes for your life—who you want to be and what you want to do. Other times they can visit you as a body-felt knowing, a waking vision, clear, compelling ideas, or an auditory calling. The following three real-life intuitive visions—examples of a body-felt vision, a waking vision, and a prayerful state vision—were the impetus for a collaborative vision event which today brings many individual intuitive visions together year after year. This behind-the-scenes story provides you with keys to understanding more about the individual intuitive vision process and preparation for a collaborative vision.

1. A Body-Felt Vision

In 1992, David Berry, a United States government official based in Washington, D.C., heard that a Hopi spokesperson, Thomas Banyacya, was

> *George Washington [expressed the opinion] that spirituality and morality are the twin pillars of a healthy national life.*
>
> ROBERT BENNE

going to speak about prophecy at a local Tibetan Buddhist Center. Berry was curious. As a student of different spiritual traditions, David was familiar with some prophecies, but he wished to become more acquainted with Indigenous teachings and prophecies.

Thomas, a colorful figure dressed in a beautifully woven vest, Indian jewelry, and a red ribbon circling his forehead, told the ancient Hopi prophecy of the "gourd of ashes" [atomic bomb] which would be let loose on the Earth and destroy all in its path until humankind learned how to live in balance on the Earth. Thomas had heard these prophecies from his elders in the mid-1940s, and he went on to talk about a "house made of mica [United Nations] which was to be built on the eastern shores of Turtle Island [North America] and where the people of the world would gather to talk." In conclusion, Thomas pleaded for all people to come together, stop hurting Mother Earth, and fulfill the ancient prophecy by choosing a better way of life. Just before he sat down, Thomas mentioned that he had accepted the responsibility to deliver this message to the United Nations, but, although he had been knocking on the U.N.'s door for decades, he'd never been received and could use some help.

Suddenly time began to slow way down for David. Molasses Time moved in. David was surprised to feel his hand rise up, seemingly by its own volition, and in the midst of being acknowledged by the crowd, the Hopi elder saw David's hand and pointed for him to get up.

David describes that moment: "I found myself standing up with no idea of what I would say or what would happen next. 'I accept your invitation and will help you get into the United Nations,' I heard myself say."

Apart from his active professional life, this pledge was the beginning of a ten-month whirlwind of travel and negotiations for David which culminated on December 10, 1992, when the elder delivered prophecies to the United Nation's General Assembly.

This is a perfect example of a body-felt visionary experience; David's body recognized a vision for his future, his intuitive voice kicked in, and he knew what to do. Of course, only David's subsequent follow-through al-

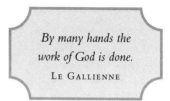

By many hands the work of God is done.

LE GALLIENNE

lowed him to fulfill the promise he made that day and to meet the partners who would eventually become part of his future. If your visionary body, like David's, appears to know something of which your conscious mind is unaware, experiment with trusting it. But exercise reason. Your visionary soul is never going to ask you to do something for the purpose of hurting another or yourself. In fact, visionary messages often have the collective good in mind.

2. A Waking Vision

Here is an example of a waking vision, a vision which arrives unexpectedly when you are wide-awake and in the middle of doing something else, like a surprise guest. During the early '90s, Betsy Stang was sitting in the Capitol gardens in Washington, D.C., with a companion who was telling her that the headdress which adorns the statue of Freedom on top of the Capitol Dome is modeled after the one given by the Cherokees to runaway slaves on the underground railroad. The bonnet signified the ability of the slaves to fly to freedom and receive shelter from Indigenous tribes in the north.

As Betsy listened to the story, a waking vision took over, and her intuitive eyes saw the headdress turn into an eagle which soared above the Capitol, filling the area with enough light to illuminate all the eagles that the nation's founding fathers had put in place. She believed the radiant eagle symbolized healing between the U.S. government and the First Nations (the Indigenous nations of North America) for all the abuse and broken agreements. In a quick flash, she thought that healing would start when Medicine people and people from all the races that call this land home encircled the Capitol in prayer.

When the waking vision ended, Betsy shared her experience with

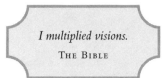

I multiplied visions.

THE BIBLE

her companion, and to her amazement her companion described a similar vision. In spite of this, skepticism set in immediately and Betsy heard herself say, "Well, we have as much chance of this happening as the statue coming alive right now and flying about!" Just then, an enormous hawk swooped down out of the sky, circled them, flew off, and landed on the statue's headdress. Betsy's and her companion's mouths flew open. They decided to talk over the waking vision with their elders and hold it in their prayers.

Waking visions can have as much power and truth as visions which arrive in more traditional settings; don't dismiss them because they happen when you are in a reverie or are wide-awake. Remember another thing: talk your experience over with someone whom you love, trust, and respect. Another person can help you evaluate your experience, judge its importance, keep your life in balance, and assess if the vision has a contribution to make to the people.

3. A Prayerful State Vision

While a waking vision usually comes as a surprise guest, a prayerful state invites visions to visit you. Ideally, you are prepared for them and they will be welcome guests. Nonetheless, it is important to exercise caution with all your visions. Don't let them take over your life any more than you would expect an invited guest to take over your home. The injunction to "weigh the spirits" can be applied equally to your visions; evaluate them. Some spiritual literature states that one way you can identify a neophyte from an adept is that the latter knows how to harness the energy of a vision for the collective good while the former, the neophyte, sometimes gets harnessed by the vision and loses perspective. Collaborative intuition and an intuitive vision process reduce these concerns because the community owns the emerging collaborative vision rather than follows the preordained dictates of someone's personal vision. The following prayerful state vision, which was to demonstrate some of these points, comes from my life.

In 1993, while standing outside praying, not too far from the Iowa corn belt which gave me birth, an inner vision began to move within me. As a professor and practitioner of intuition, I was used to these sorts of things (it was in my family blood), but the sight of fifteen or more huge, blazing-eyed, hooked-beaked visionary eagles walking straight at me was terrifying. I prayed harder and tried to bring my logical mind to the situation, but the eagles continued their fierce march toward me, collapsing into one as they came. I thought I would faint when everything seemed to disappear, and I found my visionary self riding through soft, white clouds on the back of this one eagle.

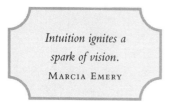

Intuition ignites a spark of vision.

MARCIA EMERY

As the clouds opened up, the eagle dove down and headed straight for the Washington Monument in Washington, D.C. I recognized it at once, of course. I followed his actions for a few moments, and, when he seemed ready to leave, I looked down on the field next to the monument and I saw a small gathering of people in prayer—people whom I seemed to recognize.

Abruptly, the vision was over. I was standing outside praying thousands of miles away from Washington, D.C., a place I'd only visited once in my life. I wasn't sure how I felt about this visionary guest; I needed to pray about it, talk it over with spiritual teachers, elders, and friends, and evaluate it. I knew enough about visions to realize I'd have to take responsibility for what I saw and be willing to consider doing something in D.C., three thousand miles away from where I lived.

Although my dad talked about politics a lot when I was growing up, I wasn't a political person, and what I remembered best was his telling me that he believed our Universe was part of a vast being's body. "What do I have to do with Washington, D.C.?" I asked myself. "I am not political."

Frankly, in spite of years of teaching people about the importance of evaluating, honoring, and responding to intuitive visions, there was a part of me that just wanted to forget about it. But one problem continued to nag me: how could I ask my students to experiment with intuitive vision

> *There is a light that shines beyond all things on earth, beyond the highest, the very highest heavens. This is the light that shines in your heart.*
>
> CHANDOGGYA
> UPANISHAD

if I didn't dare to do it myself? Everything lay dormant until I finally dared to call the National Parks Department in Washington, D.C., and follow a spiritual teacher's advice to call the woman who was destined to be my first D.C. partner, Betsy Stang.

Three Visions:
Partners Multiply Exponentially

The truth is that you must act on your visions in order to lay the groundwork for a collaborative intuitive vision. If you don't act on your personal vision, you will never meet the partners who are acting on theirs and want you on their team. When you do act and meet your partners in vision, another dimension of partnering exponentially enters your life. You know magic click, after magic click, after magic click.

In August 1993, when I called New Yorker Betsy Stang to see if she'd be interested in creating something in October in Washington, D.C., she instantly agreed and suggested I call a Washingtonian she had just met, David Berry. When the three of us began to talk on the phone, we slowly shared our visions with each other. The telling of our stories began to give collaborative visionary shape to our event. It would be an open-to-the-public, all-volunteer prayer vigil which would welcome a diverse community, respect the Indigenous nations, honor the principles found in the Iroquois Great Law of Peace and the U.S. Constitution, and pray and celebrate life on Earth. It would eventually be called A Prayer Vigil for the Earth.

Other members began to arrive with their visions. Arthur Lisch followed his intuition, flew three thousand miles to D.C., came to the Mall in the pouring rain to honor his commitment to get the Jefferson Pier realigned with the true cardinal points, and stumbled upon our first small gathering.[7] John Peterson, author of *The Road to 2015,*[8] had been called by "ideas" to work with the military on visions and strategies for the future. John arranged a meeting in the Pentagon, where Indigenous Wisdom Keepers presented their prophecies about this period in history. Amshatar Monroe, the founder of an organization called Sacred Space, was participating in a very sacred African three-to-seven-day ceremony when she was intuitively shown that her life's work is to bring the African and Native American people together. Sacred Space has offered its voices, music, drums, and traditions to hundreds of people at the

> *While I stood there, I saw more than I can tell, and understood more than I saw; for I was seeing in a sacred manner . . . the shape of all shapes as they must live together like one being.*
>
> BLACK ELK

Prayer Vigil. As partners continue to be drawn intuitively to the annual event, in addition to the sacred drums and ceremonies of Indigenous people (the host nations) the air rings out with chants of Jains, the blessings of Buddhists, the Lord's Prayer, the Muslim call to prayer, the Jewish *shofar*, the hum of people exchanging deeply with each other, and the laughter of children. Also, the event that Betsy had seen in her waking vision took place: Medicine people and people of all faiths and colors encircled the U.S.A. Capitol building in prayer.

This is one story of a successful intuitive vision in process. It brings joy, meaning, magic clicks, healing, celebration, and being "in the zone" to hundreds in the U.S.A. and around the world. There are many steps behind its creation. Knowing these steps can help you and your partners actualize an intuitive vision and, thereby, enter an amazing, shared "in the zone" space.

YOU AND THE STEPS BEHIND AN INTUITIVE VISION PROCESS

The first step in a successful collaborative intuitive vision process is for you to share with others what is sometimes a very personal vision. You may be

> The essence of ritual is that something done in the physical realm is related to the higher worlds.
>
> A'EVBEN SHIMON HALEVI

nervous, not sure your vision is "real" or meaningful. The only way you are going to find out if it is relevant is to bring it out in the open. If it is valuable, your community will intuitively recognize it and begin to work with it. Also, you don't tell your vision story to your community so that you can lead others in Joan of Arc fashion. You tell your vision story to (1) catalyze or uncover other community member's visionary experiences; (2) discover how all the visions present in your community relate to each other; and (3) help assemble the various pieces of visions together so that an overall collaborative vision is birthed. The final product aligns your personal vision and the collective vision.

For example, when Betsy told her vision of the illuminating eagle, I shared my ride on the back of an eagle, and we recognized that something larger than ourselves was at work. This provided incentive for weaving the puzzle pieces of visions, our own and many others, together in order to know what to do. As more visionary partners arrive, a new intuitive vision begins to emerge.

This brings up the second step in an intuitive vision process: community members need to leave the vision open. Your finished product needs to remain fluid, to be allowed to unfold along with time, and to emerge as you are engaged in the doing. This step is different from the traditional collective vision process used in organizational settings. There, usually everyone throws their ideas on the table, from these ideas a final vision takes shape, and then the group sets about to make it happen. In an intuitive collaborative vision process, the final vision is revealed in the doing rather than identified in the planning. This is because the behind-the-scenes convenor of an intuitive vision process is the individual and collective soul.

The Prayer Vigil community remains open in several ways. There no longer is an entity called "the Steering Committee." Everyone can belong; the new name of the same group is "the Organizational Committee." Also the program is left fluid with clusters of people being told that their offering will be sometime during a three-to-five-hour block. This allows the program to take shape organically based on the flow of events.

> *We have it in our power to begin the world all over again. . . . The birthday of a new world is at hand.*
>
> TOM PAINE

The third step in the intuitive vision process is to remember this: when you are intuitively called to a conference, party, vacation, place, or to more abstract activities such as working for the principles your nation represents, you arrive first and foremost as a soul. This means you fully show up (you're not wishing you were somewhere else at the time), you tell the truth to your fellow participants, and you pay attention to what is going on. You also recognize that sometime while you are present, you are likely to be reminded of what needs healing inside you. Your soul is always interested in that, and you remain alert to the opportunity.

At the Prayer Vigil, dancing, singing, praying, and celebrating in each other's cultures, languages, and traditions is healing. People have stumbled out of the Holocaust Museum on the Mall, run into a round dance for world unity, and burst into tears. Jewish people have prayed with Arabs; people of mixed heritage—African, Native American, and white—have participated in ceremonies from each tradition; tourists have rushed across the Mall to lift their national flag and chant, "May peace prevail in Moldovia. May peace prevail on Earth." These are healing images for more than the parties involved. And, of course, private one-to-one healing is happening as it quietly occurs.

The fourth and final step is to nourish your soul by following its advice after you arrive and while you are participating in an intuitive vision process. If you are moved to strike up a conversation with another, take a moment alone, or explore one activity over another, do so. And remember, it is not now, nor has it ever been, the number of people who gather with you which creates a successful soul community and a flourishing collaborative intuitive vision. Success is determined by the level of soul you and every other individual chooses to share while you are together. If you are shy or at a loss for what to say to others for any reason, begin by sharing what is meaningful to you. Since meaning is where intuition begins to operate fully, talking about meaning will jump-start your experience. Finally, don't be afraid to be yourself. A "like-souled" community (in contrast to a like-minded one) welcomes diversity because it recognizes that all members are committed to a common purpose: collective spiritual evolution.

Practicing these four steps moves the quality of your interactions with others in an intuitive vision context from one which is focused primarily on actualizing your vision to curiosity and investigation about the larger, collaborative intuitive vision. You and all the members of your team can employ all the skills of collaborative intuition that you've studied and experimented with in this chapter to undertake a treasure hunt. The gold that you seek is found in the creation of a diverse inner union, the joy of healing together, and the promise of soul-filled partnerships which multiply exponentially. When you have these things, you live "in the zone," know "the Force," and flow from one magic click to the next.

To begin calling your future partners intuitively, do the following meditation, which I have adapted from the work of Alice Bailey.

Exercise: Meditation, I am one with. . . .

1. Prepare yourself with the Basic Breath exercise on page 76.

2. Then say the following prayer to yourself or aloud:

I am one with my brothers and sisters and all that I have is theirs.
May the love which is in my soul pour forth to them.
May the strength of my soul lift and aid them.
May the thoughts which my soul creates reach and encourage them.

I am one with my brothers and sisters and all that they have is mine.
My I receive the love which their souls pour out upon me.
May I receive the strength of their souls which lifts and aids me.
May I receive the thoughts which their souls create as they reach and encourage me.

We are one with our brothers and sisters and all that we have is shared.
May the love of our collective soul pour forth unto all.
May the strength of our collective soul lift and aid all life.
May the thoughts which our collective soul creates reach and encourage
the wisdom of life everywhere.

3. Let yourself *be* the prayer, and when you are really comfortable, drop the words and radiate to all life on Earth and beyond.

4. Be silent for a few moments.

5. Then relax and feel yourself receiving the love of your brothers and sisters. Resonate with this love.

6. Conclude your meditation by saying the prayer again.

Final Exercise: Your Intuition To Do List

1. Complete the sentence, "Because I am accepting my soul's invitation to 'Partner Exponentially,' I already know to "attend a dance this weekend," "tell my work team my vision for our next project," "form a talking circle with my friends." List 5 to 10 things you know to do. When you've finished, read your list over, highlight the easiest activity which you believe would create a *"snow ball"* effect in your ability to partner exponentially, and do it. Record everything in your journal.

2. Go back and look at your Guiding Image for this chapter. How does it reflect what finding a "like-souled" community would be for you? Does it contain a hint about the best way for you to meet your partners? Identify the most interesting thing you learned about collaborative intuition in this chapter. How does your illustration relate to it? Record in your journal.

CHAPTER

CONNECT THE DOTS

Invitation Ten:

THE BIG PICTURE

When I was a child, every two years my family took long car trips to Iowa from our home on Long Island, New York. In those days, there were few interstate highways, and the trip seemed to take forever. To pass the time, my parents often purchased Connect the Dots coloring books for us. I remember what fun it was to guess what the final picture would be.

Of course, in later years the final picture looked obvious before I ever started to link the dots together. Intuitive development follows a similar course. In the beginning, it is difficult to discern how or if your intuition is not only correct, but if it is serving anything larger than yourself. As your intuitive life grows, you connect the dots of your life: you see the meaning behind events, and you evolve—alone and with others—a committed stance for going forward. A Big Picture view of what you already know to do starts to emerge. Over the years, I've learned from people that an effective way to explore this grand vista is through a personal, intimate, and loving relationship with the living Earth.

That's right. Many traditions teach that the Earth is alive. Most Indigenous cultures view life as a gift from the womb of the Earth, their

Mother. These people revere the Earth's teachings, and dialogue with Her inhabitants in order to gain wisdom. The idea that the Earth is alive also has European roots. The ancient Greeks worshipped the living Earth as the Goddess Gaia. Although the rise of industrial and scientific perspectives all but eradicated the belief in Gaia for many centuries, twentieth-century biologist Lewis Thomas raised the possibility again, observing:

> *The only myth that's going to be worth thinking about in the immediate future is one talking about the planet—not this city, not these people, but the planet and everybody on it.*
>
> JOSEPH CAMPBELL

What is the earth most like? . . . It is most like a single cell. . . . Aloft, floating free beneath the moist, gleaming membrane of bright blue sky, is the rising earth, the only exuberant thing in this part of the cosmos. . . . It has the organized, self-contained look of a live creature, full of information, marvelously skilled in handling the sun.

In the early 1960s, while pondering the many unlikely chemical interactions which take place continually on Earth, another scientist and inventor, Dr. James Lovelock, augmented and formalized Thomas's ideas, and proposed the Gaia Hypothesis, the theory that the Earth is alive. Although Lovelock's observations were drawn from the Big Picture perspective of science and technology, there are many comparable Indigenous, mystical, and spiritual conclusions that are reached with the Big Picture eyes and heart of the soul. The implication is that ordinary people who open their intuitive channels can access the extraordinary insights and wisdom that a relationship with the Earth offers.

This will come naturally to you because, as your intuitive skills expand, your sensitivity to larger and larger dimensions of the collective soul increases. You become more conscious of your part in the Earth community; you develop planetary consciousness and sensitivity to the heart,

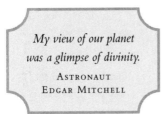

My view of our planet was a glimpse of divinity.

ASTRONAUT
EDGAR MITCHELL

mind, and consciousness or soul of the Earth.

The Earth responds to this by "talking" to you through the mechanics of the oversoul and the spiritual principle of overshadowing. To be overshadowed is to be impressed upon, beckoned from within, or "called." When the living Earth calls someone for an insightful chat, believe me, that person stops and listens. This chapter is filled with stories about such callings; these tales capture the impact of passion, power, purpose, and presence during people's interaction with the living Earth. Intuition is central to your Earth dialogues and reveals how your relationship with the Earth provides a Big Picture perspective for even small beings such as ourselves.

Before you explore the presence, passion, power, and purpose you can exchange with the Earth, select your Guiding Image for this chapter. This image provides guidance for connecting the dots of your reality in a new way so that a Big Picture perspective of your life on Earth emerges.

Exercise: Your Guiding Image for "Connect the Dots"

- Create a section of your Intuition Journal and label it "Chapter Twelve: Connect the Dots."

- Reach into your Image Vocabulary envelope and, without looking, pull out your guiding illustration for this chapter.

- Write the category of your image on the bottom of your selected page.

- Paste your illustration on this page.

THE EARTH: A SURPRISING PRESENCE

In the mid-1960s, Sy Safransky thought he knew what he was going to do with his life. He had taken great pride in the fact that, as a graduate of Co-

lumbia University's Graduate School of
Journalism, he had landed a job as a re-
porter for the seventh-largest afternoon
newspaper in the U.S.A., *The Long Island
Press.* But after a few years of work, Sy
had become disenchanted and needed a
break for many reasons. He decided on a
European vacation and, one day, lying
alone on a beautiful beach in southern
Spain, Safransky joined for the first time

> *I am part of the sun as
> my eye is part of me.
> That I am part of the
> earth my feet know
> perfectly, and my blood is
> part of the sea.*
>
> D. H. LAWRENCE

a generation of people who experimented with consciousness-expanding
substances. He was unprepared for what happened; he had not been led to
believe a direct encounter with the Earth's presence was possible with or
without substances. Nonetheless, here is how he describes what happened
next:

> I suddenly became aware that the whole Earth was a living,
> breathing, pulsating, throbbing entity. The world was alive. I
> saw the Earth breathe, I felt its rhythms, and discovered a
> missing part of myself. I felt the intuitive connection among
> all things. I knew that nothing was dead or inanimate. Basi-
> cally, from that moment forward I started to believe in God.

Safransky returned to the beach the next day to check out his impressions. Although the beach appeared normal again, Sy's consciousness
had been altered, and he began a deeper search for ways of re-creating his
experience without the use of substances. Unable to find information
about Oneness and mystical experiences in the mainstream periodicals he
was accustomed to reading, Safransky turned to spiritual literature, which
he had previously shunned. Eventually he left New York and joined a "return to the land movement" in North Carolina. The Big Picture view of
his life forever altered, Sy refocused his journalistic talents, founded the
monthly literary and spiritual magazine, *The Sun,* and has been one of its
editors for twenty-five years.

> *The exceeding beauty of the earth, in her splendour of life, yields a new thought with every petal.*
>
> RICHARD JEFFERIES

Business consultant Lee Johnson tells another story about a glimpse into the living Earth's presence. Taking an afternoon break during a business conference, Lee was loafing around on the grass and watching the clouds roll by. When an airplane came into view, she decided to follow it from one horizon to the next. An unusual feeling overcame her.

Although my body stayed on the grass, another part of me flew up and became the plane I had been looking at. I looked down and was awestruck at the beautiful Earth. Many different forms of transportation danced before my eyes, and all this activity looked like the Earth's blood stream transporting things from one corner to the next as they were needed. Next the electrical information flashing from one computer to the next around the world appeared to behave like the Earth's nervous system. The Earth was alive!

As I considered how irresponsible business could be toward the Earth who had just come alive for me, an immense sorrow began to flood me. I was immediately back on the grass. Tears swarm at the edge of my eyes. I longed for my community, which was primarily responsible for these transportation and computer activities, to practice sustainable, enduring, collaborative values for the sake of all life.

Following this vision, Lee felt ablaze with new purposes and immediately began sharing her vision with others. The role of business in the context of the living Earth was radically different from how she had previously perceived it, and, although she couldn't lay out a path before her at the moment, she knew she had peered into some aspect of her future.

Not all encounters with the Earth's presence will lead you to apply your talents in different directions as happened with Sy and Lee. Sometimes these encounters are just quietly helpful or sheer fun. The following unique example captures how two people's shared intuitive connections with one of the

> *How we are educated by children, by animals! We live in the currents of universal reciprocity.*
> MARTIN BUBER

Earth's creatures, dolphins, provided joy, assistance, and a fascinating glimpse into the potentials of interspecies visionary communication.

Lorrie, a friend and student, was in Florida with a group preparing for a chiropractic certification exam. Try as she might, she had not been able to get her intuition assignment (the love letter to herself you did in Invitation Number One) done before she got on the plane to Florida. In fact, completion had eluded her for weeks. Although the unfinished task nagged at her, Lorrie wasn't thinking about it at all as she and Julia, a colleague, decided to put studying aside and spend the afternoon swimming with dolphins. "Swimming with them was one of the best things I did in Florida. It was humorous, joyful, and even euphoric," Lorrie said. Swimming above the water, Julia described a particularly poignant moment she would never forget. One of the dolphins came right up to her, stared deeply into Julia's eyes, opened her jaws, and very, very softly closed her jaws around Julia's mask. The dolphin held Julia's mask in her mouth for a few minutes and then gently let it go. "It felt just like being held in someone's arms," Julia told me. After their swim, Julia and Lorrie returned to the motel to study, and their delightful play with the dolphins faded into the background.

Later that night, when they finished studying and turned off the lights to go to sleep, however, something odd began to happen.

"When I close my eyes," Lorrie dared to say aloud to Julia, "I see dolphins."

"So do I," Julia responded.

"They appear to be leaping in the night sky. The stars and the Milky Way are around them," Lorrie said.

> The first day we all pointed to our countries. . . . By the fifth day we were aware of only one Earth.
>
> ASTRONAUT SULTAN BIN SALMANAL-SAUD

"I see it, too. The whole ceiling has disappeared. We're living in the midst of the heavens with leaping dolphins all around," Julia shared.

"I've opened my eyes and I'm still seeing them!" Lorrie cried out.

When Julia opened her eyes and still experienced the same vision, they agreed to call out "Now!" whenever either of them saw blue lights or dolphins shooting across their heavenly ceiling. Their motel room echoed with simultaneous "Now's," a few isolated cries, and intermittent silence *all* night long. Amazingly, when daylight broke and the visionary dolphins disappeared, both women felt refreshed and ready for their exam. And, Lorrie had no trouble writing her love letter to herself later that day; it poured out of her in one sitting. The experience remains close to the hearts of both women.

Lee Johnson's and Sy Safransky's direct encounters with the Earth's presence invited them to connect the dots of their lives together in new ways, so a more authentic and creative picture of their contributions could emerge. Julia and Lorrie had a different experience; their direct encounter with the presence of one of the Earth's creatures led them to believe that, from a Big Picture view of their lives, everything was unfolding appropriately. Although the impact of the individual events was different, Sy, Julia, Lorrie, and Lee all received vivid, intuitive invitations to explore another level of reality—realities that you, too, can explore.

Obviously, the Earth has a Big Picture view of your life. Said differently, you, as a piece of the Earth, have within you a Big Picture view of your life. You have a right to pursue knowing what this part of you knows. One of the best ways to do so is to have conversations with the Earth. These conversations link your soul with the oversoul of the Earth. And, even if you don't believe something as big as the Earth could be aware of you, experiment with the possibility that your soul's communications are limited only to the extent of your imaginative willingness.

Exercise: The Earth and Presence

1. After you've read these directions, take your eyes off this book.

2. Look around you at everything. Drink your environment in.

3. Ask yourself what seems alive.

4. Love whatever evokes that aliveness right now. Continue to love it for at least 5 minutes.

5. At the end of the 5 minutes, have a "conversation" with whatever you loved.

6. When you feel your exchange is finished, take out your journal and record what has happened.

> *I am so absorbed in the wonder of earth and the life upon it that I cannot think of heaven and the angels.*
>
> PEARL S. BUCK

Of course, all these "conversations" do not have leaping visionary dolphins, or the pulsating Earth, or blood stream and nervous system insights. Students have reported profound intuitive conversations with the Earth and Her creatures while simply walking in the woods, glimpsing a flower, observing the shape of a mountain, hearing the cry of an animal, seeing the vastness of the ocean, or noting the industry of ants. As these students tell their enchanting stories to a group, they are transformed into modern scientific shamans—observers and healers whose simple images convey the wisdom of the vast, infinite Earth to the finite minds and hearts of their listeners.

Whether people recognize it or not, telling stories about intuitive encounters with the living Earth arises from the personal desire to heal our relationship with nature and our collective yearning to be whole. As a species, we desire an image of wholeness so much that we sent our emissaries, the astronauts, to photograph and send back to our ground-based eyes a picture of the blue-brown-wispy white Earth ball we call home. As they did for astronauts from around the globe, these pictures awaken great love in the hearts of many people.

> *One expects blues and greens, whites and browns, but the pinks, purples, yellows!*
>
> ASTRONAUT
> BRYON LICHTENBERG

EARTH PASSION: A MUTUAL AFFAIR

All too often people believe that their love for a favorite spot on Earth, or their joy at a sunset, or their peace in a beautiful meadow is strictly a one-way street. In such settings, they think to themselves, "I know beautiful feelings here, but the trees, rocks, animals, insects, and the Earth Herself don't know I exist unless I'm threatening them in some way." A close Native American friend widened my horizons and cured me of this attitude.

"Do you have a favorite spot of Earth near your home?" Jim asked.

Images of a nearby redwood fairy ring came instantly to my mind. Inwardly, I saw the twelve towering trees which ring the remains of a mother redwood, who must have been ten to twelve feet in diameter when she was alive. I was flooded by memories of the soft breeze which often blows up the hill onto my face, the smell of the loam, and the rustling sounds the ancient trees make as they sway in the wind. The fairy ring has one exception to its uniformity: a convenient break is on the east side. This forms a natural doorway for the morning sun.

"What feelings do you have when you go there, Sharon?" he asked.

"Warmth, love, family, joy, comfort, friendship, longevity, wisdom, laughter, sacrifice . . . ," the words came tumbling out.

"I want you to remember those feelings so well that you can feel them in your body right now."

When I reached that state and held the feelings strongly, I said so. The depth and intensity of Jim's voice surprised me as he said, "*Never* forget that as you yearn to have these moments with your spot, your spot yearns to have them with you. Love in nature is not just one-way; it is all around us, everywhere in us, and meant to be shared. When you start longing for your particular spot, know that your spot is longing for your particular presence. It's a mutual thing. The same is true for the joy which rushes you at the sight of an animal, or your pleasure in the sounds of a creek, or any other interaction you might have in nature. These are love and recognition 'greetings' between you and the Earth family. Treat them as such."

This window into passionate exchange among the Earth family had a profound effect on my subsequent experiences with nature. When I was joyfully startled by a hummingbird outside my kitchen door, I let the pleasure be mutual; the beauty of my blooming Christmas cactus on Memorial Day became a conversation between us about "right timing"; and I knew the fairy ring redwood trees loved my presence as I loved theirs.

> *A strange feeling of complete contentment suddenly overcame me when the module landed. The weather was foul, but I smelled Earth, unspeakably sweet and intoxicating.*
>
> ASTRONAUT
> ANDRIYAN NIKOLAYEV

Pondering from this perspective some of the intuition stories I'd been telling and hearing for years, I saw these stories in a completely different light. For example, one of my favorites is about Eleanor Friede, an editor for the publishing firm MacMillan. Eleanor loved East Hampton, Long Island—a town designed for living at the beach—and had taken a manuscript she'd been assigned with her to the shore for review. She knew that the submission, a children's story told from the perspective of an animal, had been rejected by twelve previous publishers. One can picture her settling down to read the story with the sound of crashing waves and calling seagulls in the background. The Earth setting was perfect.

After reading the manuscript, Eleanor had a radical intuition about the book: why not publish it as a book for adults rather than children? Her colleagues at MacMillan disagreed and nicknamed her commitment to do so "Friede's Folly." The year was 1970, and eventually Eleanor's intuitive perception triumphed. *Jonathan Livingston Seagull* went on to sell over ten million copies in twenty-seven languages.

Before I understood the importance of the Earth and its passionate pres-

> *While out in orbit,*
> *dreams were usually*
> *about Earth.*
>
> ASTRONAUT
> VLADIMIR LYAKHOV

ence, I viewed the seagulls flying around Eleanor when she read the manuscript as an interesting synchronicity. The Earth wasn't alive for me. But once my eyes opened to another perspective, I came to see that the passionate context in which Eleanor reviewed the manuscript played an important role in fostering her intuition. Eleanor's powerful intuitive flash propelled her push for publication, her advocacy for an adult market, and her determination in spite of her co-workers' derision. When your path is true, doubts which arrive from within or without are overcome. You know what to do.

Another example comes from the life of Dutch author Karen Blixen (Isak Dinesen) who wrote about the years she lived in Africa. In a well-known passage, Blixen asks aloud, "If I know a song of Africa—I thought—of the giraffe, and the African new moon lying on her back, of the plows in the fields, and the sweaty faces of the coffee-pickers, does Africa know a song of me?" Events of the last decade, particularly the internationally successful film based on her book *Out of Africa,* lead me to believe that the answer to her question is "yes."

Like human love affairs which last beyond the initial attraction, Earth love affairs have the potential to catalyze productivity. To turn this potential into reality, first identify something you yearn for but lack the passion, the inner fire, to actualize. You might focus on an activity or project (e.g., exercising, creating a Web page, saving to buy a new car), or, perhaps you are more interested in attaining a quality of being such as inner peace, self-esteem, or generosity.

Second, identify the place on the Earth you feel most passionate about at this time. Although it is wonderful if you can physically go there, this is not required. Your main criteria should be the amount of passion you feel for this spot. If you love a place enough to think about it often, keep photos of it around, or if it feels like home, this is the spot to choose. When you've identified the reason why you seek passion and the place on the Earth for which you have the greatest passion, you are ready to do the Earth and Passion exercise.

Exercise: The Earth and Passion

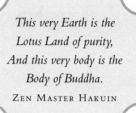

*This very Earth is the
Lotus Land of purity,
And this very body is the
Body of Buddha.*

ZEN MASTER HAKUIN

1. Take out your journal, date, and title a page "The Earth and Passion."

2. Draw two vertical lines down your page, creating three equal columns.

3. Label the first column "My Passion for the Earth," the second column "The Earth's Passion For Me," and the third "What Is Missing About My Passion?" Draw a line across the entire paper separating the titles from the columns.

4. At the top of the first column underneath the title, write the phrase "I love this spot on the Earth because . . ." As quickly as they come to mind, list all the reasons you love your identified spot.

5. At the top of the second column underneath the title, write the phrase "The Earth loves and is passionate about me because . . ." and then fill in the blank with the answers you put in column one. For example, if you've listed that you love your spot because of its spaciousness, you would fill in the blank in column two with "(The Earth loves and is passionate about me because . . .) *I am spacious.*" Go all the way down the column letting the Earth testify its love for you.

6. At the top of the third column, write the phrase "The passion that is missing for my project (activity or quality) is . . ." Then look down the attributes in column two and identify 1 to 3 attributes that you need to add to your passion to make your activity, project, or quality a reality. For example, if you filled in the blank in column two with the word *wildness,* you would know that you might not be able to accomplish your goal because you are not being wild enough.

7. On the next page in your journal, copy and complete the following sentence plugging in the answer(s) in column three.

"I will add _____ to my passion for my project by _____." E.g., "I will add *wildness* to my passion for my project by *doing something unexpected and spontaneous once a week.*"

8. When you've finished, thank yourself and the Earth for the illumination you received from this exercise and the presence of your mutual intuitive connection.

You can do this exercise several times a year, plugging in different projects and different sites. Often tears come to people's eyes when they are writing column two because they seldom recognize that what they love about the Earth, the Earth loves about them. In those moments, people realize what Jim meant when he said, "Earth Love is a two-way street."

The Power in Ordinary Earth

A spot where your passion flows eventually becomes your own private mecca or sacred site, a place where your spirit gets rekindled, reinforced, or redirected. While sacred sites have to do with particular spots on the Earth, Buddha showed us that an ordinary spot can become extraordinary. Beset within and without by overwhelming forces opposed to His spiritual evolution, He simply went outside and sat down under a tree. Buddha immortalized the moment by insisting that He would not get up until He achieved enlightenment.

To help him, He reached down, lay His hand flat on the Earth, and

BUDDHA CALLING THE EARTH

asked the Earth to bear witness to His attainment. In that moment, Buddha attained enlightenment. The Earth added Her power, bore witness to His pledge, and supported His liberation. This part of the story teaches us that the Earth is a powerful ally for ethical and spiritual evolution.

> *But ask now the beasts, and they shall teach thee; and the fowls of the air, and they shall tell thee.*
>
> THE BIBLE

The Old Testament also advises us to "call heaven and earth to witness" our activities and to "speak to the earth, and it shall teach thee." In the Christian tradition, Jesus' triumph was proceeded by being buried for three days in the womb of the Earth. It was there he surmounted death and gathered the power to resurrect life. Initiation rites in some cultures include partially burying the initiates in the Earth to help them gain mastery with issues of life and death. These teachings suggest you can turn to the Earth to receive a surge of power or communion with higher forces and that, following Buddha's model, even simple acts like sitting under a tree can yield rich rewards.

During a spring Board meeting for JFK University's Leadership and Management Program, I took a walk during lunch break with business consultant Tom Wright. Our conversation focused on the decision-making process—the various steps to good decisions, the role of intuition, and who we consulted for advice. Then Tom said something that really stuck with me: "Whenever I am facing a decision and don't know what to do, I ask the advice of the largest thing I know. . . ." Looking at me as if I should get his meaning, Tom took a long, long pause. I didn't break the silence. "If you don't know what that is, Sharon, look down at what is under your feet." It took me a few moments to understand what Tom was talking about. When I looked down, the Earth spread out before me, creeping through the sidewalk cracks, running its bright green grass border beside us, and wafting the fresh scents of spring everywhere. I was rushed with pleasure and instantly thought, "How great! Tom is speaking intuitively to the Earth and asking for Her power to help remind him of what he already knows to do."

You can ask the Earth for help, too. And the Earth's answers can pro-

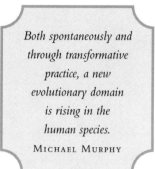

Both spontaneously and through transformative practice, a new evolutionary domain is rising in the human species.

MICHAEL MURPHY

vide the power necessary to actualize what's best for you. In fact, you may be already asking for the Earth's help without realizing it. For example, Karen placed a great deal of trust in her job as a marketing consultant and was thrilled with her advancement to a six-figure income. She and her partner settled into a wonderful house overlooking San Francisco Bay. Believing she was living a dream life, Karen didn't understand why about nineteen months later, she began suffering bouts of depression. She soon realized that her job, although lucrative, felt meaningless; her values were changing, and the products her company made were no longer aligned with them. On top of that she could never really relax at work and had to travel two to three weekends a month.

The one thing Karen had done since moving to San Francisco was walk its nature trails. The trails allowed her to disappear into nature and walk for miles, often without seeing another human being. As she walked, whether she realized it or not, Karen would intuitively ask herself, "What shall I do?"

It took some months, but eventually Karen joined a group where she could search job postings. One attracted her eye—"Wanted: The Regional Trails Association seeks a Director of Development with some marketing skills." She applied. The salary cut was large. Since her partner was still in graduate school, they were both concerned about the financial loss, but when they connected the dots of the Big Picture, it looked like the Earth itself was echoing an answer to the call Karen had uttered.

These stories demonstrate the Earth's ability to empower human beings to actualize their dreams and visions. The following exercise is designed to help you get in touch with the Earth's power.

Exercise: The Earth and Power

This work can be done for a group or organization. The group works as one to answer the questions.

> *Perhaps the earth can teach us . . .*
> PABLO NERUDA

1. In your journal, write down your first response to the question, "What is your Big Picture plan for your life?" (the organization's Big Picture plan)

2. Explore what you have written. (Discuss what you've written.)

3. Now go deeper inside yourself. If you have difficulty doing this, imagine getting inside an elevator and going to a lower, deeper level. When you get out, look around for deeper answers to the question in Step #1. Explore your answer.

4. Keep asking the question and exploring the answer from deeper and deeper levels until you arrive at an answer you find most appropriate. It should be a Big Picture plan you can get behind.

5. Go outside (individually or collectively). Find a spot you like and sit down on the ground. Place your hand on the Earth and ask Her for help and guidance with your Big Picture. (The entire group does this for one Big Picture they share.)

6. Record your activities in your journal and leave enough space so you can write *anything* of relevance in the coming six months.

   Option: Instead of putting your hand on the Earth, go for a walk, look down, and ask the Earth for help with your Big Picture insights.

Intentionally asking the Earth for Her consecration and empowerment creates a spiritual highway between yourself and the living Earth. This soul highway can produce such miraculous changes in your life that you may come to understand why author Pablo Coehlo says in his

> *Now I know why I'm here. Not for a closer look at the moon, but to look back at our home, the Earth.*
>
> ASTRONAUT
> ALFRED WORDEN

book, *The Alchemist,* "The boy reached through to the Soul of the World, and saw that it was part of the Soul of God and his own soul. And that he, a boy, could perform miracles." Often these miracles have to do with purpose.

PURPOSE AND LIFE ON EARTH

Purpose, whether it is to develop one's spiritual dimensions or achieve a professional goal, is a thread woven into the chemicals of life. We are seekers of meaning. We search the heavens for its secrets, excavate layer upon layer of the Earth's crust to know its history, develop rich traditions which set a context for our lives, and surround ourselves with the pageantry of ancestral generations. We look for the purpose behind our life on Earth.

But if we turn this description around for a moment, perhaps it is the Earth who has Her purpose, Her meaning, in choosing us for life. After collecting many intuitive stories, I've come to believe that this is true in general and particularly true for some individuals. When the Earth issues intuitive calls, the dialogue between the Earth and the individual or group is not a gift of personal insight, guidance, companionship, or joy, but rather a vocational call to work directly on behalf of the Earth. These requests for help are often so direct that I've occasionally felt like the Earth is calling certain individuals much like the body calls on white blood cells when it feels threatened.

For example, in 1985, when anthropologist Dr. Lisa Faithorn was on a teaching trip in Kashmir, she experienced a strong Earth calling. Taking a break from her heavy lecture schedule, Lisa visited a beautiful estate on the shore of Dal Lake. Surrounded by apple orchards, sweet-smelling flowers, and a sense of serenity and peace, she settled into sleep that first night profoundly grateful for the quiet seclusion. Her sleep, however, was far from restful.

At dawn I wrenched myself awake from a vivid dreamlike experience during which I heard and also became the trees all over Kashmir crying out in agony at having been cut down. My head ached and I felt like an ax was lodged deeply in it. The dream image wracked me with sobs and I couldn't stop crying for some time.

> *For the first time I saw the horizon. It was accentuated by a thin stream of dark blue light—our atmosphere. I was terrified by its fragile appearance.*
>
> ASTRONAUT
> ULF MERBOLD

Later Lisa learned that much of the area she had not seen was recently clear cut because of increasing demands for wood and agricultural land. Her telepathic communication with the trees of Kashmir moved Lisa from an abstract awareness of "environmental problems" to acute sensitivity to deep ecology issues. Today she is a radical ecologist who urges all of us to tell each other our ecostories—stories of childhood memories of the Earth, tales of environmental loss, and visions and revelations the Earth has given us.

Sue Conklin has a similar ecostory to tell. One cool spring day Sue went for a walk. The diagnosis of breast cancer four months earlier had forever altered her fast pace and fiercely independent life. After two surgeries and thirty radiation treatments, she was about halfway through her chemotherapy when her medical oncologist told her, "You need to keep your bones strong. Go find someplace quiet, out in nature, and just walk." So, there she was in a beautiful, dew-laden park she'd never noticed before, even though it was only six miles from her house.

Facing cancer alone had been an enormous challenge for Sue, so it was not surprising that when she came upon a soft, inviting, mossy knoll in one of the park's clearings she collapsed on the ground. "What is happening to me?" she cried. "I feel weak, sick, frightened, angry, and sad. My body is so full of toxins that it has become a stranger to me." Still focused on her disconnected and out-of-balance feelings, Sue was startled by the sound of honking geese as they mounted into the sky. Looking up,

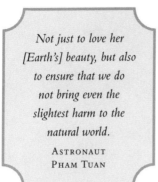

Not just to love her [Earth's] beauty, but also to ensure that we do not bring even the slightest harm to the natural world.

ASTRONAUT
PHAM TUAN

she saw the sun breaking through the clouds and then heard a voice say: "What is happening to you is happening to me and it has to stop."

Sue sat quietly for a moment, uncertain who had spoken to her and then heard it again: "What is happening to you is happening to me and it has to stop . . . it has to stop now."

The voice, gentle yet stern, was delivering a crystal-clear message. The moment Sue realized that the speaker was the Earth, she felt a huge surge of energy coming into her through the ground below. In a flash, she knew she would beat the cancer! She felt connected with the Earth who could comfort her because She knew all too well the pain of having poison pollute Her body. Her consciousness changed forever, Sue immediately volunteered her organizational talents to non-profit groups.

Stories such as Sue's and Lisa's have given birth to a new branch of psychology: ecopsychology. According to ecopsychologist and author Theodore Roszak, a psychology which implies that "the soul might be saved while the biosphere crumbles" is like a therapist trying to help a concentration camp victim adjust to what happened without acknowledging that the situation he or she was in was fraught with madness. Ecopsychology practices psychology as if the whole Earth matters, believing that intuitive experiences such as Sue's are not simply a metaphor for personal challenges but are deeply related to our connection with the Earth. In short, if our treatment of the Earth is contributing to the destruction of many species (including the possibility of our own), we must recognize that the Earth, like any other living organism, will be issuing intuitive calls on behalf of Her own wellness. Living things pursue life.

Joanna Macy, author of *World As Lover, World As Self,* asks participants in her workshops to intuit what a plant or animal might be feeling when threatened and to give voice to the creature's desire for life. Exercises such as these awaken people's sense of how their particular purpose fits into the Big Picture of life on Earth. Working by yourself or in a group, do the following exercise to get in touch with your purpose and to see how intuition might help you fit that purpose into a larger Earth pattern.

> *The earth is us, it is not ours. We are earthlings.*
>
> AMIDON & ROBERTS

Exercise:
The Earth and Purpose

1. Taking with you your journal, a pen, and a highlighter, go out in nature and find a spot to sit.

2. Look around your surroundings and find one thing that strikes you as beautiful—a leaf, a rock, a branch, bark, a view, the sunlight.

3. Name your object in your journal and then list everything you find beautiful about it.

4. Imagine for a moment that this beautiful thing was about to be unnecessarily destroyed and disappear forever.

5. Fill your chest with love for your object. Become its advocate. Imagine the purpose of your life is to defend your object's right to live. Write everything you would say to defend your object in your journal.

6. Highlight two or three of the best defenses you've just listed.

7. Now look your object over. How does it symbolize your Big Picture plan? (If you don't know what that is, look back at what you named in step #4 of the exercise entitled "The Earth and Power," on page 315.) For example, if your object was a rock, you would look to see if it has many bumps on it, indicating that your Big Picture plan is complex. If your object was a leaf, you would look to see if your plan has many intricate pathways. Use your imagination.

8. Now look back at step #6 of this exercise. Imagine your Big Picture plan was under attack by some part of yourself. Defend your plan with the same or similar arguments you used in step #6 to defend your object. This helps you to understand that your Big Picture

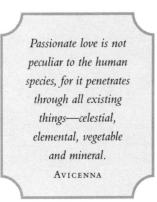

Passionate love is not peculiar to the human species, for it penetrates through all existing things—celestial, elemental, vegetable and mineral.

AVICENNA

plan also could become extinct if you don't protect it.

9. Finally, ask yourself how your plan serves the Earth.

10. Record everything in your journal.

This last exercise brings together the presence, passion, power, and purpose you've been working with. The presence of your object's beauty calls to you; it awakens a passion within you; it empowers you to take a stand; and it provides a moment of purpose for your presence. From a Big Picture perspective, the circle is complete—your presence, passion, power, and purpose have been met and augmented by interacting with the oversoul or collective soul of the Earth. Only one thing remains: to claim your tribal affiliation with the Earth community and, as a result, acquire a new level of heart.

ONE TRIBE, ONE HEART

The present level of human inner and outer development does not foster sustainable principles for our global community. As author Elisabet Sahtouris points out in *Biology Revisioned,* "We seem to intuit and practice [sustainable principles] reasonably well at the family level. Not many people starve three of their children to overfeed the fourth, for example, or beautify one corner of their garden by destroying the rest of it." Yet, when we come to consider the Earth as a whole, we do not intuit life as a family. Developed nations continue to gobble resources and spew out toxic pollutants at near-lethal rates while the rest of the world struggles to obtain the basic necessities of life. What has happened to our ability to intuit better ways of behaving?

In the first chapter of this book, pages 25–29, I talked about the

seven-level chakra model of human
evolution and spiritual development.
Without conscious awareness and development, psychic and other experiences located in the solar plexus or third
level can be based on power, emotional

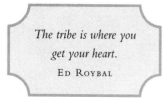

*The tribe is where you
get your heart.*
ED ROYBAL

satisfaction, greed, control, fear of loss, domination, and win/lose interactions. Unfortunately, it appears that the majority of humanity relates to
the Earth from this level of development. Therefore, the Earth is approached from the same perspective: What can we take from the Earth?
How can we control Her? What ways can She serve our material interests? Essentially, consciously or unconsciously, our inner image of the
Earth resides in the solar plexus level. When faced with challenges, responses to this inner-world attitude can lead to stockpiling food while
others go hungry, to paying poor wages in order to increase profits, and
to minimal care for others, if it detracts from what we could have for ourselves. As Sahtouris says, "We don't see ourselves as family." We don't have
our tribe; our inner psychic riches get shunted off into self-protection.

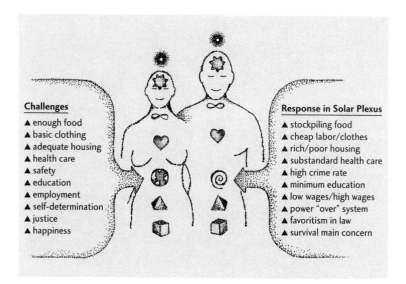

Challenges

▲ enough food
▲ basic clothing
▲ adequate housing
▲ health care
▲ safety
▲ education
▲ employment
▲ self-determination
▲ justice
▲ happiness

Response in Solar Plexus

▲ stockpiling food
▲ cheap labor/clothes
▲ rich/poor housing
▲ substandard health care
▲ high crime rate
▲ minimum education
▲ low wages/high wages
▲ power "over" system
▲ favoritism in law
▲ survival main concern

> *Only when I saw it from space, in all its ineffable beauty and fragility, did I realize that humankind's most urgent task is to cherish and preserve it for future generations.*
>
> ASTRONAUT
> SIGMUND JAHN

Challenges and Responses: Inner Image of the Earth Focused in the Solar Plexus

The heart is missing. When you consciously choose to move your inner image of the Earth from the solar plexus level to your heart, you automatically add compassion, love, and empathy to the mix. Intuitive pathways spring open. You are in soul-to-soul connection with others and aware of mutual interdependency. Responses to world challenges quite naturally shift from just self-interest to include collective interest. Your thoughts and actions contribute to what's good for the whole; you value basic food, housing, and clothing needs for all; you invest in cooperation; and you look forward to collaboration (see diagram).

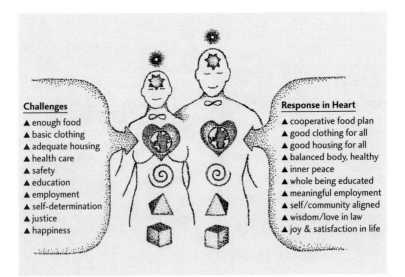

Challenges

▲ enough food
▲ basic clothing
▲ adequate housing
▲ health care
▲ safety
▲ education
▲ employment
▲ self-determination
▲ justice
▲ happiness

Response in Heart

▲ cooperative food plan
▲ good clothing for all
▲ good housing for all
▲ balanced body, healthy
▲ inner peace
▲ whole being educated
▲ meaningful employment
▲ self/community aligned
▲ wisdom/love in law
▲ joy & satisfaction in life

Challenges and Responses: Inner Image of the Earth Focused in the Heart

In this state, your intuition keeps you connected to a larger purpose through contact with the collective soul and "talks" with the Earth. You think and act like a tribal member. Although you may still face personal and collective

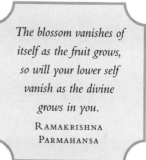

The blossom vanishes of itself as the fruit grows, so will your lower self vanish as the divine grows in you.

RAMAKRISHNA
PARMAHANSA

struggles, you are not alone, and your life has meaning. You have heart.

Gary Zukav describes this change well when he says:

> As the human species awakens to itself as a collection of immortal souls learning together, care for the environment and the earth will become a matter of the heart, the natural response of souls moving toward their full potentials.

When your heart responds like this, it is enlightened. It "gives light, provides clear views, or illuminates," and your life is illuminated from within. Because your heart has become an organ of perception, your future path is clear. You know what to do for yourself, your family, your nation, your Earth tribe, and your world.

This type of heart can, according to philosopher Dane Rhudyar, create what he calls "theosynthesis," a type of human photosynthesis. In photosynthesis, plants transform sunlight into food and in the process make a tremendous contribution to the Earth's atmosphere. Rhudyar's theosynthesis performs a similar function: the spiritual light emanating from the Source (God) is transformed by souls just as physical sunlight is transformed by plants. Rhudyar believed that the power released in this theosynthesis process (which would include the light of intuition) meant that we, too, like green plants, could change the spiritual atmosphere of the Earth. If this is true, one of the most important contributions you can

> When you let intuition have its way with you, you open up new levels of the world. Such opening-up is the most practical of all activities.
>
> EVELYN UNDERHILL

make is to move your inner image of the Earth to your heart and seek the heart's enlightenment.

Philosophy isn't the only place which may offer insight and encouragement for such behavior. The scientific research of psychologist Roger Nelson at Princeton University, Dick Bierman at the University of Amsterdam, and Dean Radin, author of *The Conscious Universe,* indicates that groups of people, from a small group to billions watching a live television broadcast, can affect the physical world. Using the impact on random-number generators (a machine that generates chance events) as a measurement, Radin's and the others' research results suggest that, when people's attention is coherently focused on things like Holotropic Breathwork, the Academy Awards, or the Opening Ceremonies of the Olympics, the odds *against* chance get higher. In other words, your collective attention matters; it impacts reality-moving events from a random state to one of greater coherence even if the group is small. Called the "field consciousness" effects, Dean states that these experiments also imply that there is a fundamental interconnectedness among all things, including individual and "mass minds."

While it is impossible from the results of these scientific RNG experiments to say with certainty that holding a loving image of the Earth in your heart will make a contribution to positive change, we can wonder what would happen if many, many people chose to lovingly hold the Earth in their hearts either all at once or separately. If it were to make a difference, you can envision a day in the not-too-distant future when Rhudyar's concept of theosynthesis, transforming the spiritual atmosphere of our planet like plants transform their physical atmosphere, would be actualized by large numbers of people and would validate through modern scientific research the value of our Oneness.

This chapter's concluding Earth Meditation, which comes from the practice of Dr. Lorrie Eaton, will help you develop your illuminated heart skills, deepen your intuitive connections with the Earth, and integrate the presence, passion, power, and purpose you have encountered throughout this chapter.[1]

Exercise:
The Earth Meditation

1. Using your imagination, place an inner image of the Earth in your heart. Fill your heart with love for the Earth. If you find this difficult, think of a place on the Earth that you love.

2. Put your hand on your heart and say the following invocation.

> *It is not primarily the unfoldment of intuition which is important. It is the establishment of a potent group interplay, intercommunication, and group relation so that an emerging world unity can be seen in embryo [that makes intuition important.]*
>
> ADAPTED FROM
> ALICE BAILY

"Let this beautiful planet be filled with loving kindness.

Let this beautiful planet be well and healthy.

Let this Mother Earth be filled with great joy, peace and understanding.

Let this beautiful planet, our home, be filled with good will and the will-to-love.

And so it shall be."

3. Repeat these words as often as you'd like, as you would a chant.

4. When you are thoroughly relaxed, focus on the love you feel in your heart.

5. Record your reactions to this meditation in your journal.

Remember that while you are doing this meditation, your intuition is connecting the dots of a very Big Picture, a view of which can only be had from beyond the stars, from the place where we all came from.

Final Exercise: Your Intuition To Do List

1. Complete the sentence, "Because I am accepting my soul's invitation to 'Connect the Dots' of my life, I already know to . . ." List 5 to 10 things you know to do such as "talk to the Earth tomorrow," "visit the ocean," "find a special spot in my yard or apartment that I want to make a sacred spot." Remember you can choose simple things such as "taking a walk," "thinking of your favorite place on Earth," or "remembering the Earth's passion and power." When you've finished, read your list over, highlight the simplest activity which *will reveal the soul's long, large view of life,* and do it. Record everything in your journal.

2. Go back and look at your Guiding Image for this chapter. How does it capture passion, purpose, power, and presence? What specific part(s) of your image are about your capacity to give to the Earth? Does your illustration make you think of a love song you'd like to sing to the Earth? Record in your journal.

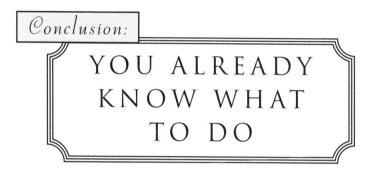

Conclusion:

YOU ALREADY KNOW WHAT TO DO

JUST YOUR IMAGINATION

In 1991, I spoke before five hundred people for the first time at the "Emerging Perspectives in Education: Opening the Intuitive Gate" conference sponsored by JFK University and the Center for Applied Intuition. I had designed an informative and entertaining speech but was not satisfied with its conclusion. Frankly, it was flat. I wanted something that conveyed the grandest principles of intuition I knew, something which would inspire us all. After much restless pondering, I made a list of the things that inspired me the most about intuition. When I did so, I discovered what I already knew to do. I came up with a mini-multimedia, ten-minute closing comprised of three parts: music, slides, and a reading.

The music was easy; I chose the victory song from the movie *Chariots of Fire*. The slide master who was serving all the presenters had a fader, so I was able to fade each of my slides into the next. The slides were graduated so that they began with grand pictures of the Universe—spectacular nebulae, the Milky Way, star bursts—and led to smaller and smaller areas of the Universe until you observed a tiny ball in the distance. The next three slides brought that ball, the Earth, closer and closer. The final images kept the Earth in the foreground and brought a beautiful, lotus-

> *I tell you these things, not because you know them not, but because you know them. All living instruction is nothing but corroboration of intuitive knowledge.*
>
> COVENTRY PATMORE

type blossom behind Her in such a way that the Earth was situated in the center of the lotus.

While the music and slides played, I read an imaginative description of what intuition can bring to a human being and the human family, beginning with the simple act of an individual vowing to live an intuitive, soul-infused life through graduated steps until humanity had achieved Universal Consciousness. I concluded my remarks by saying that intuition activates and contributes to the power which can bring humanity's seemingly impossible dreams of dynamic peace, creative health, and simple unity for all into reality. I said that, not because I believed that intuition was the only way we have to help us achieve these things, but because I was, and still am, convinced it was a forgotten, misused, misunderstood, or underdeveloped way of life in Western culture.

When my talk was over, people applauded profusely. They may have even stood up. I don't remember. What I remember was the pin-drop silence that blanketed the room when the applause died down. Not knowing how to interpret the silence, I immediately wished Jerry, my former husband, was sitting in the front row, cheering me on, and helping me through this moment. I felt all alone as I stood motionless in the front of the room for what seemed like forever.

Forgetting the teachings I believed in so much, I responded to my confusion by bolting for the bathroom. I hid out, afraid I might have gone too far, been too grandiose, or too revealing. Previous years of dedication to my field with few people interested or listening washed over me. I felt nauseated. Had I just blown it? Should I have chosen a safer, more traditional ending? Was I off on some imaginary tangent?

As I came out of the bathroom, a person from the audience came up to me and said, "I am so glad you are a woman." I thanked her, believing that she was saying something important, but I wasn't sure what. The wonderful woman who at the last moment had lent me the lotus slide (she had taken the picture) came to me and we hugged with tears in our eyes. I was beginning to think people had been touched; they had seen the potential of intuition's gifts. About twenty minutes had elapsed since the finish of my talk, and Irv, a JFK University friend who was managing the book store sales,

There will come a time when you believe everything is finished. That will be the beginning.

LOUIS L'AMOUR

came up to me and said, "Sharon, if you had a book, we'd already be sold out." I laughed and thanked him for the compliment. I had no plans for writing a book. I still hadn't started my Ph.D., one of the reasons I'd come to California.

I am sharing this story with you in part to let you know that, even after years of work with intuition, doubts can assail you. You can ask yourself, "Is this my intuition or is it just my imagination? Do I really know what to do?" Yet, even in the midst of such questions, the soul is laying seeds for the future. Ten years later I am writing the book Irv was telling me about. Years ago intuitive time used Irv's words to chart a course for me which today looks as natural as sunrise.

Intuitive time is doing this for you, too. Maybe it is has already happened today. Perhaps your soul sprinkled the seeds of your future in some side comments over morning coffee, or in last night's dreams, or in newspaper articles you read this morning, or in flashes of insight on the way to work, or in meditation.

To experience what I mean, look back at the first image you pasted in your journal. This image symbolized your intuitive journey with this book. What does it mean to you now? How does this image capture your present relationship with your intuition? What did this image tell you about your intuitive journey months before you completed it? Did it predict anything in particular? Does the image have one aspect which points to the role intuition will play in your future? Finally, look back at each chapter's Guiding Image page to see which category (passion, purpose, power, or presence) was represented the most. How does this category relate to your intuitive journey? Assume that this category is part of your intuitive long suit whether you realize it or not. What does this category

> *Verily, the hour is coming . . . that every soul may be recompensed for its efforts.*
>
> MOHAMMED

say about the intuitive journey you have just completed and your future intuitive life? Name one specific way this category will help you in the future.

Intuition is famous for pulling the threads of seemingly unrelated skills or insights together in order to produce new perspectives. Creative artists, political geniuses, inventors, healers, and people in ordinary situations experience this when they are alert to intuition's presence. This process occurs because the soul collects itself; it does not scatter. When you embrace the intuitive world, the things you do and say are not scattered randomly, but in deep connection with your soul's Big Picture perspective of your life. As you've seen, when you awaken, the soul's presence, purpose, passion, and power become an intrinsic part of your life. All you need to remember, *to know* without question, is that intuition is real; it's not just your imagination.

Now

Rumi Jalamudi, an inspirational thirteenth-century Sufi mystic and poet recognized the problem people face as they wonder if messages from their inner world are real or imaginary. He penned these words to address some of our concerns.

> *This we have now is not imagination.*
> *This is not grief or joy,*
> *Not a judging state, or an elation,*
> *or a sadness.*
> *Those come and go.*
> *This is the Presence that doesn't.*

Not only is intuition not just your imagination; it's not all instinct, limited to psychic experiences, a mere curiosity, a passing fad, fast intellect, or only the province of the mystic. Intuition is now, and always will be, the calling card of your soul, the voice of your Presence.

> *The Lord bless you and keep you; The Lord make his face to shine upon you, and be gracious unto you.*
>
> THE BIBLE

In knowing this, you can come home to yourself. You can come home to who you already know you are: an individual and, together, a community of immortal souls. Although this particular journey to intuition is coming to an end, the journey to a lifetime of application is about to begin. We are here on Earth to "play in the fields of the Lord." If we forget who we are, we play rough, we harm ourselves, others, and the Mother Earth who gives us life. When we remember who we are, though, we know intuitively that there is a better way. We commit ourselves, one by one, community by community, nation by nation, to finding that way. This intention is rock solid within us, individually and collectively, and *nothing* can deflect us from it. You turn to intuition and seek guidance for your part in the Big Picture. You already know what to do.

Now is the time.

NOTES

1. The names of some individuals and/or small details of the stories in this book have been changed to protect privacy.

CHAPTER ONE: INTUITION: TELL ME MORE

1. Author Jagdish Parikh's book *Intuition; The New Frontier of Management* contains a thorough discussion of the different ways the word "intuition" is used.
2. Whitehead's book is *Science and the Modern World*.
3. Not all scientists accept the neat delineation of the left/right brain theories. Others go beyond hemisphere studies studying the relationship of brain to mind and vice versa.
4. Part of the scientific community believes that mind—whose definition in Buddhist philosophy is close to our understanding of soul—is the same as the brain. Other parts of the scientific community believe that mind (soul) is not identical with brain but intimately connects the two. Nobel laureate in neuroscience Roger Sperry even suggests that a person's awareness or consciousness has a causal effect on reality.
5. *The Portable Jung*. Translated by R. F. D. Hull, from *The Collected Works*, Chapter 8, "Psychological Types."
6. Psychiatrist Arthur Deikman discusses this in his book *The Observing Self*.
7. *The Portable Jung*. Translated by R. F. C. Hull, from *The Collected Works*, Chapter 8, "Psychological Types."
8. Many systems refer to levels beyond these seven, but for our purposes we will focus on the traditional seven. If you want to know more, see Kirpal Singh, *The Crown of Life*.

9. The courageous scientists who study this phenomena, parapsychologists, have handled misconceptions around the word psychic by creating the broader and more useful term, *psi,* for the unknown factor which appears in psychic or intuitive experiences. Parapsychologists can now refer to a psi experiment, psi experience, or, simply, psi itself. The term is neutral, making no statement about what psi is, where psi comes from, how it operates, its interaction with spirituality, or its ethical component.

10. This discussion of Psychological/Religious-Centered models is far from complete. Christian mystics, such as Teresa of Avila, Evelyn Underhill, and St. John of the Cross, all recount the illuminated, interior world of beauty and wisdom.

11. Black Elk's book *The Sacred Pipe* is a great resource for understanding the seven spiritual rites of the Olgala Sioux.

12. This term describes living daily life in honor of Native spiritual teachings.

13. In this book, Fools Crow provides precise details on how to make yourself a "hollow bone" and many other prayers and ceremonies you can do to enhance your service.

CHAPTER TWO: PREPARATION FOR YOUR JOURNEY

1. This is an excellent resource for developing intuition and for keeping up with what is new in the field. See Resources page for how to contact them.

2. Author Louisa Rhine, author of *Hidden Channels of the Mind,* divides her massive collection of anecdotal psychic and intuitive stories into four categories. Symbolic forms of communication is one of them.

3. The psychologist C. G. Jung called events such as Verna finding a picture of a woman's head covered with snakes in a relatively small pool of magazines "synchronicities." He defined these as the "acausal connecting principle" which links people with matter or events.

CHAPTER THREE: JUST SAY "YES"

1. This story is told by James McClendon, Jr., in his book *Biography as Theology.*

2. Neale Donald Walsch's three books, *Conversations With God,* Book 1, Book 2, and Book 3, are excellent resources for establishing a direct, personal relationship with God.

CHAPTER FOUR: OPEN YOUR SENSES

1. This statement reinforces Dr. Goleman's findings about gut knowledge, which I discussed in the introduction. For more information, see *Emotional Intelligence* by Dr. Goleman.

2. This center is called the third eye or ajna center in the chakra system and the latifa *khafiya* or the luminous black latifa in the Sufi system.

3. Murphy and George Leonard founded an educational program, the Integrative Transformative Practice, for people to engage in transformational practices. The group can be contacted at P.O. Box 609, Mill Valley, CA 94942.

4. Joan Kenley's book *Voice Power* provides good explanations for the power of the intuitive power centers and speaks directly to how soul embodiment brings life and power to the voice. (Only available at 1-800-820-2010.)

5. You can find more information about these topics in *Intuition* magazine, issue #10, in an article entitled "Hearing the Unspoken in Japan."

6. Psychiatrist Jule Eisenbud has an important account of his anecdotal research with sending intuitive messages to two patients in his book *Parapsychology and the Unconscious*. He humorously entitled the chapter "How to Influence Practically Anybody (but Fellow Scientists) Extrasensorially at a Distance."

7. Psychological understandings of where this voice comes from include the supra-conscious or unconscious self.

8. This story comes from the "First Person" section of *Intuition* magazine, issue no. 12.

9. For information on these cruises, contact Dreamtime Cruises & Tours, 2911 Red Bug Lake Rd., Ste. 800, Casselberry, FL 32707.

CHAPTER FIVE: CULTIVATE SILENCE

1. Intuitive fitness is not a substitute for physical fitness. Your intuitive capacity is di-minished when you have excess toxins running around in your body due to lack of exercise or poor eating.

2. From *In the Zone* by Murphy and White. This book has a wonderful collection of anecdotal stories.

3. Confucius said this about the intuitive connections of a spiritual being: "A supe-rior [spiritually motivated] man abides in his room. If his words are well spoken, he meets with assent at a distance of more than a thousand miles. . . . If the su-perior man abides in his room and his words are not well spoken, he meets with contradiction at a distance of more than a thousand miles. . . . Must one not, then, be cautious?"

4. Some people argue that intuition is nothing more than very fast intellect. This completely obliterates the notion that intuition is a legitimate way of knowledge in its own right.

5. An example of this is found in the Hebrew tradition of the ark of the covenant. The ark contained the Shekhinah, the feminine face of God which would de-stroy anyone who accidentally touched it. Only the spiritually prepared were able to have a direct encounter and survive.

6. This meaning was taught to me by one of my elders, Ann Dosher.

7. Another style of meditation has people follow each different object as they enter their consciousness (you do not go back to object #1) until the people go beyond the endless stream and enter deep silence. The best simple book on meditation I know is Lawrence LeShan's *How to Meditate*.

CHAPTER SIX: NURTURE JOY

1. Three excellent books on intuition and your health are: *The Anatomy of Spirit* by Caroline Myss, *Awakening Intuition* by Mona Lisa Schulz, and *The Intuitive Healer* by Marcia Emery.

2. To me these addictions are coming from ego deficiency, both representing the need to be loved. One validates himself by the "good feeling" (this means I'm a good person who is doing things right); the other receives validation by working so hard, therefore, being a "good child."

3. Helen Palmer's book *The Enneagram* has tremendous insights as to how people employ intuition to serve their psychological fixations or deficiencies.

4. When you realize how interconnected events are, you no longer assume that a series of synchronicities signals right action. You know that your relationship with everything is capable of bringing forward ties at any time. Therefore, your decisions are based on many factors, and you don't give synchronicities more weight than other things.

5. This theory is based on the teachings of H. Almaas and has a strong Sufi influence.

6. A discussion about this appears in Evelyn Underhill's *Practical Mysticism*.

7. This story comes from *The Bhagavad Gita*.

8. An advanced technique of this work is to breathe in your area of concern and hurt, hold it inside you in an internal vessel of joy, and then exhale it transformed into joy.

Chapter Seven: Set Time Free

1. An excellent book for relating to time differently is Peter Russell's *Waking Up in Time*.

2. When an Indigenous spiritual leader was invited to invoke prayer as part of the opening ceremonies at a large global event with hundreds of environmentalists represented, he was surprised that the event "just started," stating, "In my way, everyone in the gathering is quiet collecting himself or herself until we all 'feel' the presence of Spirit and, therefore, right with each other. Only then can we start anything. How can anything succeed without this?"

3. Other explanations exist for this. Bohr's theories suggest that at a subatomic level things come into existence only when they are observed. Therefore, you cannot think of them as separate entities, but rather as part of an interconnected field which existed before observation. The implications of these ideas, if one can justifiably extrapolate their principles to day-to-day life, are that events in your life may also come into existence as you observe them. Your interpretation of them, therefore, becomes relevant. For books which help the lay person understand these ideas, see Gary Zukav's classic, *Dancing Wu Li Masters,* and Michael Talbot's *The Holographic Universe*.

4. This exercise is an adaptation that Frances Vaughan, author of the excellent book *Awakening Intuition*, led at the Intuition in Business Visions and Decisions Conference in Europe in 1988.

5. Parapsychologists, or psi scientists, have been working with experiments to determine this for decades. The most common experiments employ a random number generator whose actions people attempt to influence mentally.

6. From Murphy and White's *In the Zone*.

7. In *Black Elk Speaks,* Black Elk describes a very similar experience when he charged a line of soldiers at the Battle of Wounded Knee. It was only after the

charge, when he was on safer territory that he felt a wave of fear for being shot. Within a few minutes, he was shot.

8. Many years ago Dr. Penfield discovered, when operating on a patient, that if you touched certain places in the frontal lobe, the patient would have the sensation of a déjà vu. Considering that the frontal lobe plays an important part of intuitive decision-making, it might be a fruitful area for future research on the mechanics of intuition. Knowing the mechanics does *not* imply the experience is reducible to only brain functioning.

9. There is an inverse relationship between external (objective) time and internal (subjective) time.

10. As your spiritual mastery develops, the time differential between what you perceive in the future and its actualization can greatly diminish. For example, an acquaintance of mine who had lived in an ashram in India for many years discovered when she left that all she had to do was visualize something vividly (fancy jobs, cars, homes, etc.) and it would be hers within weeks or months. Others see this phenomena on a smaller scale, e.g., visualize a car space for yourself in the next block and it actualizes, need a pen and someone hands it to you, etc.

Chapter Eight: Shift Space

1. If you want to know more details of such experimentation, Dr. Russell Targ has co-authored two books, *Miracles of Mind* and *Mind Race,* which contain a wealth of information for lay people. *Foundations of Parapsychology* also has a discussion of protocols.

2. This story and much, much more is in Michael Murphy's authoritative book *The Future of the Body.*

3. The Medicine man was traveling in parallel time, not into the future. In the setting where he described this occurring, clock time would be very hard to judge.

4. This quote is from *The Psychic Side of Sports,* re-published as *In the Zone,* by Michael Murphy and Rhea White.

5. Until Robert Monroe wrote his book *Out of the Body* and established his Institute in Virginia, few people in the general population were acquainted with out-of-body experiences.

6. I still use this technique. When I feel a cold coming on, I lie down and relax deeply by inviting my spaciousness in and expanding myself outward. In my case, this helps if I'm able to release my mental tension. If I can't, I do not have such good results. Of course, I have no idea if it would be helpful with serious illness, although relaxation is good for your body.

7. For a discussion of how space is not empty, see Meg Wheatley's book *Leadership and the New Science,* Chapter 3.

8. One suggestion in the quantum physics world is that particles may come into existence, for however briefly, when two fields intersect. You can imagine the moment of greatest density as the moment of greatest intersection, if you want.

9. See the book *Dancing in the Flames: The Dark Goddess in the Transformation of Consciousness,* by Woodman and Dickson, and *The Void* by A. H. Almaas. Many of Almaas's books contain sections on emptiness, space, and the void.

10. This exercise, with an important variation, done in a group context strengthens

the collective identity. To do it with this emphasis, each group member lets the Dot symbolize the entire group (organization, nation, world, Universe) and the Circle becomes the member's Self. The members, therefore, embrace the group as core to themselves and central to their larger identity. This encourages the membership to recognize and embrace its unique oneness.

11. The quality of this information is distinctly different from that provided by unconscious interacts, projections, or wishful thinking. The latter two are often not valid, and the first, unconscious information, is not integrated into the relationship.

12. This tale is found in Michael Murphy's book *The Future of the Body*.

CHAPTER TEN: MATE WITH SOUL

1. This story comes from Jaworski's book *Synchronicity: The Inner Path of Leadership*.
2. Helen Palmer, in the book *The Enneagram*, referenced on page 335, provides specific examples of how we can utilize our budding intuitive abilities to serve our dysfunction. For example, she shows how a paranoid style utilizes intuition to identify danger; a co-dependent style utilizes intuition to know what someone else needs and uses the information to build dependency, etc.
3. The tendency to do this is called "the repression of the sublime" in psychology.
4. This story comes from an article entitled "The Inner Athlete" of *Intuition Magazine,* issue #12.
5. Professor Noddings has written the only book I know of about intuition in education, called *Awakening the Inner Eye: Intuition in Education.*
6. The foundation of this exercise was taught to me by a Tiwa man from New Mexico.

CHAPTER ELEVEN: PARTNER EXPONENTIALLY

1. Years ago when Alan Alda visited the Psychical Research Foundation in Durham, North Carolina, he mentioned that telepathy was present among performing artists and actors. Perhaps the entertainment field should be added to this list, but I'm not familiar with enough stories to do so.
2. This quote is from *In the Zone* and is augmented by Novak later when he says, "This is one of the great inner secrets of sports. There is a certain point of unity within the self, and between the self and its world, a certain complicity and magnetic mating . . . that conscious mind and will cannot direct."
3. Henry Reed of the Association for Research and Enlightenment has played a similar "game" with over 4,000 people and writes about it an article entitled "Intimacy and Psi: A Preliminary Exploration," which appeared in *The Journal of the American Society for Psychical Research,* vol. 88, October 1994.
4. Those who have made big contributions are researchers Douglas Dean and Alan Vaughan, author, scientists, and business man, Willis Harman, author and educator, Weston Agor, and practitioner, writer, and consultant, Bennett W. Goodspeed, and author Ray Rowan.
5. The seven highly developed market economies were Austria, France, Japan, the

Netherlands, Sweden, the United Kingdom, and the United States; one middle-income developing country was Brazil, and India was the one low-income developing country. I highly recommend the book this comes from. About a quarter of it is devoted to the survey and its fascinating raw data.

6. This organization, founded in the early 1970s by astronaut, scientist, and engineer Edgar Mitchell after a mystical experience which was inspired by his voyage to the moon, is dedicated to the scientific study of aspects of reality—such as mind, consciousness, spirit—that include yet go beyond physical phenomena. (See Resource List for contact information.)

7. This is the cardinal direction stone used by the architects of Washington, D.C., to design the city. Located near the Washington Monument, this stone is no longer square, having been moved many years ago and not aligned to the true axis when it was put back in place. We continue to support Arthur's dream.

8. I recommend this book highly if you want to explore your future and the future as a whole in useful ways.

CHAPTER TWELVE: CONNECT THE DOTS

1. If you want to do a long version of this meditation, here's the first part. Begin by visualizing the core of the Earth, the water, the crust, or the highest mountains. Then visualize the molecules that make up your chosen place adhering to each other, bound by the Creator's love. For example, imagine the molten core of Mother Earth resonating with the heartbeat of creation. Moving from the place you have chosen, envision the oceans, the ground water, the lakes, waterfalls, the rivers, etc., all filled with loving kindness. As you are doing so, imagine all the molecules dancing with joy.

   Then see everything that lives in the waters, the coral, seahorses, trout, algae, etc., purifying the water, living in total harmony. Express thankfulness to those in the unseen world who are helping clean and purify the water. Then move onto the air, the crusts, the mountains, and whatever has your attention, radiating love as you go.

   Next send love to all beings who are friends of the Earth, who are helping Her in any way. Then imagine the unseen spiritual masters and teachers, the incarnated spiritual leaders, political leaders, and others flooded with loving-kindness and overshadowed by love for the soul. Move on to the geographical areas of the world that are suffering (Bosnia, Russia, Rowanda, etc.) and imagine all the people shaking hands and circling the globe as one family. Finally, see loving-kindness within and surrounding your friends, family, professional life, and community.

   Close with thankfulness to the Earth for the gift of life.

RESOURCES

Sharon Franquemont
Intuition Works
6114 La Salle Ave. #175,
Oakland, CA 94611
(510) 531-3842 (510) 531-7478
www.intuitionworks.com

Colleen Mauro, Pub.
Intuition Magazine
275 Brannon, 3rd Fl,
San Francisco, CA 94107
(415) 538-8171 (415) 538-8175
www.intuitionmagazine.com

Jeffrey Mishlove, Dir.
Intuition Network
369-b Third St.,
San Rafael, CA 94901
(415) 456-2532 (same)
www.intuition.org

Roger Frantz, Conf. Chair
Intuition 2000
Dept. of Economics, SDSU,
San Diego, CA 92182
(619) 594-3718
(619) 594-5062

Marcia Emery
Intuitive Management
1502 Tenth St.,
Berkeley, CA 94710
(510) 536-5510 (510) 526-9555

Nancy Rosanoff
Nancy Rosanoff & Assoc.
109 Sunnyside Ave.,
Pleasantville, NY 10507
(914) 769-7226 (914) 769-4473
www.intuitionatwork.com

Helen Palmer
CRII
1442A Walnut St., #377,
Berkeley, CA 94709
(510) 843-7621 (510) 540-7626

Patricia Einstein
765 Greenwich St.,
New York, NY 10014
(212) 627-3810 (212) 989-1615

Sherry Noone
Intuitive Concepts
300 N. Rampart St. #117,
Orange, CA 92868
(714) 939-9336

Intuition: Audiocassettes

Patricia Einstein
Uncommon Sense:
Total Intuition Program
Available at (212) 627-3810

Marcia Emery
Intuition: How to Use
for Greater Power, 2 tapes
Simon & Schuster, Inc.
1230 Ave. of the Americas,
New York, NY 10020

Marcia Emery
Intuition: How to Use for Greater
Power, 6 tapes
Nightingale Conant
1-800-323-5552

Sharon Franquemont
You Already Know What to Do,
2 tapes
Sounds True 1-800-333-9185
www.soundstrue.com

Sharon Franquemont
Intuition: The Electric Self, 6 tapes
Sounds True 1-800-333-9185
www.soundstrue.com

Caroline Myss
Energy Anatomy
and Spiritual Madness
Sounds True 1-800-333-9185
www.soundstrue.com

Helen Palmer
Intuition Training
Shambala Publications,
300 Massachusetts Ave,
Boston MA 02115

Nancy Rosanoff
Use Your Intuition
Nancy Rosanoff & Assoc.
1-914-769-7226
www.intuitionatwork.com

Alan Vaughan
The Path of Channeling
and the Path of Healing
260 S. Lake Ave. #101,
Pasadena, CA 91101

Intuition and Travel

The Inner Voyage:
A Spiritual Experience at Sea
Dreamtime Cruises
1-800-546-7871

Sacred Sites School
of Conscious Evolution
Intuition Network
(415) 456-2532
www.intuition.org

Intuition: Television and Videocassettes

Jeffrey Mishlove
Thinking Allowed, PBS program
Call (510) 548-4415 for list of
over 170 tapes of interviews
or visit Web site:
www.thinkingallowed.com

Sandra Martin, Producer
Intuition: The Spark That Ignites
Paraview, Inc. Call (212) 489-5343
Fax (212) 489-5371

Caroline Myss
and C. Norman Shealy
Vision, Creativity & Intuition
Fax (417) 467-3102

Caroline Myss
The Energetics of Healing
Sounds True 1-800-333-9185

Victoria Weston, Producer
*The Intuitive Factor:
Genius or Chance?*
(404) 876-7149

Research Organizations

(IONS) The Institute of Noetic
Sciences (offers many services)
475 Gate Five Rd., Ste. 300,
Sausalito, CA 94965
(415) 331-5650

The Rhine Research Center
402 N. Buchanan Blvd.,
Durham, North Carolina
(919) 688-8241

Business and Intuition

Verna Allee
Integral Performance
500 Ygnacio Valley #250,
Walnut Creek, CA 94596
(510) 825-2663
Fax (510) 825-1515

Alan Gauthier
Core Leadership
1 Fernhoff Ct.,
Oakland, CA 94619
(510) 530-5500
Fax (510) 530-5510

Susan Greene
Greene Alliance, Inc.
9550 Ella Lee Lane,
Houston, TX 77063
(409) 249-3355
Fax (409) 249-3124

Madeline Hughes
4211 Pitt NE #14
Albuquerque, NM 87111
(505) 292-8505
e-mail: bizcoach@earthlink.net

Sharon Lehrer
slehrer@nnbn.com

Jagdish Parikh
c/o Blackwell Publishers,
108 Crowley Road,
Oxford, OX41JF,
United Kingdom

John Peterson
The Arlington Institute
1501 Lee Highway, Ste #204,
Arlington, VA 22209
(703) 812-7900
www.arlingtoninstitute.org

World Business Academy
P.O. Box 191210
San Francisco, CA 94119-1210
(415) 227-0106

Crosscultural Work with Intuition and Wisdom Technologies

Lisa Faithorn
21 Jeanette Ct.,
Walnut Creek, CA 94956
(510) 938-4097
Fax (510) 933-8205

Betsy Stang
The Wittenberg Center
188 Wittenberg Rd.,
Bearsville, NY 12049
(914) 679-9764
www.wittenberg.org

Elisabet Sahtouris
www.ratical.org/lifeweb

The Circle, *One People, One Planet, One Life*
6114 LaSalle Ave #166,
Oakland, CA 94611
(510) 336-0223 West Coast
(703) 620-2577 East Coast
www.oneprayer.org

Sacred Space, *Where Indigenous Paths Meet*
P.O. Box 26426,
Washington, DC 20001
(202) 232-6158
(202) 232-4220

Related Organizations

Michael Murphy
Integrative Transformative
Practice
P.O. Box 609,
Mill Valley, CA 94942

Rhea White
EHE Network
44 Rockledge Road,
New Bern, NC 28562
(919) 636-8734
http://ehe.org

Barbara Marx Hubbard
The Foundation For Conscious
Evolution
(415) 454-8191
Fax (415) 454-8805

Joan Kenley
The Kenley Group
1-800-820-2010
e-mail: joankenley@earthlink.net

Nancy Rivard
Airline Ambassadors
P.O. Box 11732m
Burlingame, CA 94011-7321
(650) 685-6262
(650) 685-6263

Sy Safransky
The Sun
107 North Roberson St.,
Chapel Hill, NC 27516
(919) 942-5282

Wisdom Network
www.wisdomnetwork.com

Intuition and Games

PSI Explorer
Author, Mario Varvoglis
A breathtaking, state-of-the-art
interactive CD-ROM focused on
psychic & intuitive abilities.
Call 1-800-266-5766 Books Now

BIBLIOGRAPHY

Adams, Cass, editor. *The Soul Unearthed*. New York: Jeremy P. Tarcher/Putnam, 1996.

Adrienne, Carol. *The Purpose of Your Life*. New York: William Morrow and Company, Inc., 1998.

Agor, Weston H. *Intuitive Management: Integrating Left and Right Brain Management Skills*. New Jersey: Prentice-Hall, Inc., 1984.

Allee, Verna. *The Knowledge Evolution*. Boston: Butterworth-Heineman, 1997.

Almaas, A. H. *Essence—The Diamond Approach to Inner Realization*. Berkeley: Diamond Books, 1986.

————. *The Pearl Beyond Price*. Berkeley: Diamond Books, 1988.

————. *The Void—A Psychodynamic Investigation of the Relationship Between Mind and Space*. Berkeley: Diamond Books, 1986.

Bailey, Alice. *Discipleship in the New Age, vol. 1 & 2*. New York: Lucis Publishing Co., 1995.

————. *The Light of the Soul*. New York: Lucis Publishing Co., 1995.

Bartlett, John. *Bartlett's Familiar Quotations*. Boston: Little, Brown and Company, 1980.

Becker de, Gavan. *The Gift of Fear: Survival Signals That Protect Us from Violence*. New York: Dell Publishing Co., 1998.

Bhahtivedanta. *The Bhagavad Gita, As It Is*. New York: Collier Books, 1968.

Black Elk. *The Sacred Pipe*. New York: Penguin Books, 1953.

Bohm, David, edited by Lee Nicol. *On Dialogue*. New York: Routledge Press, 1996.

Bolen, Jean Shinoda. *Goddesses in Every Woman*. New York: Harper & Row, 1984.

Buber, Martin. *I and Thou*. Translated by Walter Kaufman. New York: Charles Scribner's Sons, 1970.

Bucke, M.D., Richard Maurice. *Cosmic Consciousness: A Study in the Evolution of the Human Mind*. New York: University Books, Inc., 1961.

Burress, Charles. "Listening Between the Lines." *Intuition* magazine, issue 12, April 1996.

Campbell, Joseph. *The Masks of God: Creative Mythology*. New York: Penguin Books, 1968.

———. *The Power of Myth with Bill Moyers*. New York: Doubleday, 1988.

———. *The Hero with a Thousand Faces*. New York: Bollinger Foundation, Inc., 1948.

Campbell, Joseph, editor. *The Portable Jung*. New York: Viking Press, 1971.

Castenada, Carlos. *Journey to Ixlan: The Lessons of Don Juan*. New York: Simon & Schuster, 1972.

Chopra, M.D., Deepak. *Ageless Body, Timeless Mind, The Quantum Alternative to Growing Old*. New York: Harmony Books, 1993.

Coehlo, Paulo. *The Alchemist*. San Francisco: HarperSan Francisco, 1993.

Corbin, Henry. *The Man of Light in Iranian Sufism*. Boulder: Shambhala Press, 1978.

Cousineau, Phil, editor. *Soul: An Archaeology*. San Francisco: HarperSan Francisco, 1994.

Covey, Stephen R. *The Seven Habits of Highly Effective People: Restoring the Character Ethic*. New York: Simon & Schuster, 1989.

Deikman, Arthur J. *The Observing Self, Mysticism and Psychotherapy*. Boston: Beacon Press, 1982.

Dimasio, Antonio R. *Descartes' Error: Emotion, Reason, and the Human*. New York: A Grosset/Putnam Book, 1994.

Dossey, M.D., Larry. *Space, Time and Medicine*. Boulder: Shambhala Press, 1982.

Edge, Hoyt L., Robert L. Morris, Joseph H. Rush, and John Palmer. *Foundations of Parapsychology*. Boston: Routledge & Kegan Paul, 1986.

Eisenbud, M.D., Jule. *Parapsychology and the Unconscious*. Berkeley: North Atlantic Books, 1983.

Eliade, Mircea. *Cosmos and History: The Myths of the Eternal Return*. New York: Haper Torchbooks, 1954.

Emery, Ph.D., Marcia. *The Intuition Workbook: An Expert's Guide to Unlocking the Wisdom of Your Subconscious Mind*. New Jersey: Prentice Hall, 1994.

———. *The Intuitive Healer: Accessing Your Inner Physician*. New York: St. Martin's Press, 1999.

Faithorn, Lisa. "Building Alliances Across Differences: New Forms of Partnership." *Vision/Action*, Winter 1995.

———. "Ecostories: Reawakening Our Kinship with the Natural World." Paper presented at the Southwest Anthropological Association Annual Meeting, Pasadena, April 1996 (unpublished).

Fox, Matthew. *The Coming of the Cosmic Christ*. San Francisco: Harper & Row Publishers, 1980.

Franquemont, Sharon. *Do It Yourself Intuition*. Oakland: self-published, 1997.

———. "Psychic Awakening." Interview with Jeffrey Mishlove, Ph.D., for television program, *Thinking Allowed*.

Franz, Roger, and Alex N. Patakos, editors. *Intuition at Work*. San Francisco: New Leaders Press, 1996.

Gandhi, Mahatma K. *Gandhi, An Autobiography: My Experiments with Truth*. New York: Dover Publishing, 1983.

Gerber, M.D., Richard. *Vibrational Medicine*. Santa Fe: Bear & Company, 1988.

Goldberg, Philip. *The Intuitive Edge: Understanding and Developing Intuition*. Los Angeles: Jeremy P. Tarcher, Inc., 1983.

Goldman, Joseph. *The Experience of Insight*. Boston: Shambhala Press, 1983.

Goleman, Daniel. *Emotional Intelligence*. New York: Bantam Books, 1995.

Goodspeed, Bennett W. "Different Style of Analysis Imperative to Business: More Often Than Not, Intuition, Not Numbers, Tells the Real Story," *American Banker*, November 9, 1981.

Govinda, Lama Anagarika. *The Way of the White Clouds*. Berkeley: Shambhala Press, 1971.

Hampden-Turner, Charles. *Maps of the Mind*. New York: Collier Books, 1981.

Harding, M. Esther. *Woman's Mysteries, Ancient and Modern*. New York: Harper & Row, Publishers, 1971.

Harman, Willis. *Global Mind Change*. Indianapolis: Knowledge Systems, Inc., 1988.

Harman, Willis, and Rheingold, Howard. *Higher Creativity, Liberating the Unconscious for Breakthrough Insights*. Los Angeles: Jeremy P. Tarcher, 1984.

Harman, Willis, and Elisabet Sahtouris. *Biology Revisioned*. New York: Berkeley, North Atlantic Books, 1998.

Hillman, James. *The Soul's Code*. New York: Random House, 1996.

Houston, Jean, and Robert Masters. *Mind Games*. Wheaton: Quest Books, 1998.

Hubbard, Barbara Marx. *The Revelation: A Message of Hope for the New Millennium*. Navato: Nataraj Publishing, 1995.

Iyengar, B. K. S. *Light on the Yoga Sutras of Patanjali*. Great Britain: Thorsons, 1993.

Jackson, Edgar N. *Understanding Prayer*. New York: W. Clement Stone, 1968.

Jacobi, Jolande. *The Psychology of C. G. Jung*. New Haven: Yale University Press, 1973.

Jaworski, Joseph. *Synchronicity: The Path of Inner Leadership*. San Francisco: Berrett-Koehler Publishers, 1996.

Jung, C. G. *Alchemical Studies*. New Jersey: Princeton University Press, 1967.

———. *Aion*. New Jersey: Princeton University Press, 1959.

———. *Memories, Dreams, and Reflections*. New York: Vintage House, 1961.

Kavanaugh O.C.D., Kieran and Rodriguez, O.C.D., Otilio, translators. *Teresa of Avila: The Interior Castle*. New York: Paulist Press, 1979.

Kelly, Kevin W. *The Home Planet*. Reading, MA: Addison-Wesley Publishing Company; Moscow: Mir Publishers, 1988.

Kenley, Joan. *Voice Power*. New York: Henry Holt and Company, 1989.

———. *Whose Body Is It Anyway?* New York: Newmarket Press, 1999.

Kunkel, M.D., Fritz. *In Search of Maturity*. New York: Charles Scribner's Sons, 1943.

Lane, Phil, and Michael and Judy Bopp, and Community. *The Sacred Tree*. Lethbridge, Canada: The Four Worlds Development Project, 1988.

Laskow, M.D., Leonard. *Healing with Love*. San Francisco: HarperSan Francisco, 1992.

LeShan, Lawrence. *Clairvoyant Realities* (formerly *The Medium, the Mystic, and the Physicist*). New York: The Viking Press, 1974.

———. *How to Meditate: A Guide to Self-Discovery*. New York: Bantam Books, 1984.

———. *From Newton to ESP*. Northamptonshire, England: Turnstone Press Limited, 1984.

Lytle, Clyde Francis. *Leaves of Gold*. Pennsylvania: The Coslett Publishing Co., 1948.

Mails, Thomas E. *Fools Crow, Wisdom and Power*. Tulsa: Council Oak Books, 1991.

Mann, Harriet, Siegler, Miriam, and Humphrey Osmond. "The Many Worlds of Time," *Journal of Analytical Psychology*. 1968, 13(1).

Mauro, Colleen, "Lightning Bolts and Illuminations." *Intuition* magazine, issue 8, 1995.

McClendon, Jr., James. *Biography as Theology*. Nashville: Abingdon Press, 1974.

Mishlove, Jeffrey. *The Roots of Consciousness*. Tulsa: Council Oak Books, 1993.

Mitchell, Stephen. *The Enlightened Heart: An Anthology of Sacred Poetry*. New York: Harper & Row Publishers, 1989.

Moore, Thomas. *Care of the Soul.* New York: Harper Collins Publishers, 1992.

Murphy, Edward F. *The Crown Treasury of Relevant Quotations.* New York: Crown Publishers, Inc., 1978.

Murphy, Michael. *The Future of the Body.* Los Angeles: Jeremy P. Tarcher, Inc., 1992.

Murphy, Michael, and Rhea A. White. *In the Zone* (formerly *The Psychic Side of Sports*). Reading, MA: Addison-Wesley Publishing Company, 1978.

Myss, Caroline. *The Anatomy of the Spirit.* New York: Harmony Books, 1996.

Neihardt, John G. *Black Elk Speaks.* New York: Pocket Books, 1959.

Nelson & Sons, Thomas, editor. *The Holy Bible: Revised Standard Version.* New York: 1952.

Nisker, Wes "Scoop." *Crazy Wisdom.* Berkeley: Ten Speed Press, 1990.

Noddings, Nel, and Paul J. Shore. *Awakening the Inner Eye: Intuition in Education.* New York: Teachers College Press, 1984.

Novak, Michael. *The Joy of Sports.* New York: Basic Books, 1976.

Palmer, Helen. *The Enneagram.* San Francisco: Harper & Row, Publishing, 1988.

Palmer, Wendy. *The Intuitive Body: Akido as a Clairsentient Practice.* Berkeley, California: North Atlantic Books, 1994.

Parikh, Jagdish. *Intuition: The New Frontier of Management.* Oxford: Blackwell Publishers, 1994.

Perry, Whitall N. *A Treasure of Traditional Wisdom.* New York: Simon & Schuster, 1971.

Peterson, John L. *The Road to 2015, Profiles of the Future.* Corte Madera, California: Waite Group Press, 1994.

Potter, R. L. "Psychology in Silence." *Journal of Esoteric Psychology, vol. 3, no. 2.* Jersey City Heights: 1987.

Radin, Dean I. *The Conscious Universe: The Scientific Truth of Psychic Phenomena.* New York: HarperCollins, 1998.

Ray, Michael, and Rochelle Myers. *Creativity in Business.* New York: Doubleday & Company, 1986.

Redfield, James. *The Celestine Prophecy: An Adventure.* Hoover, Alabama: Satori Publishing, 1993.

Rhine, Louisa E. *Hidden Channels of the Mind.* New York: William Morrow and Company, 1961.

Rinpoche, Sogyal. *The Tibetan Book of Living and Dying.* San Francisco: Harper San Francisco, 1992.

Rodman, Selden. *A New Anthology of Modern Poetry.* New York: Random House, 1946.

Rosanoff, Nancy. *Intuition Workout.* Boulder Creek, California: Aslan Publishing, 1995.

Rowan, Ray. *The Intuitive Manager.* Boston: Little, Brown and Company, 1986.

Rudhyar, Dane. *Astrology and the Modern Psyche,* Davis: CRCS Publications, 1976.

Russell, Peter. *The Global Brain.* Los Angeles: Jeremy P. Tarcher, 1982.

———. *Waking Up in Time, Finding Inner Peace in Times of Accelerating Change.* Novato, California: Origin Press, 1998.

Sahtouris, Elisabet. "The Biology of Globalization," Monograph, 1997. Later published in *Perspectives on Business and Global Change,* September 1997, Vol. 11, #3.

Schwenk, Theodore. *Sensitive Chaos: The Creation of Flowing Forms in Water and Air.* New York: Schocken Books, 1976.

Sider, Marlene. "Spinning the Wheel of Fortune." *Intuition* magazine, issue 12, August 1996.

Singer, June. *The Boundaries of the Soul.* New York: Anchor Books, 1972.

Stribbe, Bill. "The World as Self, the Self as World," *Intuition* magazine. issue 12, August 1996.

Talbot, Michael. *The Holographic Universe.* New York: Harper Perennial, 1991.

Targ, Russell, and Jane Katra. *Miracles of Mind.* Navato: New World Library, 1984.

Thompson, Keith. "The Inner Athlete." *Intuition* magazine, issue 12, August 1996.

Thompson, Trisha. "Feeling Smart: A Talk with Author Daniel Goleman." *Intuition* magazine, issue 9, February 1996.

Tyndale House Publishers & Coverdale House Publishers Ltd., *The Living Bible, paraphrased.* Illinois & London, 1971.

Walsch, Neale Donald. *Conversations with God,* book 1. New York: G. P. Putnam's Sons, 1996.

Wheatley, Margaret J. *Leadership and the New Science.* San Francisco: Berrett-Koehler Publishers, 1992.

————. "The Unplanned Organization." *The Noetics Science Review,* Spring 1996.

Whitman, Walt. *Leaves of Grass and Selected Prose.* New York: Holt, Rhinehart and Winston, 1962.

Whitmont, Edward C. *Return of the Goddess.* New York: Crossroad, 1982.

Wilber, Ken. *The Atman Project.* Wheaton, Illinois: The Theosophical Publishing House, 1980.

Wilhelm, Richard, translator. *I Ching.* New Jersey: The Princeton University Press, 1950.

————, translator. *The Secret of the Golden Flower.* London: Routledge & Kegan Paul, 1979.

Vaughan, Alan. *Incredible Coincidence.* New York: J. B. Lippincott Company, 1979.

Vaughan, Frances E. *Awakening Intuition.* New York: Anchor Press, 1979.

Zukav, Gary. *The Seat of the Soul.* New York: Simon & Schuster, 1989.

INDEX

ABOUT THE AUTHOR

A former professor of intuition at John F. Kennedy University, for twenty-eight years Sharon Franquemont has been an intuition teacher, coach, speaker, and consultant. Addressing the role of intuition in business, education, psychotherapy, and daily life, she is a regular speaker and educator at national and international conferences and has been interviewed on national television and radio. Franquemont sits on the Advisory Board of *Intuition* magazine, and is a member of the Intuition Network. She lives in Oakland, California.